Globalization
EAST AND WEST

Bryan S. Turner and
Habibul Haque Khondker

Los Angeles | London | New Delhi
Singapore | Washington DC

First published 2010

SAGE Publications Ltd
1 Oliver's Yard
55 City Road
London EC1Y 1SP

SAGE Publications Inc.
2455 Teller Road
Thousand Oaks, California 91320

SAGE Publications India Pvt Ltd
B 1/I 1 Mohan Cooperative Industrial Area
Mathura Road, Post Bag 7
New Delhi 110 044

SAGE Publications Asia-Pacific Pte Ltd
33 Pekin Street #02-01
Far East Square
Singapore 048763

Library of Congress Control Number 2009932565

British Library Cataloguing in Publication data
A catalogue record for this book is available from the British Library

ISBN 978-1-4129-2852-6
ISBN 978-1-4129-2853-3 (pbk)

Typeset by C&M Digital (P) Ltd, Chennai, India

CONTENTS

ACKNOWLEDGEMENTS

We owe a great debt to many for their support and inspiration while writing this book. In many ways, Roland Robertson has been a mentor to both of us.

Some of the arguments in Chapter 4 appeared in H. H. Khondker (2008) "Globalization and state autonomy in Singapore", *Asian Journal of Social Science*, 36 (1): 35–56. The argument of Chapter 5 first appeared in Bryan S. Turner (2008) "Does anthropology still exist?", *Society*, 45 (3): 260–6 and has been developed extensively for this chapter. Aspects of Chapter 6 first appeared in Bryan S. Turner (2003) "Class, generation and Islamism: towards a global sociology of political Islam", *British Journal of Sociology*, 54 (1): 139–47; (2006) "Religion", *Theory, Culture & Society*, 23 (2–3): 437–44; and "Revivalism and the enclave society", in Amyn B. Sajoo (ed.) (2008) *Muslim Modernities. Expressions of the Civil Imagination*, London: I.B. Taurus, pp. 137–60. These passages have all been extensively revised for this book.

Chapter 8 was first published in Bryan S. Turner's *The New Medical Sociology* and has been rewritten for this study of globalization. Chapter 9 draws upon the discussion of Norbert Elias in Bryan S. Turner (2004) "Weber and Elias on religion and violence: warrior charisma and the civilizing process", in S. Loyal and S. Quilley (eds), *The Sociology of Norbert Elias*, Cambridge: Cambridge University Press, pp. 245–64. An extended and slightly modified version of Chapter 10 appears in Bryan S. Turner (ed.), *Handbook of Globalization Studies,* (2009). Aspects of Chapter 11 first appeared as Chapter 1 in Bryan S. Turner (2006) *Vulnerability and Human Rights*, University Park: Pennsylvania State University Press. It has been rewritten for this study. Chapter 12 first appeared in Chapter 1 of Bryan S. Turner (ed.) (2008) *Religious Diversity and Civil Society. A Comparative Analysis*, Oxford: Bardwell Press, and has been revised for this work. Aspects of Chapter 13 first appeared in Bryan S. Turner (2007) "Religious authority and the new media", *Theory, Culture & Society* 24 (2): 117–34, and in Chapter 10 of Chris S. Rojek and Bryan S. Turner (2001) *Society & Culture, London*: Sage. These passages have been extensively revisited and revised.

FOREWORD: THIS MILLENNIAL MOMENT
Roland Robertson

More than fifty years ago the novelist Philip Roth wrote that actuality is continually outdoing our talents and the culture tosses up figures daily that are the envy of any novelist. This observation is even more relevant at the end of the first decade of the twenty-first century than it was in the middle of the twentieth century. Moreover, the comment applies far beyond the realm of novelists. In particular, it certainly applies to many of those who write about globalization. Indeed, by the time this book is published it will, to some extent, inevitably be outdated. This is well demonstrated by the fact that the extent of the so-called economic downturn has only recently become fully evident, in the early months of 2009.

We live at a time when across the globe there are millennial outbursts concerning particular aspects of the human condition, indicating that we are at the beginning of the end. This, in spite of many proclamations, particularly those issuing from medical and pharmaceutical sources, that individual lives can be infinitely extended and most, if not all, diseases cured. The idea of the perfect global storm encapsulates much of this end-time, apocalyptic rhetoric. Among the most important components of the global storm are global warming, water shortage, salination, fuel depletion, pandemics, famine, "natural" disasters, and demographic changes on a global scale, with attendant problems arising from rapid and extensive migration and the production and reproduction of global diasporas.

In the present book Turner and Khondker seek to provide a new perspective on – indeed, a new theory of – globalization. This is a highly promising and much needed venture. Here I am concerned primarily to highlight the main contours of the project of theorizing the concept of globalization. Much is made in the literature on globalization of the pivotal significance of interconnectedness – sometimes called connectivity. In spite of this clearly evident feature of the modern world, its newness should not be exaggerated. The theme of global interconnectedness is now to be seen in the work of an increasing number of historians. This is a classic example of what David Edgerton has called the shock of the old.

On the other hand, in light of recent global fears and disasters, we can readily agree that connectivity is not the only major dimension of long-term globalization. Specifically, what is missing in this regard is the pivotal feature of increasing – or, better, increasingly reflexive – global consciousness. While many sociologists – if not historians and anthropologists – might argue that the latter is a relatively recent characteristic of globalization, this view is not at all realistic. Of particular importance here is the insistence that isolated societies have had no conception of "the world". To the contrary, an increasing number of anthropologists have shown that so-called primal peoples have had sophisticated views of the world beyond. The increasingly important theme of alterity is demonstrating this, if only in abstract terms. On the historical front the last few years have seen an increasing number of books by major historians, demonstrating that the world was much more global than recent history has suggested, in the sense of both extensive connectivity and reflexive global consciousness.

In any case, the principle of the shock of the old applies equally to the present global fashion for talking in apocalyptic terms. This can be seen through the ever-growing genre of historical literature claiming that particular periods were more or less unique in their millennial dreams.

The input of historians and the revival of interest in world, or global, history suggests that the major "contribution" of sociology has, in fact, been to *negate* globality as a major theme in the understanding of the world; even though, paradoxically and ironically, sociology has been at the forefront of reviving concern with the global, thereby overcoming its classical methodological nationalism, which arose after the deaths of Comte, Saint Simon, and Marx. It must be stressed that this revival has had a relatively long prehistory, exemplified in much of the work of sociologists in the 1960s, in spite of the latter rarely having a full-on interest in "globalization". Here again we have another example of the shock of the old, although in this case the old is not very old.

A particularly important feature of contemporary global consciousness is its fractured nature. Currently we find a great mixture of groups arguing for their own interpretations of the world's planetary troubles. For example, in the G20 demonstrations in London of March 2009 many, often rival, groups were protesting – against climate change, against particular kinds of energy, against transnational corporations, against banking systems, inequality and so on. Even though some participants may well have been concerned with the overall picture of a planet in peril, it appears that, on the other hand, each group was, in a certain sense, fundamentalistic. In other words, the tendency seems to have been to reduce a big issue to a much smaller dimension. This is, in fact, what is most plausibly meant by the word fundamentalism – the reduction of a cluster of themes to one particular, allegedly master theme. This feature of global consciousness was well demonstrated in the old nuclear disarmament movement, when adherents seemed to believe that if there were a world consensus on the evils of nuclear arma-ments then all the problems of the world would be solved. Indeed, this reductionist worldview is still to be found in those who argue that glob-alization is the cause of all of the problems in the world – teenage preg-nancy, rising rape rates, drug addiction and trafficking, prostitution, gang warfare, even traffic accidents etc. Thus, if present trends continue, we may expect global consciousness to increase but only in this heavily fractured form.

A major but paradoxical element of contemporary global conscious-ness has to do with the much vaunted idea of late capitalism – one which has been used almost incessantly in the decades since Ernest Mandel first used it. Just as David Harvey has examined neo-liberalism as, in the first place, an ideology (rather than a direct apprehension of a material con-dition), so has capitalism acquired a similar kind of significance. It is now regarded much more as a cultural phenomenon than it is an eco-nomic-material one. Moreover, anti-capitalism is now subject to the same kind of fracturing processes as are the other phenomena that threaten our planetary world – indeed, the universe(s).

The fractured nature of global consciousness is to a large degree the result of, or is consolidated by, the disciplinarity of contemporary knowledge: sociology, international relations, geography, meteorology, astronomy, surveillance and security studies, biomedicine, comparative literature and cultural studies, and numerous others. It might well be said that these are times of increasing transdisciplinarity – that is, disci-plinary mutations that involve considerable overlap of, and interpene-tration between, heretofore separate disciplines. One increasingly finds people in a particular discipline more or less duplicating work of roughly the same kind as those in other disciplines. Much of this overlap and interpenetration tends to be overlooked and, thereby, much intellectual effort is wasted. To this it should be added that, in spite of disciplinary globalization, we still live in a world of intellectual nationalism, that is, one in which nation-states compete with each other for intellectual credit and global matters are seen in national terms.

Turner and Khondker are particularly concerned with the East–West distinction, and rightly so. On the other hand, this geocultural comparison should not lead to sociological neglect of the rapidly crystallizing and aggressive controversy relating to the North and the South Poles. Much of this has emerged via the problem of global warming, with an increasing number of states laying claim to Antarctic and or Arctic territory. Indeed, this may well be the site of the next "world war". Add to this the threat of cyber wars and the great proliferation of nuclear weapons and we see that risk, uncertainty and fear are among the principal emotive factors in the contemporary world as a whole.

Returning to the East–West issue, it must be remarked that, to all intents and purposes, the sharpness and prominence of such a distinction primarily derives from the work of Hegel, to be consolidated by such major scholars as Marx, Troeltsch, Max Weber, Spengler and Heidegger. More recently, Said's much celebrated – but increasingly criticized and misleading work – on orientalism has consolidated this old way of thinking. In contrast, Turner and Khondker appear to be working in the relatively new tradition of the increasing number of historians and anthropologists – Goody, Jardine, Colley and numerous others – who have been showing that there has been much more sociocultural interpenetration of the old geographical distinction between East and West, or Orient and Occident. We can now see more clearly that the "East" and the "West" are equal and mutually amplifying "inventions" or constructions. In any case, the numerous historical interpenetrations between cultures "distributed" across the entire world are increasingly the subject of major scholarly contributions.

It would be a great omission were the global South to be overlooked in any "mapping" of the world as a whole. Thus the debate about black Athena – that is, the impact of black Africa upon Hellenic cultures – is an excellent example. This, however, fades into insignificance compared with the global significance of the Third World – or, in politically correct terms, developing countries. Here again we encounter geopolitical difficulties, particularly with regard to whether Latin America is in or out of the Third World, not least because of the increasing prominence of Brazil and smaller countries, most problematically Venezuela. In the world that we live in imperialism is now taking a very sharp turn, with China, Russia and India becoming the imperialists. In addition – and to complicate matters further – the increasing global prominence of South Africa (along with Brazil) is of great significance. Needless to say, some Southern Hemisphere countries – particularly Australia and new Zealand – have never been regarded as Third World or developing societies, in spite of rather meagre attempts to speak of a "Southern" sociology.

The attention given to religion in this book is greatly to be welcomed, in spite of numerous and fashionable but clearly wrong arguments that religion is in decline. To cogent scholars of the contemporary global human condition it is exceedingly clear that the world as we know it is and would not be possible without a conception of something "out there". Herein lies much of the intellectual danger that threatens us. Moreover, the global religious revival is closely bound up with what I call the totalitarian drift. In saying this I have in mind the theocratic, millennial – not to say apocalyptic and eschatological – tendencies which are to be found in the proliferation of novels, computer games, films, pictorial and photographic art, scholarly books and the like. None the less, we must be very wary of the historical record that illustrates that the decline of economic "fortune" leads, paradoxically, to the increasing importance of economics. It is ironic that a significant branch of the study of globalization has amplified – in the form of world-systems theory – this unfortunate tendency.

Turner and Khondker introduce and dwell on many facets of globalization and illustrate the all-encompassing nature of the study of these global processes.

Roland Robertson
Scotland
June 2009

INTRODUCTION: PROSPECTS FOR A NEW SOCIOLOGY OF GLOBALIZATION

INTRODUCTION

Over the last three decades, social scientists have taken the fact of globalization – the increasing interconnectedness of the world as a complex system – for granted. The processes of globalization, including its often negative consequences, have appeared to be inevitable and all-embracing. No society, however small and remote, could escape entanglement with such global cultural, political and economic processes. Any sociological analysis of a single society, region, city or village that did not take into account the global context was seen to be inadequate. Yet suddenly from September 2008 the unfolding of a global economic crisis that appeared to fan outwards from the problems in the American housing market to undermine the financial stability of whole societies such as Iceland brought into question many of our comfortable assumptions about the world and its economic foundations. There were rumours in the corridors of university social science faculties that the facts of globalization were perhaps not as secure as we had been led to believe. Why had economists in general failed to understand the fragility of the global financial system? Do we need as a result new perspectives on globalization? Will globalization as we know it come to an end? However, by the middle of 2009 the financial world appeared to have achieved some equilibrium and by September 2009 there were signs of a recovery in Europe and the United States which followed the recovery in Asia on the heels. A study commissioned by the United Nations (2009) revealed that there are deep and systemic problems with the global economy, the most important of which was social inequality. The Report recommended long-term solutions in addition to short-term stabilization measures. These questions about the economic character of globalization represent simply one dimension of our approach to globalization which we consider from the perspective of the East and from the West. Although the financial crisis has already brought misery to many thousands of families in the developing world, we see new democratic opportunities within this crisis, but we also detect the need for some major rethinking of the actual nature of globalization.

In the wake of the global financial crisis of 2008 which developed into a global economic crisis in 2009 with a bleak prognosis for the future (World Bank, 2009; United Nations, 2009),[1] many writers are understandably blaming globalization for our economic difficulties. The extreme turbulence in the global economy and the snowballing of the crisis from one country to another have indeed raised questions about the sustainability of the world economic architecture. Is globalization – viewed as the unbridled free market at play – to be replaced by a return to managed or state-centred economic systems? While some commentators recommend protectionism as the most appropriate strategy to stabilize the global economy, other economists suggest a comprehensive rearrangement of the global economic system as the only long-term solution. A leading economist, Jagdish Baghwati (2007), was confident that further economic globalization will in fact be the cure, but the challenges that the world faces are largely rooted in the gap between economic and political institutions. While the world has in economic terms become sufficiently global to emerge as a loosely integrated global economic system, the global economy is not matched by the institutional development of a global polity. Inadequate and ineffective coordination between the global economy and regulatory institutions has given rise to the possibility of a deep and prolonged economic crisis extending into the future, despite President Obama's huge injection of funding into the American economy as a recovery strategy. Yet in both the diagnosis and the cure of the crisis, policy-makers, as well as large sections of the public, continue to equate globalization only with economic globalization. It is imperative that we broaden our perspective on globalization as a multidimensional process in which economic globalization is only one of the important factors.

Globalization, viewed as a macro-social process, inevitably gives rise to questions about its future. Do social processes come to an end, or do they change course according to newly emerging social and economic conditions? If we highlight the structural or systemic features of globalization alone, then the conclusion becomes inescapable. All systems – ecological and economic – are in a constant process of transformation and change. However, if globalization is seen as an all-encompassing social condition, the processes of globalization will continue to shape the lives of people in the foreseeable future both at the level of everyday reality and at the level of social systems. The globalization process must change and adapt to newly emerging conditions if we are to plan more effectively for global pandemics, financial crises, economic inequality and imbalances in population movements through migration. As various writers in the last decade of the twentieth century celebrated the coming of the age of globalization, they also stressed the plurality of the processes of globalization, and hence it was important to speak in the plural of "globalizations". In the first decade of the twenty-first century, other critics have started to talk about the possibility of some disengagement from globalization, referring to new concepts such as "assemblage" and "re-assemblage" to describe the possibilities of disconnecting and disaggregating the components of global systems. In addition, it is well known that the processes of globalization do not preclude certain parallel processes such as regionalization and that in fact the two are interrelated (Therborn and Khondker, 2006). Disengagement from globalization, entailing the temporary repositioning and redirecting of trade flows, is often an aspect of the trading strategies of nations and regions, but these processes should not be seen as incompatible with globalization. Although globalization cannot be seen as an example of Max Weber's irreversible "iron cage", it is perhaps better described in the words of Ernest Gellner as a "rubber cage". While nation-states have some degree of flexibility in relation to globalization, they cannot enjoy complete independence from global constraints.

Will a new global catastrophe make people want to return to the secure boundaries of the nation-state? We are sceptical about the openness of social systems – at least in the medium term. While the idea of a "borderless world" has become somewhat tired as a result of excessive overuse, we see the erection of walls and fences separating borders between nations as evidence that the porosity of state boundaries should not be exaggerated. The world is only borderless for the privileged few, but for the great majority of humanity it is a tightly bordered and highly regulated world. We see as a consequence of such "gated communities", "gated" or "walled" countries, the emergence of what Bryan Turner (2007) calls the "enclave society", characterizing modernity in terms of immobility in opposition to the claims supporting ideas about global mobility and "flexible citizenship" (Ong, 1999). With the growth of widespread urban terrorism from New York to Mumbai, we believe that the need for securitization by modern states will limit the possibilities for human mobility and porous state borders. We follow Roland Robertson (2007) in believing that transparency and surveillance are simply the opposite sides of the same coin of this global condition. Given these assumptions about the emphasis on security as a priority concern of the modern state, we need to ask whether some major catastrophe – environmental, political, or biological attack on a state or states – will bring an end to globalization as we know it. Such a catastrophe would not be confined to the developed world. Based on recent trends, most of the future pandemics of global scope would origi-nate from the developing world.

The 9/11 attacks on New York and Washington and the fear of terror-ism took a heavy toll on tourism and the travel industries but obviously did not halt global tourism. Soon after the attack, one commentator pre-maturely declared that globalization was over. Because of the physical impact on Wall Street in New York City, the financial market stalled tem-porarily but bounced back in full vigour in a matter of weeks. Yet 9/11 has become a template for understanding other acts of terrorism. The attacks in London in July 2005 were immediately labelled as the "7/7 terrorist attacks" and the Mumbai terrorist attacks on 26 November 2008 were equally quickly labelled as the "26/11" attack or "India's 9/11". The deeper processes of globalization did not rest for a moment as a result of such devastating attacks, despite the scale of the trauma, the collective sense of fear and the prospect of military conflict between India and Pakistan. The 9/11 attack itself could of course be seen as a global attack in its perceived causes, methods, and strategies as well as its conse-quences. Modern terrorism is a menace to the normal functioning of civil society, rather like "low intensity wars", pestilence and pandemics, but the consequence so far has not been to halt or even necessarily to trans-form globalization. These disturbances are indeed the unpleasant under-belly of globalization that is often masked by the alluring world of global consumerism, tourism, popular culture and sport.

We are throughout this study struck by the deeply contradictory nature of globalization. In Chapter 4 we will argue that globalization points to the contradictory processes of wall removing and wall build-ing. The modern world witnessed the dismantling of the Berlin Wall as part of the collapse of the Soviet system and at the same time there was the emergence a new ideological Berlin Wall – between the East and the West – as a negation of the historical transactions and exchanges between cultures and civilizations over the centuries. The international relations perspective of Samuel Huntington, who coined the phrase "the clash of civilizations" in which world-views, cultures and values remain incommensurable, has not been borne out either by recent history or by the opinion polls. A recent book based on Gallup surveys, where the authors analyzed 50,000 face-to-face interviews in 40 Muslim countries, found that only 7 per cent justified the 9/11 terrorist attacks in terms of political reasons. The study also found that what Muslims most admired about the West was its technological progress and its democratic politics.

What both Muslims, and a large number of Americans, admired least about the West was its moral decay and the breakdown of traditional values (Esposito and Mogahed, 2008).

Although in everyday usage and in political rhetoric, as well as in some popular social science discussions, phrases such as "East versus West" and "the Christian world versus the Islamic world" are freely used, we argue that such simple binaries fail to capture the actual complexities of the contemporary world. One of the deeper consequences of globalization is in fact the obliteration of such differences. Although our study is called *Globalization East and West*, our main aim is to question such traditional geographical divisions. Contrary to other popular views, the world has not become flat; far from it. Globalization has rendered the world more complex and hence more difficult to understand, and therefore we need to abandon simple slogans about globalization such as "the world is flat". In an interview on CNN's chat show *Global Public Square* hosted by Fareed Zakaria and aired on 28 September 2008, the Chinese Prime Minister Wen Jiabao, not only referred to Adam Smith's *The Causes of the Wealth of Nations* as a guide to economic development, but also alluded to the *Theory of Moral Sentiments* in order to buttress the importance of ethical considerations in a market-driven world. He stressed moral questions and raised issues relating to social equity and justice. Whether Marxist idealism can coexist with market-driven capitalism is an issue that only the future of China's development can settle. In fact one could see the spread and survival of the socialist ideas of Karl Marx and Friedrich Engels, and their continuing hold on the global, as a concrete historical example of globalization. However, Wen identified Marcus Aurelius's *Meditations* rather than Marx's *Capital* as the principal inspiration for his moral and ethical position. Surprisingly, he did not quote from either Confucius or Mencius. In fact the Chinese leadership is slowly abandoning references to Marxist-Leninism and favouring a restoration of neo-Confucianism as a state ideology with its powerful emphasis on respect for order and social peace. It is far from self-evident that globalization will bring about the hegemony of neo-liberal ideas as the necessary underpinning of a market economy.

Another feature of globalization is that the leadership of global processes is constantly changing. Several writers have, for instance, commented on the shifting centres of global economic power. In the theories of Immanuel Wallerstein (1974), the core economies of the world system in the past were never permanent – their fates changed with historical circumstances. In the contemporary world, the economic powers of the twentieth century – North America, Europe and Japan as represented in the G7 and G8 (with Russia) – are increasingly being forced to take notice of the emerging BRIC countries (Brazil, Russia, India and China). The rise of these new centres of economic power is illustrated by the fact that, of the 500 firms listed by the business magazine *Fortune*, 62 are from the BRIC countries (*The Economist*, 20 September 2008, p. 3). Some of these firms, such as Lenovo of China and Tata of India, have also displayed remarkable creativity and innovative styles.

CAN SOCIOLOGY EXPLAIN GLOBALIZATION?

While books on globalization grow like conceptual mushrooms, the quality of theories of globalization is often poor, and research often scanty and inadequate. In fact, is there a distinctly *sociological* perspective on globalization? Our answer is affirmative. However, most sociological theory deals with micro–macro relations but typically within the nation-state, the region or the city. There seems to be some difficulty in thinking analytically about global processes, despite the encouragement and example of a minority of sociologists such as Roland Robertson. The main exceptions showing how we might develop genuinely sociological perspectives are probably George Ritzer on McDonaldization, Ulrich Beck on the risk society and cosmopolitanism, Anthony Giddens on distantiation theory, and Manuel Castells on the network society. From each of these sociological viewpoints, they make important contributions to our understanding of some selective aspects of globalization but do not provide a complete or comprehensive picture. Castells's work, however, makes significant strides in linking the role of communication in a networked society of capitalism and outlines several critical processes in which globalization can be challenged. Furthermore, he does not prematurely make a judgement about the outcome of globalization, because he sees the control and ownership of the global media as the outcome of endless struggles between various elites.

There is nevertheless a lot of theoretical speculation but little genuine research. For example John Urry (2000) talked about "sociology beyond societies", but just how mobile are the majority of people? How many people globally make at least one international flight per year? How many have international holidays, own a holiday home, have a passport, migrate to secure a higher income, marry a foreign person, or send their children overseas for education? What little research we have suggests people have strong subjective ties to their local town, city or region and do not exhibit strong cosmopolitan values. This emphasis on locality in people's lives was illustrated in *Globalization and Belonging* (Savage et al.,

2005). What are the implications of high mobility for elites? How does this impact on the concept of the self? Under what conditions could we anticipate the emergence of cosmopolitan identities? Do only cultural elites qualify for cosmopolitan status? What about the underclass of globe-trotting, undocumented, casual workers? Is there a cosmopolitanism from below as well as from above? Against the processes of geographical mobility, the crisis of terrorism and the emergence of new wars – which are also genuine examples of globalization – have produced a new emphasis on security, surveillance and the sovereignty of the state. Unfortunately, the outbreak of a pandemic, which many public health officials believe is inevitable, would certainly place significant limits on human mobility. The swine flu pandemic of 2009 may be less severe than originally predicted, but it provides a clear if chilling example of how rapidly such infections would spread from society to society.

One might argue that the scale of the issues relating to globalization appears to be too large to undertake adequate social science research. Hence, most global studies are in fact comparative and historical rather than global in orientation. Most social scientists appear to work happily with old methodologies of single-sited research. We need new methodologies, innovative theories and almost certainly revised epistemologies to do good research on globalization processes. We do not pretend to escape from this criticism and we do not have ready-made answers to these various questions. Multi-sited, comparative and collaborative research will address some of these issues. However, it is ironic that at a time when the frontiers of methodological nationalism need a certain erasure, some social scientists are bent on reverting to a methodological parochialism under the guise of promoting indigenous social science.

Most sociological theories of globalization, despite the call from C. Wright Mills and the example set by sociologists such as Immanuel Wallerstein and Charles Tilly, remain historically shallow. It is naïve to suggest, for example, that globalization started with the rise of the modern media or with the spread of American consumerism. These claims ignore the historical role of the missionary work of the world religions or the role of trade and merchant cultures since the fifteenth century or the global reach of ancient empires. Many sociologists continue to employ crude explanatory models that are typically based on some form of technological determinism such as the rise of the Internet. Understanding globalization almost certainly requires a high degree of interdisciplinarity, but sociologists too frequently fail to reach outside their own disciplinary assumptions. Unsurprisingly, much of the most interesting recent work has been undertaken by human or social geographers such as David Harvey. Creative reconfigurations of the sociological discipline would be a timely step towards redesigning methods appropriate to understanding global processes.

Except perhaps in journalistic writings, little sociological attention is paid to Asian globalization or to the impact of Asian commodities and cultures on the modern shape of globalization. Much globalization theory is based on narrow Western assumptions, for example, that modernization and globalization inevitably produce secularization. In short, globalization is normally understood from the viewpoint of some Western issue, process or location. Little attention is paid to the impact of a Japanese aesthetic on car design or fashion or the impact of Korean film on global culture. These West-centric assumptions are still persistent despite the changing global circumstances that are consequences of the economic and political rise of China and India – two societies that account for one-third of the world's population.

TRACKING CHANGES IN THE FIELD OF GLOBALIZATION STUDIES

THE SPATIAL TURN

Theories of globalization have been the dominant paradigm in sociology for at least two decades, but certain features of the globalization debate have been part of sociological discourse for much longer. In mainstream academic sociology, one of the earliest publications on the topic was W.E. Moore's (1966) "Global sociology: the world as a singular system". He argued that sociology was becoming a global science and that "the life of the individual anywhere is affected by events and processes everywhere" (Moore, 1966: 482). "Globalization" in this framework refers, then, to the process by which the "world becomes a single place" (Robertson, 1992), and hence the volume and depth of social interconnectedness are greatly increased. Globalization can also be seen as the compression of social space (Giddens, 1990). Giddens's definition of globalization was influenced by the so-called "spatial turn" which involved a revival of human geography which came to have a significant impact on the debate about globalization. In particular, there has been an important emphasis on the study of the global city. Globalization in this respect is treated as urban or city globalization in which a series of mega-cities (London, New York, Paris, Delhi, Tokyo and so on) became the principal sites of globalization – especially financial globalization. Cities such as London, Paris and Tokyo dominate the political and

economic life of their own societies, and as a result the chief political officers of such global cities (or "lord mayors") are often dominant political
figures within the national landscape. The linkages and flows between
these mega-cities are thought to be more important than the linkages
between states. In her major publication *The Global City: New York,
London, Tokyo*, Saskia Sassen (1991, 2001) has been concerned to illustrate the mobility of capital and people within the network of such sites.
These cities pose interesting political issues with respect to the national
sovereignty of their own societies.

ECONOMIC AND FINANCIAL GLOBALIZATION

While it is often difficult to measure or describe social and cultural globalization, economic globalization is often relatively visible, obvious and to some
extent uncontested. What is frequently debated is the actual impact of neo-
liberal globalization. What needs some attention, however, is the fact that
neo-liberal globalization is not historically the only form of economic globalization. Social Keynesianism based on the economic ideas of J.M. Keynes, the
Cambridge economist, had been a dominant but certainly contested orthodoxy in the period 1950–70. This strategy had emerged in the post-war
period as a policy to improve the level of employment by directing state
expenditure towards building infrastructure such as roads, railways and ports.
Because Keynesianism involved major state intervention in the management
and direction of the economy, it was often thought to be incompatible with
liberal (and more recently neo-conservative) ideas. Towards the end of this
period, economists and sociologists started to talk about the profit crisis of
capitalism – falling profits, rising taxation, expanding state expenditure,
declining investment, increasing strikes, high wages, and eventually stag-
flation. The state was now thought to be inimical to economic growth
because it was assumed to impede private investment and to depress entre-
preneurship. This produced new economic theories and strategies such as
Reaganomics, Thatcherism and neo-liberalism, which promoted low personal
taxation, rolling back the state, low corporate taxation, enterprise culture,
consumer sovereignty, free trade, and the end of state subsidies. These strategies became global partly because the Cold War came to an end with the collapse of the Soviet Union in 1989–92. The collapse of communism revealed
a number of societies suffering from corruption, low investment, industrial
stagnation and inefficiency. With socialism in retreat, neo-liberal ideas became
the dominant global orthodoxy and were often propagated by the Bretton
Woods institutions as mantras for economic success. An efficient market
became the main criterion of social development.

State socialism, despite its inefficiencies, had represented an alternative form of economic and political globalization. These communist social movements had not been given the adjective "International" for nothing. This history of global socialism (from Cuba to Vietnam and China) has been largely suppressed in the mainstream globalization literature which has concentrated on the period since the 1970s. Economic globalization has been largely seen as essentially liberal economic globalization, and hence anti-globalization movements have been largely against liberal capitalism, against free-trade orthodoxy, and against privatization and free markets. Of course, in the late twentieth century, some communist states began to liberalize their economies. In China, the Eleventh Congress of 1977, in the wake of the death of Chairman Mao in 1976, unveiled four modernization programs in four sectors – industry, agriculture, science and the military – to make China an industrial giant by the late 1980s. In modern-day Cuba and Vietnam there have been similar experiments to attract foreign capital, develop markets and diversify financial institutions such as banks.

The pros and cons of this economic debate about global capitalism are difficult to assess. What is clear is that this aspect of globalization has increased inequality both within and between societies. Liberal economic globalization has also had very negative effects on the environment, increasing political conflicts over basic resources. On the other hand, the old centralist, state-dominated programs do not appear to have worked either. Towards the end of its historical centrality, the Soviet Union became excessively corrupt and inefficient, developing an oversized and suffocating bureaucracy. The lack of political freedom, which was part of the trade-off for economic security, became unbearable in the face of ongoing economic deprivations. Bread-lines became a common sight in the Soviet Union of the 1980s. Chronic underemployment, underinvestment and industrial inefficiency and technological backwardness came to characterize these socialist societies. In addition, the powerful Soviet state had not solved its ethnic divisions and had brutally repressed its ethnic and religious minorities. With the re-establishment of the eastern Orthodox Church after the fall of communism, religious divisions and repression have resurfaced in recent years along with the growth of political authoritarianism. The collapse of the Soviet Union had been perceived by some commentators in the United States and Europe as the final victory of the liberal-democratic consensus. Francis Fukuyama's "end of history" thesis gained widespread notoriety in which he claimed that the old struggle between liberalism and socialism was over, and hence history had come to a conclusion in which liberal ideas were finally triumphant. Thus the continued unflagging and apparently unstoppable march of liberal cap-italism and democracy was taken for granted.

The global economic crisis of 2008–9 was a rude awakening for these champions of unfettered market capitalism and has exposed hitherto hidden forms of corporate corruption and ineptitude. Bernie Madoff in the United States was sentenced to 150 years' imprisonment for his cor-rupt financial practices in June 2009. The crisis in the United States and other heartlands of liberal capitalism has had significantly negative effects as far afield as Singapore, China and Vietnam, and some coun-tries such as Iceland are now bankrupt. These catastrophic developments are inevitably raising questions about market-driven strategies and the deregulation of financial services. These economic difficulties cannot be understood within an economic framework alone, because these eco-nomic problems have multiple causes. It is thus imperative to reconsider the non-economic bases of globalization.

THE CULTURAL TURN

In mainstream sociology, the most influential writer on the impor-tance of religion (or more generally culture) in globalization has been Roland Robertson (1992), who has complained with some justification that social scientists had overstated the economic nature of globalization (free trade, neo-liberalism, financial deregulation, and integrated produc-tion and management systems), to the neglect of its social and cultural characteristics, especially its religious dimensions. Theories that empha-size the technological and economic causes of globalization (such as computerization of information and communication or economic and fiscal deregulation in the neo-liberal revolution of the 1970s) show little appreciation for long-term cultural, religious and social conditions. These theories of economic globalization tend to be somewhat simple versions of economic or technological determinism. Whereas Ulrich Beck (1992) and Anthony Giddens (1990) have approached globalization as an aspect of late modernity (and therefore as a feature of the risk soci-ety and reflexive modernization), Robertson has been concerned with long-term cultural developments. These include the unification of global time, the spread of the Gregorian calendar, the rise of world religions, the growth of human rights, values and institutions, and the globalization of sport. In short, we also need to attend to the various dimensions of glob-alization and their causal priority: such dimensions as the economic and technological (including global markets in goods, services and labour); the informational and cultural (such as global knowledge, religious revival movements and radical fundamentalism); the legal and political (human rights, legal pluralism and legal regulation of trade), and the environmental, medical and health aspects (such as pollution, ageing populations, and the market in organs and epidemics). We can simplify this discussion by suggesting that globalization has four major dimensions: economic, cultural, technological and political. Any comprehensive analysis of the future of globalization would have to consider all four dimensions and their interaction.

In the 1960s Marshall McLuhan (1967) had introduced an influential vocabulary to describe the role of "the global village" in the analysis of culture and mass media in order to understand how the world was shrinking as a result of new technologies of communication. In more recent years, Castells's research on information technology and its role in shaping the world has also made a significant contribution in understanding the media in the global world. Castells's analyses touched on the globalization of information and knowledge. He also dwelt on the problems of democracy and information. The growing capacity of the Internet as knowledge provider marked a new chapter in the communication of ideas. For example, the digitalization of all library-based knowledge opens up new possibilities of a globalized knowledge society. At the same time, the issues of intellectual property rights become hugely complex. The impact of communications technology on work, as well as the growth of new types of consumerism and popular culture, are all areas of great importance in a globalized world.

The globalization literature grew apace in the 1970s and 1980s. Within the sociology of religion, religious revivalism or fundamentalism was increasingly seen as a global process (Beckford and Luckmann, 1989; Robertson, 1987a). By the 1990s globalization had been identified as the "central concept" of sociology (Robertson, 1990). Religious dimensions of globalization have, however, been somewhat neglected, and most explanations focus broadly on technological and economic causes (Beyer, 1994). For example, while Ulrich Beck (2000: 53) clearly recognizes the importance of cultural globalization and "ideoscapes", his *What is Globalization?* contains no discussion of fundamentalism, Islamic radicalism, or religion in general.

Sociologists have, in addition, had little to say about military globalization or about warfare. The impact of war and militarism on the origins and development of globalization has thus been neglected (Black, 1998), and yet military conflict has played a crucial part, especially with the rise of world wars, in transforming the international order into a global system. In the globalization literature, there has developed an unfortunate gap between sociological and international relations theory.

Religion and military violence are therefore important but somewhat neglected causal aspects of globalization processes.

GLOBALIZATION AND ITS CRITICS

Social sciences are known to be windows on the present. Some fields in social sciences are too engrossed with the present to take either the past or the future seriously. In this book, because we have tried to situate the forces and processes of globalization historically, it is also incumbent on us to attempt to predict the future of globalization processes. What is the future of globalization both as a phenomenon and as an intellectual framework? Does the historical process of globalization come to an end at some point in the future? What are the chances of the world retreating into autarchic nation-states? Or is the world moving into a post-globalization phase? What would the world look like in the post-globalization phase? What kind of intellectual tools should be brought to bear to understand such hypothetical processes?

As the chapters in this study try to show, globalization theories broadly deal with the state of the affairs of the world as a whole and seek to explain the functioning of the world and its future. There are several other intellectual traditions in social sciences that also aim to understand the same processes. In examining the future of globalization, we also consider those theories that compete with the globalization paradigm. In mainstream sociology, theories of multiple modernities may, for example, present an alternative to (monocausal) globalization theories. A number of writers on the Left have always been suspicious of globalization theories, accusing them of being simply an aspect of the neo-liberal project. Critical theory was more inclined to advance versions of the theory of imperialism or what we might call empire studies against orthodox assumptions about liberal globalism. Others have advanced versions of dependency and world-system theories, which they believe are more adequately grounded in modern political economic realities. Yet there are other writers who bring to the study of globalization a vision of an interdependent world by invoking the ideas of Gandhi and other visionaries who refused to abandon hope in human creativity and their passion for a better world.

Some of these competing theories have emerged out of anti-globalization protests or have even been proposed by the global institutions themselves. At the World Social Forum held in Mumbai in 2004 the popular slogan was: Is another world possible? The answer to this rhetorical question was affirmative. Various writers have promoted the use of an alternative terminology such as "globalization with a human face" or "just globalization" or "ethical globalization". Related expressions such as "fair trade alongside free trade", or notions such as sustainable development, more inclusive development, and democratic governance have made a fruitful contribution to public discussions.

Globalization has certainly created its detractors. Now there are clearly pro-globalists and anti-globalists. These critiques of globalization have already formed the basis for a social movement against globalization in which the anti-global movement itself has become a global movement. From Porto Alegre to Mumbai, the movement has grown in strength. In subsequent chapters, we examine the origin and future of the anti-globalization movements in greater detail. Some of the critical views of globalization have been translated into ideas of action and protest, especially targeted at the World Bank, the International Monetary Fund (IMF) and related institutions. Organizations such as ATTACK, a French non-governmental organization (NGO), and similar organizations have emerged in mobilizing protests against rapacious economic globalization.

In two important books, *Empire* (2000) and *The Multitude* (2004), Michael Hardt, an American Left intellectual, and Antonio Negri, an Italian radical social activist and philosopher, have provided their critical assessment of the world. In the first book, they developed a theory of empire which is very different from the empires that were collections of subordinated states. In the modern empire, multinational corporations and other non-state organizations work together and often assume some kind of sovereignty. In *The Multitude* they argue that the grip of the empire cannot last for ever and that it is increasingly being challenged by the people from below with their own democratic aspirations. These masses – the multitude – seek true emancipation and can mobilize an enormous emancipatory power.

Here we raise two sets of questions. At the theoretical level what comes after globalization? Post-globalization, glocalization, or neo-globalization, or the world of new empires? At the empirical level we must deal with the question of the fate of the earth as an ecosystem, as a place where all can live in peace, minimally defined as the absence of war and violence and an end to hunger and social insecurities in an environment of freedom. The idea of development as freedom is a powerful one and a goal that all can pursue without allowing the issue of cultural relativism to stifle debate. A minimum set of welfare provisions such as food for the hungry, shelter for the homeless, and medical care for the sick must be made available and such aspirations can be satisfied within the resources of the world. Gandhi was surely right when he said that the earth has enough to meet everyone's need but not everyone's greed.

In the 1970s a number of writers studied the finiteness of the resources of the earth. Their views, represented in the Club of Rome reports, identified the limitations of the ecosystem. In order to save the earth, one has to limit consumption. On the theme of the survival of humanity, *North–South: A Program for Survival* (1980), also known as the Brandt Report, and the subsequent Earth Summit report, *Our Common Future* (1987), made valuable connections between environment and development issues. Not only was the idea of sustainable development promoted, but the report also underscored the ecological interdependence among nations.

The last decade of the twentieth century saw the failure of a social experiment that created the false impression and an equally ideologically charged belief that the market would solve all the problems of the world, provided the market was allowed to function without interruption, interference or distortions. Serious problems of inequality, social disorganization, violence and ecological decay marked the first decade of the twenty-first century, leading to a world-wide economic crisis.

The United Nations has taken bold, visionary and often effective measures towards dealing with global poverty and various life-threatening epidemics. In the Millennium Development Goals, the UN charted a plan of action to reduce the problems of hunger and gender inequities. Regrettably little progress has been made in exercising the collective will and taking concrete actions against war and global violence. However, the UN role is limited to dispatching blue-helmeted soldiers who under the auspices of the United Nations play the role of peace keepers but not peace makers.

It is now widely accepted that the global public must take a more active and collective role in stemming the tide of social dislocation and violence. The goals of a liveable-in and peaceful world are not only desirable but also achievable if the public or the people have the will to make the necessary changes. True empowerment will only come from such shared knowledge and real change can only come with collective action against pollution, sex tourism and poverty. We need new values and effective institutions to combat these shared problems, and in this volume we attempt to describe some of these values as a form of "cosmopolitan virtue" in which recognition and respect for others are key components.

As we write these lines in the first decade of the twenty-first century, the world is under the shadow of a growing economic crisis and is faced with mounting violence resulting from ethnic and religious intolerance. Terrorist attacks have grown out of local conditions, which have often been neglected by international agencies such as the UN, to spawn as global conditions. There is a need for renewal of certain basic, universal values such as the right to life for all. Rights to life and dignity must be cornerstones for the creation of a peaceful and compassionate world. A peaceful world must be guided by human rights and a tolerance for diversity, creating institutions to provide collective security against vulnerability. The forces of globalization must be harnessed to build solidarity and peace rather than war and destruction. An important starting point, which can itself be seen as a consequence of globalization, is to recognize our mutual vulnerability in an interconnected and interdependent world. In a world of scarcity, failure to work towards collective solutions to global problems must inevitably lead to our mutual destruction.

This book will explore those themes in conjunction with the role of the global civil society and mobilization of people across cultures in charting a more comfortable future. Our expressed hope is that by reading this book, students and other readers will not only have a better understanding of the complexities – both conceptual and practical – of the world we live in but also be able to contribute to the peace that we need.

NOTE

1 According to the World Bank (2009) press release, "Amidst global economic recession and financial-market fragility, net private capital inflows to developing countries fell to $707 billion in 2008, a sharp drop from a peak of $1.2 trillion in 2007. International capital flows are projected to fall further in 2009, to $363 billion." The UN (2009) revised its already pessimistic scenario published earlier in mid-2009, projecting that "the world economy is expected to shrink by 2.6 per cent in 2009, after an expansion of 2.1 per cent in 2008 and nearly 4 per cent per year during the period 2004–7".

2 CONCEPTUALIZING GLOBALIZATION

INTRODUCTION

Is globalization simply a euphemism for concepts such as Americanization or Westernization? Can there be an "Asian globalization"? What about the plausibility of "alter-globalization", a term that was popularized in the World Social Forum? In discussing concepts in social science, it is obviously important to ask whether the concepts at hand add anything new or valuable to the understanding of social reality. Social scientists have used various concepts – such as modernization, modernity, late modernity, post-modernity, development, post-development, imperialism – to describe a range of related social transformations. Does globalization as such add value to our conceptual repertoire? This chapter argues that, although these diverse intersecting concepts provide varied frameworks to analyse the processes of social change, globalization provides a more inclusive and comprehensive intellectual framework than any of these alternative concepts. Globalization, for us, is a historical process or a set of intertwined processes with certain structural properties. At one level it is a macro-historical process, *a process of processes;* at another level, namely, the micro level, it deeply affects human beings directly, including their consciousness and everyday life.

In providing a brief conceptual history, we challenge two popular notions: that (1) globalization refers *only* to economic unification of the globe, integrating all the countries of the world under a single market grid; and (2) globalization is a euphemism for "Westernization", that is, the discourse of globalization is a Western hegemonic imposition on the rest of the world in the mode of cultural imperialism. Rather than viewing globalization as a narrow, economic and exploitative process, we recognize globalization as a multidimensional process. We look at the various

dimensions of globalization in terms of various complexities and contradictions. We also challenge yet another popular myth that, as a mega-
process affecting all aspects of our life, globalization unleashes destructive
consequences by erasing differences and creating a uniform and homogeneous world. We do not see the flattening of the world through common communication systems as an immediate outcome. We critically
evaluate the popular understanding of globalization as "global pillage" and
examine in some depth the notion of the "global village", which Roland
Robertson once remarked looks more like a "global town". A caption in
the *International Herald Tribune* (20 May 1999) summed up the popular
understanding of globalization neatly. It said simply "Bhutan Joins the
Global Village". The newspaper covered the story of the legalization of
television and the Internet in this mountainous, remote and devoutly
Buddhist kingdom in South Asia. The coming of television to Bhutan connected this hitherto aloof society into the global system. Bhutan had
resisted television for quite some time, while neighbouring Bangladesh and
India had had television since the early 1960s. Being connected with satellite television and the Internet is indeed the popular conception of globalization and certainly this form of globalization raises the possibility of a
transformation that has both far-reaching and complex implications.
However, the popular understanding has to be complemented by a more
penetrating sociological investigation. For example, one could argue that
in neighbouring India television has been as much an instrument for preserving Indian tradition as it has been a harbinger of global modernity.
Some writers tend to conceptualize globalization as world-wide modernization, often seeing it as posing a threat to local cultures and traditions,
while others see globalization as a historical outcome made up of a variety
of local traditions. In this perspective, locality becomes a site for a
dynamic confluence of various cultures. It would, however, be too early
to assess the impact of these exposures on Bhutan.

Considering the fact that nearly half the world population now lives
in urban rather than rural areas, the global village metaphor is likely to
become quickly anachronistic. The heterogeneous and multicultural features of the processes of globalization are more likely, following
Robertson, to create a global city. Such an image opens up possibilities
for further theoretical and empirical explorations.

The main task of this chapter is to present a brief history of the concept
of globalization. By conceptual history, we mean simply the exploration
of a concept over time. It is neither the history of an idea nor a narrative of
the empirical processes. In recent years the term "globalization" has obviously become widely and promiscuously used in popular culture. Business
leaders, politicians and lay public have used it so frequently that it has

lost much of its analytical rigour. There is more to it. In the global politico-ideological discourse, it has become a highly controversial term, so much so that now there are both *globophobics* and *globophiles*. The former group embraces a doomsday scenario of the consequences of globalization, while the latter group welcomes globalization with enthusiasm, seeing it as a universal panacea.

By tracing the history of the concept of globalization, we argue that globalization does not simply mean the creation of a world-embracing economic system paving the way for cultural homogenization on a worldwide basis, and it is not just a new variant of so-called cultural imperialism. Globalization is neither a menace nor a panacea. It is a complex process of social, cultural, economic and political connectedness that has to be approached at a high level of complexity and abstractness.

It is important to conceptualize globalization in relation to cognate concepts such as modernization and Westernization. Globalization is viewed by some as Westernization in general and Americanization in particular. In order to develop this discussion, it will be useful for the purpose of conceptual clarity analytically to separate the concept of globalization from such categories as internationalization, cultural diffusion, homogenization, and universalization. Although many of these concepts are overlapping, it can be stated rather forcefully that globalization is *not* internationalization, even though many social scientists use these two terms interchangeably. It is *not* Westernization in the sense that the world is becoming more homogeneous and the non-Western world looks increasingly like the West. Its relationship with cultural diffusion is also somewhat problematic. If one conceives of cultural diffusion as a process of mediation rather than a simple unidirectional overpowering of one culture by another, then diffusion can be seen to resemble the general process of globalization.

Globalization is sometimes equated with modernization. Modernization as a concept in sociology has had a chequered history. It has been criticized for its lack of historical awareness and sensitivity as well as for its lack of empirical validity. A revised view of modernization would have to take into account the fact that historically modernization does not mean the entire elimination of the deadweight of tradition, but on the contrary modernization can mean the incorporation of tradition into the actual constitution of modernity. The historical possibilities of multiple trajectories of modernization persuade us to look at globalization in a similarly multivalent manner. One failure of an early generation of writers on modernization was their inability to understand the actual tradition that modernity was supposed to replace. Tradition, rather than being dissolved, remains alive, so much so that it can set the agenda for modernization. The notion of "multiple modernities" that was outlined by Goran Therborn (1995) made a seminal contribution in this regard. Some sociologists now argue that a second wave of modernity is marked by its reflexivity (Therborn, 2000a; Beck, 2000). In a similar vein, globalization as a process has been referred to as "reflexive cosmopolitanization" (Beck, 2000).

The multidimensionality of this concept and the heterogeneity of the phenomenon of globalization have led to a plurality of theories and discourses about globalization (Robertson and Khondker, 1998). In addition to a number of disciplinary approaches to globalization in the contemporary social and cultural sciences, there are also various regional and national debates on globalization from Asia, North America, Europe, Latin America, the Middle East and Africa. More to the point, these discussions do not share a common understanding of the meaning of globalization. Although in defining globalization the majority of authors tend to emphasize the economic interconnectedness of the world, globalization, we will argue, is a much more comprehensive and complex process. The three dimensions of globalization that need to be considered are techno-economic, socio-political and cultural/civilizational.

A PROBLEM OF DEFINITION

Against the background of an optimistic if not triumphal mood with the presumed victory of capitalism and liberalism at the end of the Cold War, "globalization" as a concept made its original appearance to capture this changed social reality. A large number of writers began to view globalization as resurgence of capitalism where market, capital, investments, enterprise and technology would not encounter any national boundaries. Certainly economists, marketing and business strategists as well as the custodians of the international financial and development organizations applauded such a view. However, the response in many liberal and left quarters was exactly the opposite. They approached this situation with a sense of concern and apprehension. Concerns were (and continue to be) raised over the fate of the environment, local cultures and cultural differences when confronted with the march of globalization. Many of the recent critics, such as James Mittelman (1996, 2004) and James Petras (1993), and possibly some supporters of globalization ground their position on a simplistic and reductionist understanding of globalization, equating it simply with the irreversible march of capitalism. Peter Smith (1997: 174), for example, sees it as merely "a shift from the rubric of modernization toward the geographical euphemism globalization". Smith (1997: 175) continues in the same critical mode to say that "Globalization is as much a script for U.S. corporate boardrooms as a strategy for national economies, simultaneously a diagnosis and prescription." For Ray Kiely (1998: 96), "the globalization thesis contends that we live in a world economy dominated by transnational corporations (TNCs) that invest wherever they like in a footloose manner". Empirically speaking, however, there is no denying the fact that there was a proliferation of transnational corporations by the late twentieth century and the extent of the reach of those corporations was matched by their enhanced political and economic clout. According to a UN Report, there were 60,000 TNCs which, together with their half a million affiliates, accounted for over 25 per cent of the global output and combined sales of over US$11 trillion (*The Straits Times*, 28 September 1999, p. 57). Others tend to see globalization as a form of "cultural imperialism" that accompanies the march of transnational capitalism.

Globalization as a concept made its appearance in the sociological literature towards the end of the 1980s (Waters 1995). Although the genealogy of the globalization perspective can be traced back to the earlier works of Marshall McLuhan (1964), William Moore (1966), and Peter Nettl and Roland Robertson (1968), serious theoretical discussions began in the mid-1980s, especially in the United States. Sociologists who took the lead in this discussion were Roland Robertson and his students (Robertson and Chirico, 1985; Robertson and Lechner, 1985) at the University of Pittsburgh, Albert Bergesen (1980) at the University of Arizona who was responding to the somewhat economically deterministic view of Immanuel Wallerstein at that time, and John Meyer (1980, 1992) who, along with his students at Stanford, was examining the globalization of state and education in light of institutional isomorphism. The notion of isomorphism clearly points to structural similarities while the contents, that is, people with their culture, collective memory and history, are different. A common theme in those discussions was the abandonment of a simplistic convergence thesis which was an outgrowth of the earlier modernization theories that predicted a convergence and withering away of the differences. Robertson's (1992) conceptualization of globalization insisted on heterogeneity and variety which are the hallmarks of the increasingly globalized world.

The emergence of the discourse of globalization itself signalled the intensification of globalization as a social/economic/political/cultural process. Globalization refers "both to the compression of the world and to the intensification of the consciousness of the world as a whole" (Robertson, 1992: 8). This definition takes into account both the empirical aspect (that

is, the *compression* of the entire world into a single, global system) and
conceptual ideas about the ways in which the world as a whole should be
mapped in broadly sociological terms (Robertson, 1990). David Harvey
(1989) argues that the process of time–space compression is rooted in the
flexibility of the new forms of capitalism. Globalization, for Anthony
Giddens, "is really about the transformation of space and time". He
defines it as "*action at distance*, and relate[s] its intensification over recent
years to the emergence of the means of instantaneous global communication
and mass transportation" (Giddens,1994: 4). John Tomlinson (1999: 2)
defines globalization as "complex connectivity", because it "refers to the
rapidly developing and ever-densening network of interconnections and
interdependences that characterize modern social life". Globalization also
means an increased awareness of the world. In the words of Malcolm
Waters (1995: 3), it is a "social process in which the constraints of geography on social and cultural arrangements recede and in which people
become increasingly aware that they are receding".

One writer used the survival of Kuwait as a state after its physical
takeover by Iraq in 1990–91 as an evidence for the "deterritorializa-
tion" thesis. As he commented:

> The occupation and subsequent liberation of Kuwait has shown that
> in the age of globalism, physical space is not central to the state's
> survival…When the territory is occupied, the state can become
> diffused in the financescape and the mediascape or transformed
> into what might be called, following Baudrillard, a "hyperreal state",
> "hyperreal Kuwait" survived as a state in the global flow even when
> it was occupied physically. (Fandy, 1999: 125).

Such analysis was perhaps a little overdrawn. Geography continues to
remain important since the project of state-making always hinges on a
land mass of one's own.

GEOGRAPHY AS PROBLEMATIC?

During the heyday of the Cold War, many critics of capitalism around the
world invoked both a non-Western and a Marxist intellectual position at
the same time. The emergence of Marxist discourse on Western soil by no
means makes it a "Western" theory, much less an apologia for the capitalist world system. The relative autonomy of these discourses should be
accepted and should supplement the view of the embeddedness of social
thought. From an epistemological point of view, a convenient starting

point for us would be the middle ground between the "strong program" and the radical non-foundational position, such as the epistemological position of the American pragmatist Richard Rorty. The post-modernist discourse (or anti-discourse), which has paradoxically turned to Rorty's anti-foundationalism for its own foundation, has made an important contribution in terms of shaking any paradigm-centred, universal orthodoxy and thereby creating an open-ended quality for debate. Our approach to globalization hopefully incorporates some of that open-endedness, especially the notion of the non-linearity of development. This globalization approach has also moved away from a rigid progressivist view that continues to characterize many of the conventional social theories of modernization. Yet, it is important to recognize that a moral compass for measuring progress is still necessary and possible.

If we create a broader meaning for the term "discourse", then we can say that in the post-Cold War world there now exists a world-wide discourse on the benefits and failures of the free market economy. Though initiated by the economists of the Bretton Woods Institutions (IMF, World Bank and so forth), this market discourse is no longer confined merely to the economists or to those governments that are dependent on the World Bank or IMF framework. Other social scientists, opposition politicians, leaders of NGOs, journalists and the "thinking public" are all participants of this discourse. Those who are opposed to or are less enamoured of these free–market ideas are also criticizing or are expressing their reservations in response to this neo-liberal doctrine, thus being implicated in this discourse. This point needs further elucidation. We are saying that in order to participate in a discourse one need not be simply a follower of it. One can affirm a discourse even by criticizing or rejecting it. In this sense, Immanuel Wallerstein's view of the contributions of the criticism of the capitalist world system provides a close parallel. Commenting on the historical anti-Western tendencies among Russian intellectuals, one writer stated that "The more Russian thinkers distanced themselves from the West, the more they used it as a point of reference. While criticizing it, they observed it, if anything, even more closely than did the westernizers" (Laszlo, 1993: 103). Similarly, protagonists of so-called "Asian values" cannot help but use the West as a necessary foil. Following the disputed presidential election in Iran in June 2009 when several European and US officials criticized the Iranian government for suppressing public opinion, the Iranian government was quick to turn it into a "bully West" trying to impose its hegemony on the "East", neglecting the fact that a large number of Iranians both within and outside the country were shocked at the derailment of democratic rights in their own country and many of them put their lives at risk at the altar of freedom.

The discourse of globalization incorporates those who affirm it, partially accept it, or even reject it. It is in the last sense that the whole movement towards indigenization – provided its point of reference is the global society – can be seen as the opposite side of the coin to globalization, thus becoming inevitably a part of the globalization discourse.

The idea of a world literature developed by the famous German literary figure Goethe provides another example of this process. As Homi Bhabha (1994: 11) points out, for Goethe, "the possibility of a world literature arises from the cultural confusion wrought by terrible wars and mutual conflicts". "Nations could not return to their settled and independent life again without noticing that they had learned many foreign ideas and ways, which they had unconsciously adopted and came to feel here and there previously unrecognized spiritual and intellectual needs" (Bhabha, 1994: 11). In a similar vein, it can be said that in today's world of so-called conflicting civilizational standards, multiculturalism, and the overall sense of chaos and political disorder, a new awareness of the globe and global culture is taking shape. Globalization is the shorthand name for these complex processes and the discourse of globalization is an intellectual response to these processes.

THE PROBLEM OF HEGEMONY

Hierarchy, historically formed and culturally negotiated, is one of the central features of the complexities of the modern world. The problem of hegemony captures the varieties of dominating, exploitative and repressive hierarchical relationships that characterize the world. We maintain, however, that there is an important difference between the hegemony at the politico-economic level and the hegemony at the cultural and intellectual levels. It is in the latter sense that Antonio Gramsci, the influential Italian Marxist intellectual, used the word "hegemony". The concept is important and relevant in helping us to understand the question of consent. There is, for example, an important difference between voluntary acceptance of certain procedures, often for pragmatic reasons, and involuntary subjugation.

Colonialism provides a good example of involuntary subjugation and of hegemonic globalization. Yet during the colonial period, we find examples of how social changes in one place had important unintended consequences elsewhere as a consequence of global connectivity. Let us take the example of indigo cultivation and its impact on the decolonization process. In the late eighteenth and early nineteenth centuries, Bengal (present-day Bangladesh), following its colonial incorporation, was selected for indigo cultivation. As Bengal became a major exporter of low-cost, high-quality indigo for the European market, the earlier suppliers of indigo in South and Central America became less competitive, which came to have a disrupting influence on their economies. Unemployment eventually led to political unrest, thereby paving the way for anti-colonial movements. Most of the South American countries overthrew the colonial powers in the early nineteenth century; for example, Argentina in 1816, Venezuela 1821, Brazil in 1822, Uruguay in 1825, and Guatemala in 1839. In short, economic changes in Bengal had unintended political outcomes in South America.

Many of the Asian and African colonies became independent after the Second World War when the colonial powers were too weak to retain a political grip over their former colonies. The impact of the Second World War on national liberation movements in Asia and Africa provides another example of the role of unintended consequences in history. Political independence in Indonesia in 1945, India and Pakistan in 1947, Burma in 1948, Malaysia in 1963, Sudan in 1956, Nigeria in 1960 and Senegal in 1960 was in part the product of changes in the global position of the so-called Great Powers. The decline of British imperial power after the Second World War created a general global context in which African and Asian countries could successfully press for independence. These developments were recognized overtly in, for example, the British Prime Minister Harold Macmillan's famous "wind of change" speech in Africa in February 1960, in which he acknowledged the inevitable movement towards a post-colonial world.

At the military, political and economic levels, it is not difficult to demonstrate the existence of the hegemony of the United States or NATO or the G8 countries, including Japan. This hegemony is often made manifest in overt domination very much in the vein of earlier imperialism. But that form of hegemony does not mean that the theoretical approaches and the intellectual currents that are being produced in that milieu are mirror images, embodying the same hegemonic intent. Let us take the example of the globalization of knowledge in medical science. In a world dominated by large and powerful multinational pharmaceutical companies, one can argue that, although there are occasional examples of enforced implementation, much of the diffusion of medical knowledge now takes place in the context of open voluntary acceptance. We clearly recognize the importance of indigenous medicine and alternative healing techniques in the developing world. However, one can argue that in the event of a massive flood in Bangladesh, which often brings in its wake epidemics such as cholera, both officials and critical intellectuals will unconditionally accept vaccines from Germany or the USA without debating the possible hegemonic quality of "Western" medical science. A less dramatic example is the popularity of certain "indigenous" types of Chinese medicine (Tiger balm, for example) in countries such as India and Bangladesh; these provide further evidence of the same pragmatic actions. When it comes to intercultural borrowing and the diffusion of knowledge, people often make choices that are based on pragmatic calculations; they are not simply cowed into ideological submissiveness by hegemonic medical regimes. An illustration of pragmatic borrowing from Western medical technology can be found in the case of Japan, a process that preceded both the Meiji Restoration and the arrival of Commodore Perry in 1853, when Japan started to borrow Western (in this case Dutch) knowledge of medical science to combat an epidemic of cholera. At the same time, Japan was embracing Western military technology – mainly gunnery – as early as the 1840s (Najita, 1993: 26). An even earlier example of such borrowing of medical knowledge can be found in the popularity of the work of Ibn-Sina, or Avicenna as he was known in Europe. Born in present-day Uzbekistan, some of his important contributions included discerning meningitis as a distinct illness, the contagious nature of tuberculosis, the real cause of asthma, the significance of the optic nerve, and the discovery of various drugs through experimentation (Nasr, 2003). In 1980, UNESCO celebrated the one-thousandth anniversary of Ibn-Sina's birth.

The view that social theories reflect certain politico-economic designs in a linear fashion is patently naïve. James Petras (1993: 145) asserts that "One of the great deceptions of our times is the notion of 'internationalization' of ideas, markets and movements. It has become fashionable to evoke terms like 'globalization', or 'internationalization' to justify attacks on any or all forms of solidarity, community, and/or social values." Even if one overlooks the irony that Petras is arguing for the protection of "community" and "social values", it is clearly evident that he is taking a simplistic and unproblematic slogan rather than the notion of globalization to task. The imperial role of the United States, which has become more glaringly obvious in the post-Cold War world, also has its apologists. We are not ruling out the official "diplomatically correct" points of view. But they are points of view that often embellish quasi-official publications in the United States. They are surely not objective theoretical statements. The disjuncture between the space where discourse takes place and the theoretical or, more generally, intellectual tendencies themselves is also a feature in the process of globalization. For example, Noam Chomsky's critical works abundantly document the imperialistic ventures of the US government and business in the so-called "new world order" (Chomsky, 1994). It is, however, at the same time worth stressing that such a critical discourse is possible in the United States (but not everywhere) and this ironic fact indicates a certain autonomy on the part of intellectual culture. Edward Said was also a vocal critic of the imperialistic designs of the United States and used his enormous intellectual force to expose the underlying assumptions of Orientalism. Now to hold Said's location in the centre of world capitalism against him – as Ahmad (1992) does – would be a denial of the possibility of some distance between geographical space and the intellectual world. Homelessness and fluidity are the essence of contemporary – post-colonial – intellectual practices and praxes. The very mobility of modern intellectuals means that they do not invariably speak from or on behalf of a specific domain.

However, we are not saying that the possibility of intellectual hegemony does not exist. It does. But such ideas as "cultural imperialism", "colonization of mind" and "enslaved imagination" are to be treated with more care than they have in the past. Leonard Binder (1988) makes a distinction between "good", "bad" and "pragmatic orientalism" in Said's "oriental discourse". Clifford Geertz's study of Islam might be taken as an example of "good Orientalism". The problem is that a wholesale attack on Orientalism has led to the development of a "reverse orientalist discourse" which can sometimes manifest in what Abaza and Stauth (1990) call "going native". The counter-discourse which we can refer to as Occidentalism is often a mirror image of the Orientalist discourse. In attacking the moral high-handedness of the metropolitan intellectual, it situates itself on an equally high moral ground.

An Orientalist from a metropolitan location or a nativist from the periphery can no longer be easily located within a specific geographical grid. A spatial definition of knowledge is predicated upon the creation of a "good us" versus "bad them" dichotomy which rules out the possibility of home-grown or indigenous fascists and other such odious reactionary tendencies. Yet those tendencies are too glaring to overlook. They include the Hindu fundamentalists in India such as Bajrang Dal, a party credited with a whole range of activities from moral policing to attacking Christians, or Shiva Sena, whose leader Balasaheb Thackeray publicly glorified Adolf Hitler. The negative and violent role of Talibans in Afghanistan and some parts of Pakistan is well known.

The attendant problem of cultural relativism, which such binary distinctions create, leads eventually to a more pernicious political and moral relativism. An escape from a binary framework to a more pluralistic understanding of the social, cultural milieu is a necessity even for political/moral reasons. Relativism disarms us from criticizing each other, thereby fore-closing the possibility of learning from each other (Jarvie, 1983). Relativism might allow one to repudiate the Other – as both the colonial and now the reverse colonial discourses indicate. In the binary world-view *difference* is the root metaphor which entails competing rationalities. As S.P. Mohanty (1989: 13) argues:

> But the issue of competing rationalities raises a nagging question: how do we negotiate between my history and yours? How would it be possible for us to recover our commonality, not the ambiguous imperial-humanist myth of our shared human attributes, which are supposed to distinguish us all from animals, but more significantly, the imbrications of our various pasts and presents, the ineluctable relationships of shared and contested meanings, values, material resources? It is necessary to assert our dense particularities, our lived and imagined differences; but could we afford to leave untheorized the question of how our differences are intertwined and, indeed, hierarchically organized? Could we, in other words, afford to have *entirely* different histories, to see ourselves as living – and having lived – in entirely heterogeneous and discrete spaces?

One prominent weakness of Orientalism has been its tendency towards conflation. Amartya Sen (1993) suggests that there are, at least, three modes of non-Indian discourses on India: the exoticist, the magisterial and the investigative. It is important to stress the varieties and nuances of the so-called "Western discourse" about non-Western societies so that the pernicious condescending and insulting (mis)representations can be separated from the more plausible and positive approaches.

The history of colonialism demonstrates various examples of cultural subjugation and violence, and yet one primary objection to the simplistic and unreflective acceptance of the notion of "cultural imperialism" is that it denies the role of agency. Moreover, notions of imperialism and domination entail intentionality, whereas globalization as a process is more unintentional and amorphous. In the words of John Tomlinson (1991:175):

> Globalization may be distinguished from imperialism in that it is a far less coherent or culturally directed process. For all that, it has an ambiguous location between the economic and political senses: nevertheless the idea of imperialism at least contains the notion of a purposeful project, namely the intended spread of a social system from one centre of power across the globe.

The idea of globalization suggests the interconnection and interdependency of all global areas rather than their purposeful organization. It comes about as the result of economic and cultural practices which do not, of themselves, aim at global integration, but which nonetheless in some sense produce it. This is, however, not to suggest that the whole process is teleological – a history unfolding itself towards a predetermined endpoint such as a global and even homogeneous world.

It can be argued that a spatial or geographically specific hegemony has been supplanted by a disciplinary hegemony. The hegemonic rise of the discipline of economics over other social sciences has taken place concurrently with the definition of the world in primarily economic terms (Markoff and Montecinos 1993). The rise of economics as a discipline and of economic presuppositions in sociology illustrates the force of economic globalization. Rather than advancing a defence for the Western social sciences, we are simply trying to establish that a globalization approach is not a camouflaged attempt to establish the hegemony of "Western" social theory, culture or ideology. And this can be done by turning to the so-called "non-Western" part of the world. The use of the quotation marks suggests that we are using yet also underscoring the essentialist qualities of these categories. In the world today, we are all implicated by and in globalization.

THE PROBLEMATIC RELATIONSHIP BETWEEN UNIVERSALIZATION AND GLOBALIZATION

Can the expansion of the global field be equated with the march of universalization in the traditional Enlightenment sense? The idea of the march of universalization in both spatial and cultural terms was one of the clarion calls of modernization theories, which unfortunately also turned out to be its theoretical Achilles' heel. Many critics pointed out that what was billed as the "universal" was in reality the "particular" culture of the West. Universalization was, in that sense, the world-wide spread of Western particularistic culture. The idea of universalization was an accompaniment to the notion of progress that had been nurtured by the idea of Enlightenment. A critical evaluation of the Enlightenment project provided another opportunity to challenge universalistic ambitions. A simplistic, yet popular, view of globalization tends to conflate globalization with homogenization. For example, one writer claims that:

> Cultural globalizing tendencies are most evident in the common core syllabuses that have spread across the globe. Schoolchildren,

whether they be in Islamic Iran, Croatia, or the Basque Country, learn
to master the same basic mathematics, physics, chemistry and
biology. As an orientation to the world, this common global socialization
provides strong constitutive elements for a core commonality.
(Goonatilake, 1995: 229)

This is a clear and empirically valid statement, but then to conclude
from this that "[t]hese ongoing processes of cultural globalization are
tending to wipe out local cultural identities" (1995: 229) is an unwarranted
exaggeration.

There is no denying the fact that there are certain homogenizing
tendencies at work at the global level, but one need not equate globalization theory with earlier homogenization theory, a theory that has its
Marxist as well as liberal varieties. The duality and the conflictual relationship between *locality* and *globality* that a misreading of globalization
theory yielded have been largely redressed by the introduction of the
concept of *glocalization* by Robertson (1995). To what extent globalization theory embodies a universalist position is an issue that cannot be
discussed here in any great detail. We share the minimalist theory of universality of (moral) values – "truth" and "justice" – proposed by Michael
Walzer (1994) as a take-off point. In a more philosophical sense, Walzer,
while retaining the duality of "particular" and "universal", seeks to transcend it by advancing both the notion of minimal morality and the politics of difference at the same time. Drawing upon the difference
between society and humanity, Walzer (1994: 8) writes:

Societies are necessarily particular because they have members and
memories, members with memories not only of their own but also of
their common life. Humanity, by contrast, has members but no memory, and so it has no history and no culture, no customary practices,
no familiar life-ways, no festivals, no shared understanding of social
goods. It is human to have such things, but there is no singular human
way of having them. At the same time, the members of all the different
societies, because they are human, can acknowledge each other's different ways, respond to each other's cries for help, learn from each
other, and march (sometimes) in each other's parades.

Here obviously Walzer proposes a pluralistic world-view in conso-
nance with the ideals of liberalism. Although we do not want to deviate
too much from this pluralistic intent, we suggest that a number of the
common concerns of humanity can be shown to have a "shared understanding", if not some shared festivals or celebrations. Issues such as ecological degradation, epidemics such as AIDS, gender equality, cultural

rights, etc. have clearly become common concerns of humanity. Earth Day and United Nations Day are also celebrated world-wide. Global conferences on the environment (the Rio conference of 1992) or the World Conferences on Women in Nairobi in 1985 and in Beijing in 1995 illustrate these common underpinnings of a global consensus. The impact of globalization on local contexts cannot be seen to be simply an erasure of local traditions, nor can the local be recreated as an imaginary land. Even those who are concerned about the adverse effects of globalization on the local are quick to issue warnings against the fabulation of the local, because such an attempt might resurrect and legitimize primitive oppression and exploitation. The local can be the site of resistance and liberation, but also a predicament (Dirlik, 1997: 85). When ideas of resistance are invoked, it raises the need for a moral compass to separate a life worth living, and thus fighting for, from what is unacceptable and loathsome. The idea of measuring progress does not become entirely inappropriate or obsolete.

One problem with earlier modernization theory was its inability to conceptualize progress adequately, including its uncritical acceptance of a unilinear view of progress. In the face of endless theoretical onslaughts against the idea of progress, it is a challenging task to salvage it. In our opinion, Therborn's (1995) discussion of four routes towards modernization – the European, the New World's, self-imposed, and modernization by conquest – is helpful in its emphasis on the plurality of the concept. On the issue of progress, Sztompka's (1990) view of a progressive theory of progress based on the principles of self-evaluation and self-correction can be incorporated into a globalization approach. The problems concerning the universal versus the particular and rationality versus relativism can also be negotiated intellectually by adhering to the minimalist position that Walzer recommends or by arguing for a position of weak or flexible absolutism, or what may be called a reflexive universalism. A reflexive universalism must be based on an adherence to a minimum set of common ground rules which would allow for sensitivity to the local traditions, norms and institutions. A reflexive universalist position would allow for negotiation and rational discussion among competing claimants of rationality. Such debates and discussions are pivotal for ensuring some minimal conditions for social justice on a global basis. A reflexive universalist position takes the local context very seriously. Though sensitive to local context, it is not context-dependent rationality.

Let us take the example of recent discussions of women's rights in the so-called Islamic societies. Now to talk about "Islamic society" as a single category would be an error and empty of reflexivity. The so-called Islamic societies are so varied in terms of both time and space, as are the conditions of the women who live in those societies, as to render any generalization almost meaningless. Women in Libya undergo military training, whereas their counterparts in Afghanistan are literally excluded from public life. Yet in such diverse conditions, one can find the presence of a global discourse of women's rights. Under the rule of the Taliban, Afghan women stand to lose their basic rights to education. In Saudi Arabia, Amnesty International is involved in helping Saudi women to gain basic rights. Saudi women remain socially and politically excluded, yet economically engaged. The negotiation process is complex and can only be done if a good deal of sensitivity is shown towards these local conditions. In Iran – which presents a very interesting case – while the Islamic guards prowl the streets to enforce a ban on lipstick (Milani, 1999), some of the high-level leaders write essays on women's emancipation. The debates around democracy and women's rights in Iran command particular attention because of their autonomous nature. Reformist leaders in Iran draw inspiration from their indigenous religious and cultural traditions. Milani (1999) makes the interestingly ironic statement that "In Iran, nothing is what it seems to be. There are layers upon layers of meaning attached to every word, to every gesture, to every action." This observation is applicable to a wide range of societies, not only Muslim societies, under global conditions.

CONCLUSION

Plurality and reflexivity are not only key attributes of the contemporary world that we inhabit, but also the hallmarks of the concept of globalization that we employ to make sense of that world. The availability of multiple discourses, controversies, debates and new intellectual battle-grounds on globalization points to a complex and non-linear reality. Recognition of and respect for disparate discourses of globalization demonstrate anything but its hegemonic intent. Globalization does not mean the removal or erasure of local culture. Local cultures under the conditions of globality have become as important as global culture itself. Local culture does not surrender itself unproblematically to forces from outside; rather it absorbs as it valorizes its own distinctiveness. At the turn of the twenty-first century, what is local and what is global are becoming increasingly uncertain. The near-erasure of the distinction between the local and the global as spatial categories has given way to a disjuncture between conceptual and spatial polarities.

How globalization as a process works out both institutionally and culturally depends to a large extent on local conditions. The reconstitution of locality takes place in due recognition to the fact that local culture, like any culture anywhere, is not a timeless structure; it changes, gathering strength by incorporating and indigenizing traditions from far and near in the truest spirit of cosmopolitanism.

To conceptualize globalization in a more meaningful, and thus useful way, we must transcend binary modes of thinking. It is no longer either tradition or modernity, but the fusion of the traditional and the modern. It is no longer either global or local, rather it is global and local simultaneously (or "glocal" in Robertson's terminology). Cosmopolitanism, hybridity, pastiche, *mélange* and "multihistoricality" are the terms that come to mind in describing this process. A national citizen, whether of Singapore or South Korea, today has the potential to become a truly cosmopolitan citizen, to borrow a Kantian phrase. And that very possibility is courtesy of globalization. Robertson (1987b), in his original formulation, conceptualized the global circumstance as the global-human condition which includes individuals, societies, relations between societies and (in the generic sense) humankind as the major contemporary components or dimensions of that condition. This conceptualization very adequately captures the liberating potential of globalization without being naïve about its destructive qualities. In short, one must remain open-minded about the direction of the unfolding process of globalization.

3   STRUCTURES AND PROCESSES OF GLOBALIZATION

INTRODUCTION

In order to discuss the structures and processes of globalization, the topic of this chapter, we need to secure some minimal agreement on what globalization is. Many discussions of globalization do not even define globalization, at least directly, assuming that its meaning is self-evident. A study of attitudes towards globalization by Gallup International viewed globalization as "the increased trade between countries in goods, services and investment". Many people unfortunately use this simplistic economic definition without any elaboration. In an opinion poll released in October 2007, the Pew Global Attitudes Project (2007) found that "The publics of the world broadly embrace key tenets of economic globalization." Support for free trade ranged from 59 per cent in the United States to 90 per cent in Bangladesh and 91 per cent in China and Malaysia. Seventy per cent in the USA, 72 per cent in Britain, 75 per cent in China and 76 per cent in India agreed with the statement that "people are better off in a free market economy". In the Pew survey, the definition of economic globalization was based on favourable views on trade, the positive role of foreign companies and the free market economies.

According to another index, from Switzerland's Zurich University's Centre for Research in Economics, Management and the Arts, that measured economic openness and attractiveness as well as political dimensions of globalization, it was found that the United Arab Emirates is the most globalized Arab country, ranking 35th in the world. Belgium is the world's most globalized country, followed by Austria, Sweden, Switzerland, Denmark, the Netherlands and the United Kingdom (*Gulf News,* 13 January 2008, Business, p. 37). *Foreign Policy* magazine ranked Singapore as the most globalized country in the world in 2007, followed by Hong

Kong, the Netherlands, Switzerland and Ireland. In all these rankings, economic openness, business-friendliness and other economic indicators dominate, thereby reinforcing the notion that globalization is, in the first instance, an economic process.

Both protagonists and critics of globalization often see it as the global spread of capitalism. The critics who see globalization as the march of neo-liberal capitalism devoid of moral restraints and destroying everything in its path seem to have the upper hand in the debate in view of the economic crisis of 2008–9. By contrast, the protagonists who support globalization as the last hope for civilization and as the march of modernization and rationalization appear to be on the defensive. Unsurprisingly, globalization is one of the most contentious terms in the first decade of the twenty-first century. It is blamed for everything from environmental degradation and religious fundamentalism to the global economic crisis of 2008–9 and the earlier Asian economic crisis of 1997. Both crises have been associated with market fundamentalism. To blame globalization for both of these crises and at the same time to give credit to globalization for economic growth at breakneck speed in China or India before the current economic crisis is not very convincing. It would be easier to agree with Karl Marx that periodic economic crises are built into the very nature of capitalism. Hence an economic crisis is not so much a crisis of globalization as such but a crisis of global capitalism. Equating globalization simply with global capitalism is reductionism and does not help us to understand the complexities of this process.

It may be useful to examine these processes both at the level of the whole society as well as at the levels of various spheres of society. For example, one could talk about the impact of the open-door trade policy on the American economy, which of course has several social and cultural effects, or one could keep the discussion strictly at the level of economics (as most professional economists do). Or one could discuss the impact of Eastern religion such as Buddhism or the Hare Krishna movement on American spirituality, or the impact of Chinese cuisine on contemporary American food habits. In recent years, Bollywood movies in London have been enjoyed not only by diasporic Indians and Pakistanis but also by an English audience. Chicken tikka has become a household food in Britain, while "sushi" has become the choice of the New York elite. Yet evidence of early transactions in culture and economy is visible though not often featured in the discussion of cultural globalization.

We propose the following schemas arguing that globalization is an old process, but the twenty-first-century version of globalization has certain nuances that need to be recognized. There are several journalistic contributions that ignore the historical roots of the structures and processes of globalization. Many see globalization as nothing but runaway capitalism or 'casino capitalism' dominated by the United States. It is not surprising, then, that globalization is often used – at least, by its critics – to mean Americanization. Furthermore, many critics of globalization equate it with the spread of US imperialism. Such images are not helpful for a deeper understanding of the structure and processes of globalization. Suffice it to say here that globalization is a multidimensional process of change that involves increased connectivity across economies and societies, creating a greater awareness of the globe as a common point of reference. It is a process that makes the world a single place (Robertson, 1992).

Making the world a single place or society involves both objective or material changes on the one hand and subjective or non-material changes on the other. At one level we need to consider the technologies, social institutions, economic processes and the movement of people as driving forces of globalization. At another level we need to take into account changes in awareness, ideas, ideologies and norms that influence societies in various regions of the world. Even in thinking about local and national development, we cannot avoid keeping our focus on the larger global framework. In other words, globalization is a process which can be defined abstractly or concretely. An abstract definition is provided by Robertson as "a compression of the world and an awareness of that com-pression". John Tomlinson (1999) calls it "complex connectivity" and Goran Therborn (2000b) calls it a social process encompassing the world. A concrete definition is provided by Immanuel Wallerstein who looks at that world as a system which has been in the making for the past 600 years. The world has been economically integrated and has become a highly interconnected and interdependent system through these historical developments starting in the seventeenth century.

We view structures in the sense of historian Fernand Braudel, not after some fashionable notions in social science where one often encounters terms such as "structuralism", "post-structuralism" and so on. By "social structure" we mean the durable features of society such as the institutions shaping the everyday life of people. We explore both the durable relations between insti-tutions and the ways in which those institutions have shaped the everyday life experience of people – their mentalities, habits, values, preferences, choices and actions. In this sense, globalization is a process but it is also a condition (Harvey, 2000). It is important to identify the processes as well as the struc-tures of globalization in order to understand the dynamics of this condi-tion. Minimally, we can consider globalization at two levels: abstract and concrete. At the concrete level changes that have been taking place over centuries are quite tangible; these include politico-economic transformations that Immanuel Wallerstein (1974), following Karl Marx and Fernand Braudel, calls the world systems; technological and scientific diffusions that have taken place in both directions from the East to the West and back to the East; and changes in the social institutions. Transformations in the abstract relate to changes at the level of consciousness (Robertson, 1992) and the capacity to widen the cultural repertoire that led to the idea of "world civilization", "one world" and such notions as universality, and "our common future as human society".

The processes of globalization can also be conceptualized as occurring both at the superficial or surface level as well as at the level of the deep structure of society. Most writers tend to focus on the perceptible, surface-level phenomena, such as contemporary borrowings of everyday practices, life-styles, habits, aspirations, "best practices" of corporate management and elements of popular culture which run the whole gamut from fast food to healthy food, from "Facebook" to "Twitter". What is less often discussed in the popular discourse is the transformation at the deeper structures of society formed in layers of cultural and institutional exchanges over time. These include historically embedded, localized, indigenized, imperceptible sharing of rationality and the technology of social organization, ideas of nation-state, systems of jurisprudence, sports, and systems of education, arts and literature.

It is too easy intellectually to use the spread of McDonald's or Disney cartoons – products of popular culture – as examples of the consequences of globalization, while at the same time failing to see Islam in China and India or Christianity in Africa and South America as examples of globalization. The same can be said about trade. Of course, the Arab traders came to sell their wares in Southeast Asia several centuries ago. The Silk Route was discovered and used by traders to go to China, and later the maritime Silk Route paved the way for the spread of Islam. Cross-cultural migrations of people, ideas, technology and religion are some of the historical examples of globalization affecting the deep structures of society. It is important to draw a distinction between inter-societal connections of the past and modern globalization. After a period of treating globalization in some ahistorical fashion by many writers who date these global phenomena from as recently as the 1990s, there are now a number of authors who offer a more adequate history of globalization in which, for instance, they identify the origins of these movements with preachers, traders, warriors and adventurers (Chandra, 2007). We suggest that, although it is useful to look at globalization in phases, the earlier, pre-capitalist phase of globalization should be more adequately understood as a form of cultural diffusion preparing the foundations of subsequent globalization. Here, the critical cultural variable of globalization, a consciousness of the globe as a whole, was yet to be formed.

The drawing of early maps of the world by the seafaring traders can be seen as an early encounter with the idea of the globe, but it is not evident that such encounters gave rise to a global consciousness. Besides, the carto- graphical map itself was often limited by the mental map. The sense of glob- ality encompassing the entire globe and our membership of a global community had to be a later development:

> Two dates – 1494 and 1969 – stand out as important moments in the history of the world as a global place. ... Since the fifteenth century, people have slowly come to think of the world as a global place. This process was aided by the widespread use of maps and globes in schoolrooms. ... [In 1969] the astronauts' photographs of the earth gave currency to the idea of the world as a global place. (Schaffer, 1997: 10–11)

ON THE COMPLEXITY AND DIVERSITY OF THE GLOBAL WORLD

It is important to weave into the analytical framework the blending of the abstract and the concrete and to integrate the deep structures with surface- level phenomena. The following examples will illustrate these processes where structures or institutional linkages and global flows reinforce each other. Let us take the example of the globalization of sports. Football, in particular, provides the intersection of both "increasing subjective aware- ness of the world as a single place" (Robertson, 2002) and global inten- sification of social and cultural connectivity through telecommunications and international travel (Tomlinson, 1999; Giulianotti and Robertson, 2004). Some writers have examined the spread of cricket and its impact on diverse social contexts both as a civilizing process and as subverting the local divisions and hierarchies. Although the spread of cricket was part of an imperial project, it played a role in mobilizing nations to oppose colo- nial domination and in creating grounds for democracy. Sport as a marker of globalization presents both the complexities and intermingling of culture and economy, as well as culture and politics. In the colonial set- ting, the colonial elites, comfortable in their privileged social location, allowed the lower classes to play the "game that paid symbolic homage to British cultural and political hegemony; in fact, elites tended to regard cricket as a good means of 'civilizing' natives in their own image" (Kaufman and Patterson, 2005: 99). In post-independence India, cricket, though originally an elite game, became a national sport to the extent that

Ashish Nandy went so far as to claim that cricket is an Indian game, accidentally invented in England.

The dominance of England, the putative birthplace of cricket, has been challenged successfully by former colonies such as Australia, the West Indies, India, Pakistan and Sri Lanka. The sport's governing body, the International Cricket Council, founded in 1909 in England, was moved to Dubai in 2005 in part for tax reasons. With the growing commercialization of the game, as a result of its increased audience through television and big-budget television advertisements, the centre of cricket has moved to India, where professional cricket players earn huge sums. A shorter version of the game, known as "Twenty20", which is more suited to the fast pace of a modern lifestyle today, is played in India under the banner of the Indian Professional League where players from all over the world come to play for various glocal teams. In the early days with this new format, the high-budget game, in which many of the clubs are owned by Bollywood movie stars or the business tycoons of India, was criticized by puritan cricket lovers, who raised all kinds of objections to the "glamorization" of a classic game. Virulent objections were raised to the introduction of cheer-leaders in the style of American football, and many cricket devotees in India thought it was sacrilegious.

Growing awareness of the process of globalization is the result of the intensification of many social processes and transactions which have become increasingly visible as a result of modern technology. Take the example of migration. In traditional societies, people did migrate from one place to another but mobility was limited by very practical issues of transport. In the contemporary world, people come and go relatively frequently; some return to their point of origin and others move on to new places. The number of migrants has increased as much as the frequency of travel. Earlier theories of migration with an economic slant have been supplemented by in-depth, ethnographic understanding of the process (Constable, 1997, 1999; Gamburd, 2008). The neo-classical economic theory of migrant behaviour observed that migrants move short distances, they move from agriculture to commerce and industry, migration increases with industrialization and improvements in transport, and the main cause is economic. Migration is typically a consequence of (negative) push and (positive) pull factors. In this economic framework, migration was seen to be voluntary and rational: high-wage economies attract workers from low-wage economies. Marxist economic explanations saw migration as mobilizing cheap labour for capitalism. These theories not only fail to account for the cultural and human dimensions of migration but also neglect (a) government policies on the flow of migration, ranging from total exclusion and differential exclusion to assimilation and pluralism; and

(b) the role of migration chains and how networks shape individual choices. It is also useful to distinguish types of migrants: (a) economic and voluntary (migrant workers); (b) political and involuntary (Jews to Israel and Palestinians out of Palestine); (c) economic and involuntary (famine and ecological disaster); and (d) political and voluntary, as migrants often escape oppressive regimes for democracies.

However, the character of migration is changing rapidly with globalization, the partial liberalization of the labour market, protection of workers through the International Labor Organization (ILO), and the greying of the populations of the advanced societies. Globalization is creating new opportunities for trafficking in persons, such as the sexual enslavement of women from the former Soviet satellites and the trafficking of women in Southeast Asia. A new form of slavery characterizes the condition of migrant labourers in some parts of the world.

Migration is associated with the development of multiculturalism, because migration tends to create cultural diversity, especially where migrants come together in more or less stable enclaves or ghettos. Multiculturalism, for instance, was part of the political doctrine of liberal America for much of the twentieth century, and during the Cold War America emphasized the cultural significance of the Statue of Liberty which has for decades welcomed the alienated, exploited and dispossessed peoples of the world. In recent years this creed has been seriously challenged by neo-conservatives, because black Americans suffered so profoundly in the past from slavery, they have not experienced the same social mobility enjoyed by other ethnic communities who have prospered in the American Dream. Some conservative critics argue that repairing this historical problem of black America is beyond the scope of current social policy. The election of President Obama may help change some of these deep-seated attitudes. Yet history cannot be sidelined and its role cannot be downplayed in our understanding of the contemporary world with its multitude of problems.

As a process, globalization is often associated with financial deregulation and the neo-liberal revolution of the late 1970s. The collapse of communism around 1989–92 appeared to support the triumphal claims of capitalism and its necessary association with democratic reforms. However, the Asian financial crisis, growing inequality between societies, economic crises in Latin America, environmental pollution, the collapse of the e-economy bubble, the Enron scandal and the contemporary financial crisis raised major questions about the neo-liberal strategy and its champions (the World Bank and the IMF). Joseph Stiglitz's *Globalization and its Discontents* (2002) articulated widespread anxiety about the negative effects of economic globalization. Many societies that accepted IMF guidelines (or had them imposed) appeared to fail – Argentina and Venezuela. By contrast, India and China, which avoided the "Washington Consensus", have enjoyed sustained economic development. Opposition to globalization has given rise to many social movements expressing concerns over the environment, the decline of public institutions and the negative social and health consequences of privatization.

Economic historians have often reminded us of the volatility of commodity prices and its impact on economies far away. The Tulip crisis of Holland in 1636–7 presents a classic case. The price of tulip bulbs soared due to a frenzy among speculators, and when it collapsed in 1637 it ruined many. The impact was felt not only in the Netherlands but also in the rest of Europe, jeopardizing the entire credit system. In the context of a globalized world, soaring prices of fuel and food – two essential commodities – affected the entire world in a remarkably short period in 2008-9. The extreme volatility in commodity prices is one of the features of contemporary economic globalization. Unlike in the past, the effects of volatility are felt world-wide in a globalized economy. Although at the beginning of 2008, there was a huge increase in oil and wheat prices, by the end of 2008 and into 2009 there was a global slump in basic commodity prices. For example, soybean prices plunged by around 40 per cent between July 2008 and February 2009. In Argentina, where soybean production became a successful component of agricultural exports, there were several years of good harvests and rising prices between 2003 and 2008. The growth rate in Argentina was on average around 5 per cent, creating the basis for significant foreign investment, but the eventual collapse in prices was also accompanied by the worst drought in seventy years. The collapse in soybean prices was followed by those of copper and oil, bringing about a sudden end to economic development. This combination of environmental disaster – in this case drought – and problematic price volatility is likely to remain a feature of developmental problems for the foreseeable future.

When, in the name of maintaining cultural purity, right-wing religious groups such as the *Ram Sena* (soldiers of the Lord Rama) in India attack Valentine's Day celebrations, beating up love-birds for allegedly transgressing Indian culture, they insult the rich Indian tradition of the display of intimacy memorialized in the Indian religious lore of the flute-playing Lord Krishna and his exploits with Radha, or the amorous cave paintings of Elora and Ajanta. The historical spread of the world religions, which was the first globalizing force, explains why there is Hinduism in Bali, Islam in Indonesia and Buddhism in South Korea. Historical inter-cultural communication (sometimes through colonial institutions) in some instances has changed the deep structure of society. The spread of Victorian moral values in many colonial societies provided the basis of gender segregation as much as older religions do. The institutionalization of the rule of law and acceptance of the principle of equality in a deeply hierarchical society are some important examples. The idea of equality has been widely embraced, giving rise to movements for democracy and feminism in many cultures around the world. The traffic has been mostly from core to periphery, but sometimes reverse traffic has also occurred, as in the case of democracy. Consider the fact that women in New Zealand could exercise their voting rights long before their counterparts in the United States or that women in India could vote before women in Switzerland (Markoff, 1996).

The Conditions of Globalization

There are many accounts of the conditions of globalization. Perhaps the most influential has been concerned to understand the spread of information technology, especially the Internet, and its impact on finance, economic development, education and the military. Marshall McLuhan in the 1960s anticipated contemporary debates in his *Understanding Media* (1964), seeing the world as "the global village". In contemporary sociology, the most general and important theory in this field has been produced by Manuel Castells (1996). What are the implications of global knowledge for the economy, social networks and higher education? What are the implications of new forms of pedagogy for technologies of the self? The Internet creates new opportunities for political participation, and social theorists have studied the possibility of global civil society and global governance. One important dimension of globalization has been the development of human rights institutions and human rights culture. Early theories of democratic globalization were optimistic, but 9/11 and its aftermath have presented an alternative, pessimistic future. The so-called "war on terror" undermined the spread of the idea of respect for human rights globally.

Some theories emphasize globalization as standardization or rationalization. George Ritzer's theory of McDonaldization is perhaps the classic example. Standardization theories are often seen as Americanization, but anthropological research (Appadurai, 1996) indicates that local cultures survive globalization, occasionally producing syncretic or hybrid cultures. Other authors such as Roland Robertson (1995) and Jan Nederveen Pieterse (1995) draw attention to the hybridity and heterogeneity of global/local cultures. In part we can see this debate as a conflict between Ritzer's emphasis on standardization and growing conformity, and Ulrich Beck and others who see late modernity or globalization producing more risk, uncertainty and complexity. In part, this apparent contradiction is resolved by looking at the interaction between the local and the global in the concept of "glocalization" (Robertson, 1995). One can at one level celebrate globalization as a cultural *mélange* by showing examples of a Latin American banker in New York with a liking for sushi. It may be pointed out that to equate "sushi" with Japanese food or "chicken tikka" with Indian cuisine also involves what some critics call "essentializing" (a reductionist or overly simplified view) a culture. Japanese cuisine is surely more than just "sushi", just as Indian cuisine is more than "chicken tikka". Both Indian and Chinese cuisine have many regional and local varieties. A Chinese visitor to Dhaka, the capital of Bangladesh, would not recognize Chinese food as Chinese food because it has been so much indigenized that it has lost its Chinese authenticity.

As globalization creates new opportunities, it also brings forth new challenges. The globalization of disease provides a dramatic illustration of the dangers of global social change. The globalization of transport and migration means that diseases no longer have specific geographical locations. The spread of HIV/AIDS from the 1980s is a major example. The SARS outbreak in 2003 and the H1N1 (so-called swine flu) pandemic of 2009 illustrated the speed of modern infections, but there have been less dramatic but equally deadly outbreaks of Ebola, West Nile virus, Marburg virus and Lassa fever. There has been a return of traditional conditions such as tuberculosis and malaria. These new health problems clearly demonstrate the interconnected nature of global society. In order to understand these changes, we also need to examine the impact of local circumstances on these global developments.

We will explore the prevalence of disasters and their consequences in the context of globalization. The forces of globalization may exacerbate or help alleviate consequences of disasters, depending on social and political contexts. Empirical references will be drawn from famines and famine response in Ethiopia, and the tsunami in South and Southeast Asia.

WARS AND MILITARY CONFLICTS

In the recent sociology of the military, there has been an important debate about the distinction between old and new wars that provides a valuable insight into ethnic cleansing and genocide. In particular, the concept of new wars is helpful in thinking about the increased vulnerability of women in civil conflicts. In the old wars waged between states, the majority of casualties were military personnel; in new wars, the casualties are almost entirely civilian. New wars often involve the merging of sexual excitement and physical violence; this merger has been described as the "sexualization" of violence. The other characteristic of such wars is the growing use of children as cheap combat troops. These wars are in part the product of failed states and the reduced cost of military equipment, such as the widespread use of the Kalashnikov rifle. New wars have occurred in Afghanistan, Bosnia, Darfur, Rwanda, Burma, East Timor and the Sudan. There is also a rethinking of civil–military relations. In Western democratic states, military and civilian sectors of society maintain a clear-cut separation. There is another globalizing feature of such conflicts, namely the fusion of fact and fiction. Many films such as *Deer Hunter* (1978), *Apocalypse Now* (1979), *First Blood* (1982), *Platoon* (1986) and *Full Metal Jacket* (1987), in fusing violence, subcultural transgression and sex, provide models and images for real-life violence.

The globalization process is often made visible by its consequences. Events taken almost randomly from the crisis of Darfur in Sudan, the war in Afghanistan, the global economic crisis of 2008–9 or the earlier Asian economic crisis of the late 1990s, the Asian tsunami, the AIDS epidemic or the looming environmental crisis in China cannot be adequately analysed without reference to globalization. This is not to suggest that the only unit of analysis is the global process. Nation-states or local contexts are our immediate points of empirical contact with social reality. For example, as a consequence of the financial crisis originating in the United States with the collapse of some major banks in 2008, several mega-construction projects in Dubai have been scaled down, laying off a large number of temporary construction workers from Bangladesh and India who upon returning to their homelands have joined the ranks of multitudes of unemployed workers. These unemployed workers now returning to their countries of origin are exacerbating the problem of poverty. Thus the crisis is passed down from region to region, and from nation to nation, thereby devolving the responsibility for tackling the crisis to the respective national governments.

The world today is visited by wars, epidemics, disasters, religious and civilizational conflicts not unlike the problem of violence in the past. The main difference is that when, for example, in 1857 *sepoys* (soldiers) in India were revolting against their colonial English masters, it took several months for people in Britain and North America to find out what was happening. Today, satellite television channels such as CNN or Al-Jazeera would cover such a rebellion in a matter of hours with webcams beaming out the footage of rampaging soldiers. Yet this nineteenth-century rebellion – the so-called Indian Mutiny – was not just a local or national event. It also clearly had a global dimension since it was an uprising against the colonial rulers who came from another part of the world. The rebellion created a lively debate in the British Parliament, forcing changes in the policies of colonial administration and in the management of the British army. The framework of globalization helps us understand both contemporary as well as past issues. The difference lies in the immediacy, speed and volume of reportage and reactions.

GLOBALIZATION AS AMERICANIZATION

In any discussion of globalization, almost inevitably the point of reference is taken from the West. This has led to the mistaken notion that globalization is another name for so-called "Americanization". Amartya Sen (2002) argues that globalization is neither Western nor Eastern. He provides examples of the contributions of Indian mathematics and Arab sciences in the making of global scientific knowledge. Even if one considers everyday realities, in their general knowledge of the world American school students would be at a disadvantage *vis-à-vis* their counterparts in India or Egypt. A typical high-school student in India will have more knowledge about the world and America than an average American student possesses about the world and India. An Indian student is more likely to know the name of the US President than an American student is to know the name of the Indian Prime Minister or, for that matter, the Canadian Prime Minister next door. Herdsmen on the border of Tibet and villagers in Indonesia know about Obama from their mobile phones, but few Americans will know much about the military leadership of Burma or the name of Singapore's Prime Minister.

America is a major power, but in the foreseeable future that supremacy is likely to be overshadowed by other emerging economic and political powers. America may still have the largest bombers and the largest arsenal of nuclear warheads, but it does not produce the world's best or fastest cars. Nor does America hold the largest share of the automobile market in the world; China passed the United States in 2009 as the largest car market in the world. America may still be home to the world's largest corporations (Wal-Mart, Exxon and so on) but the fastest trains and the tallest buildings are all outside America's borders. Yet America has the world's best universities and continues to attract the world's brightest engineers, scientists and scholars to its shores. This knowledge dominance notwithstanding, the USA may be the least globalized country in the industrialized world.

Yet, in measuring social globalization even a highly regarded index such as the KOF of Switzerland employs indicators such as the presence of McDonald's and IKEA, and not knowledge and awareness of the world. It is only since the tragic events of 9/11that many Americans have taken a more active interest in the affairs of the world, especially of the Muslim world. But America continues to be provincial in its concerns and outlook when compared to European nations. A national football competition in the USA (which, by the way, is different from what is meant by "football" in the rest of the world) is called the World Championship. Many Americans also look at the United Nations with suspicion without realizing that, though falling short of many of its goals, the fumbling UN is based on the principles that are enshrined in the US Constitution.

Globalization is neither simply Americanization nor merely an economic process. Those who see the United States as the fount of global capitalism and neo-imperialism also locate Seattle, Washington, as the birthplace of the anti-globalization movement in 1999. These views deserve careful evaluation. Whether imperial or not, the USA has been the most dominant nation of the world since the end of the Second World War when the British Empire was already in its last throes, and it will remain so well into the present century. After the meltdown of the Soviet Union, the US became the sole superpower in the world. In fact, the process of US domination began to take shape at the end of the nineteenth century. Especially in the areas of scientific knowledge, technological innovation, cultural creativity and general innovation, the USA has no match. The phrase "Yankee ingenuity" is a truism. Yet America gets a lot of bad press – first locally and then internationally – for its inadequate medical system, failing schools, dysfunctional communities, homelessness and poverty – some of which was exposed during the lashing of Hurricane Katrina in Louisiana in 2005.

Yet, there are many other images of the United States in the world. The US Constitution and the Bill of Rights incorporate some of the best legal traditions and ideals of human freedom and dignity drawn from Enlightenment philosophies. These traditions remain models for peace- and freedom-loving people around the world. If one uses any of the major science indicators – whether research publications, patents for new innovations, or number of Nobel prizes, the USA enjoys the predominant position in the world. And if one examines carefully the dominance of the USA in the world of science and technology, it is a direct product of American openness to certain aspects of globalization, particularly migration. Of all the industrialized countries, according to international opinion polls, Americans are most tolerant of migrants. Yet, at a superficial level the US public often presents itself as suspicious of globalization. For example, in late June 2006 the United Nations organized a conference on small arms to highlight the problem of the illicit arms trade and the devastating effects on crime, narco-terrorism and terrorism. Although the UN General Secretary at that time, Kofi Annan, gave the reassurance that they were concerned with illegal weapons and were "not negotiating a global gun ban or denying law-abiding citizens their right to bear arms in accordance with their national laws", the National Rifle Association organized opposition to the conference by portraying it as an attack on the Second Amendment (*Washington Times*, 27 June 2006) and alleging that the UN was conspiring to take away the weapons of the American people, which led to an outpouring of patriotism in which the organizers received hate mail.

These attitudes are ironic given the importance of America in the development of human rights. Discussions of the historical growth of human rights often fail to give due credit to President Woodrow Wilson, who so well articulated the main ideas in the early twentieth century. The failure of the League of Nations was one of the main reasons for the subsequent debacle that led to genocide in Europe and the wars that followed. Although American statesmen like Abraham Lincoln and Woodrow Wilson, or writers like Mark Twain, or social activists like Martin Luther King are held in high esteem by the rest of the world, America has remained provincial in many respects and often backward in responding to globalization. America's parochialism has been most strongly criticized by American writers, columnists and thinkers themselves. America has been host to some of its most virulent critics, which indirectly shows the deeper pro-globalization that the USA represents. This observation is not to absolve the US role in world-wide wars, and American cruelty such as in Vietnam, Indo-China or more recently in Iraq, Afghanistan or in Guantánamo Bay. Yet, the anti-war movement, a social movement that questioned the actions of government, began in America. The torture and prisoner abuse at Abu Ghraib and Guantánamo Bay, the killing of civilians in Haditha in Iraq, and the My Lai incident in Vietnam were exposed by the American media such as the *Washington Post*, thanks to the actions of the late Seymour Hersh, an outspoken journalist, and the intervention of the US Supreme Court in calling the US President to account. One problem in these cases of cruelty was the suspension of the principle of the separation of powers, the corner-stone of American democracy. However, American democracy itself was sufficiently robust to check such derogation in the course of time with the election of new leadership.

GLOBALIZATION AS FLATTENING, SPIKING OR GOUGING

For Thomas Friedman (2005) the latest phase of globalization which he calls "globalization 3", began in 2000 with the Internet as the driving force, the catalyst. What are the main consequences of globalization? Again, for popular writers the answer is simple. For Friedman, the world is becoming flat, or, as another writer says, fat (Popkin, 2008). The world is becoming flat because now individuals are using the Internet to connect with each other globally. Richard Florida (2005), however, finds that the world is "spiky". The big cities around the world, which are home to com-puter geeks, corporate headquarters, universities and so on, are well con-nected with one another. However, many regions are located in valleys. The mountains and their peaks are well connected and becoming flat at the top. The Internet has created a veritable information revolution, which we can call information revolution 2. In the sixteenth century, information revolution 1 was caused by the invention and use of the print-ing press, which was accompanied by widespread literacy. According to the historian, Robert Darnton (2000), in eighteenth-century Paris, an early information society, information arrived through word of mouth and recording of news and gossip in Parisian cafés. For Darnton, each era in fact has its own information revolution. Alongside the metaphors of flatten-ing or spiking, gouging might be used to highlight many of the negative aspects of globalization. By "global gouging" we mean various cultural processes which disrupt, dislocate and occasionally expunge local or folk cultures by incorporating or reconceiving and reconstructing them. Through such gouging, local cultures can be lost or destroyed, not neces-sarily by direct or consciously brutal attacks but by subtle and gradual means. Gouging, then, is not an example of glocalization but rather a simple destruction of a dialect, or language, or religion. To coin a phrase, we might talk about total gouging as an example of "culturecide" as the cultural parallel of genocide. Cultural destruction has often occurred in many aboriginal societies in South America and Australia, but in the con-temporary world there are often processes to redress such cultural cata-strophes, normally through the work of UN agencies such as UNESCO or similar bodies.

CONCLUSION: GLOBALIZATION ISSUES

The discussion of globalization can best be framed in terms of a number of debates. Is globalization good or bad? Is it a curse or a blessing? It may seem somewhat simplistic, but this strategy would flesh out the complexities of the processes and the condition of globalization with all their contradictions. For example, is globalization leading to cultural standardization, erasing all the indigenous cultures in its path? Or, is globalization creating new syntheses of cultural forms in more pronounced and visible forms? Historically, cultures have been always admixtures. In terms of cultural products, the boundaries of the East and the West have become highly blurred. Yet, one of the major debates of our time, the social inequality debate, rages on and assumes renewed relevance in the face of our awareness of globalization. The critics of globalization put the responsibility for increasing inequality and poverty on the condition of globalization. Yet, others see globalization as a panacea for poverty and inequality. The solution to poverty and economic degradation for them lies not in less but in more globalization. Similar debates rage with regard to the relationship between globalization and the environmental crisis. Those who lead the alter-global movement (the alternative to globalization, rather than anti-globalization) denounce the idea of limitless, unsustainable economic growth. Others do not see it as a problem. In *Making Globalization Work* (2007), Stiglitz provides some useful public policy suggestions to help achieve global justice. After the euphoria of economic globalization and much of the discussion revolving around it, several writers are presently raising the issue of global justice, globalization with a human face, and an ethical economic system where markets will be moderated by democratic states and where global public institutions will offset the neo-liberal economic rampage.

Sociological theories have concentrated on the cultural causes and consequences of globalization. In recent years, the analysis of the cultural dimensions of globalization has been increasingly concerned with "civilizational conflicts", fundamentalism and religion. We will address the rise of "Islamic extremism" and the global debate over the relationship between religion and politics in our later discussion. The wars over these issues may stop but the tensions and conflicts will remain and will be recast in the language of multiculturalism, rights of citizens, gender issues and the broader issue of democratization at a global level. Globalization theory is likely to dominate sociology and related social sciences as the key perspective for much of the remaining decades of the twenty-first century. Social science views of our future are varied and complex. Some sociologists analyse globalization as global networks and social flows. Others focus on the structural properties of the world social system. Some see globalization as a relatively recent development (that is, from the late twentieth century). For others, it is a consequence of financial globalization in the 1970s, the increasing dominance of the Internet, the growth of the global labour market, and the erosion of the sovereignty of the nation-state. Others, such as Immanuel Wallerstein (1974) and Roland Robertson (1992), provide a more complex and historical narrative of globalization.

Neither the awareness of the world nor its system-like features are new. Greek philosophers had a keen interest in the issues beyond the local or the polis. The idea of *cosmopolis* is found in the Greek philosophers (Holton, 2009; Turner, 2009). When Ibn Khaldun, a Tunisian-born historian, philosopher and sociologist, attempted to write a universal history, he foreshadowed Niccolò Machiavelli, Karl Marx, Emile Durkheim and many other sociologists. The vision of the German poet Goethe was truly universal, and Tagore the Indian Nobel laureate was known – adoringly – in his own country as Bishwa Kabi or "global poet" long before the discussion of globalization began in Western academic writing. Amartya Sen points out that ideas such as tolerance, pluralism and secularism were the basis of the rule of Akbar, the Mughal emperor in the second half of the sixteenth century. At that time, in many parts of Europe, women accused of witchcraft were regularly burnt to death. Christopher Hill, the noted British historian, tells us that the rate of witch burning increased in the next century. One can find enlightened rulers like Darius I of Persia who made it his duty to look into the welfare of his subjects. Or we can mention the Andalusian ruler Mohammed I who was open to ideas and believed in pluralism. Without a sense of history, many take a crude, short-term and narrow view of social change and fail to see how many excellent ideas from the past have been ignored or suppressed. Many centuries later, we are still trying to say the things that have been said so eloquently in the past.

One of the problems with globalization studies is that now that it has become a fashionable subject, books on almost any topic from fashion to food are being given "globalization" or "global" as a prefix. The number of books with the title "Globalization of ..." is staggering, with titles ranging from *Globalization of Anti-trust* to the *Globalization of Martyrdom* and so on. We suggest that although globalization is a central force, a social process *par excellence*, everything that is happening in the world is not necessarily or automatically global. There are many issues that are strictly local or national or regional and yet some issues have become truly global. What is important about globalization is that it behoves us to recognize that today even a local or regional issue must be examined in the context of globalization. By 2009 it was clear that the river system running through the Murray-Darling basin in Australia might collapse leaving the final outlet in South Australia without water. This water crisis is local in the context of Australian politics, but it is global in the sense that Australian droughts have a profound effect on global wheat prices and an environmental crisis in Australia is not simply a national problem. This Australian example might be a perfect example for the slogan "Act locally, think globally".

In conclusion, a number of writers have returned to the theme of empire to understand the present situation, especially the place of the United States in theories of globalization. These empire studies draw heavily on political economy and the historical sociology of Marx and Weber to conceptualize the peculiarities of American power in the context of globalization.

4 GLOBALIZATION AND THE NATION-STATE

INTRODUCTION

The financial crisis of 2008, which unfolded with a dramatic bank collapse and the historic rescue of various financial institutions by governments, was preceded by a food crisis and an unusually sharp rise in the oil price. In July 2008 oil reached US$147 a barrel, but fell back to US$40 at year's end, exemplifying the precariousness of the global economic system. For Joseph Stiglitz (2008), this outcome was an American economic downturn exported to the rest of the world. In the middle of 2009 the IMF cautioned that the worst of the global economic crisis was not yet over. According to the prognosis of the IMF the world output would contract by 1.3 per cent in 2009, the first negative growth since the Depression, and spring back to 3 per cent growth in 2010 (*Financial Times*, 22 April 2009). The United Nations estimates that between 73 and 103 million more people would remain poor or fall into poverty in 2009 as a result of the global economic slowdown (http://daccessdds. un.org/doc/UNDOC/GEN/N09/414/02/PDF/N0941402.pdf?OpenElement, p. 2, accessed on 19 September 2009). Several analysts, such as George Soros (2008), put the blame on market fundamentalism – an extreme version of neo-liberalism – and the lack of adequate regulation of financial systems. Thus the crisis also demonstrated once again that even the powerful economies are not immune to crises at the global level. At the same time, the task of tackling crises of a global scale fell on the states that needed to act in a coordinated fashion. All major states came forward with economic packages to bail out ailing firms in various countries where they could afford to intervene, and turned to the IMF and World Bank where they could not. The crisis proved both the fragility as well as the salience of the nation-state under conditions of globalization.

Variations in the effectiveness and in the speed of recovery pointed out the relevance of the role of the state and differential state capacities.

The involvement of the state in the management of the crisis and its growing salience had its detractors as well. In an ironical twist, the former leader of Russia turned out to be a defender of the market against the state. In his speech at the World Economic Forum in Davos in 2009, Vladimir Putin advised world leaders against isolationism and state control:

> Excessive intervention in economic activity and blind faith in the state's omnipotence is another possible mistake. True, the state's increased role in times of crisis is a natural reaction to market setbacks. Instead of streamlining market mechanisms, some are tempted to expand state economic intervention to the greatest possible extent. The concentration of surplus assets in the hands of the state is a negative aspect of anti-crisis measures in virtually every nation. In the 20th century, the Soviet Union made the state's role absolute. In the long run, this made the Soviet economy totally uncompetitive. This lesson cost us dearly. I am sure nobody wants to see it repeated. Nor should we turn a blind eye to the fact that the spirit of free enterprise, including the principle of personal responsibility of businesspeople, investors and shareholders for their decisions, is being eroded in the last few months. There is no reason to believe that we can achieve better results by shifting responsibility onto the state. (*Wall Street Journal*, 27 January 2009)

Debates and doubts over centrality and effectiveness notwithstanding, the empirical fact that the world is made up of nation-states is a truism. If one picks up the daily newspaper or tunes into television news, one will find most of the news stories concern nation-states. Let us look at random at the *International Herald Tribune* of 22 September 2007. The major news reports included political unrest in Burma led by the Buddhist monks, news on the Darfur crisis in Sudan, cholera in Baghdad and violence in Iraq. Another newspaper, the *Gulf News* of 21 September 2007, reported political turmoil in Pakistan, nationalization of oil in Venezuela and an economic crisis in Mozambique. These are all stories involving nation-states. Some news stories will deal with inter-state relationships; for example, tensions between Lebanon and Syria over political control. Yet there are news stories that concern the whole world. There will be news about the world, such as the global financial crisis or global warming. Most often the news of the global whole will be linked to the events of the nation-state. For example, Iceland went bankrupt in the face of global financial crisis. The comprehensive collapse of the state in Somalia is the main cause of the rise of piracy in the African coast, threatening maritime trade that may have global consequences. It can be said without much hesitation that there are nation-states, there are inter-state relations, and there are global matters; all of these realities coexist and interact.

States remain central, not despite but because of globalization. According to Rotberg (2003: 2), "States are much more varied in their capacity and capability than they once were. The number of states has also increased in the last century. In 1914 there were fifty-five recognized national polities. In 1950, that number had reached sixty-nine. In 2002 that number rose to 192." In a recent World Bank study, 212 states and territories were identified (Kaufmann et al., 2007). These entities were evaluated in terms of their governance and were given scores. States could be categorized as strong, weak, failed or collapsed states "according to the levels of their effective delivery of the most crucial political goods" (Rotberg, 2003: 2). Surely there are collapsed states struggling to regain their statehood, but what is interesting to note is that even strong and effective states encounter serious setbacks and near-collapse situations. The *Foreign Policy* magazine publishes a yearly list of the failed or failing states. According to the 2008 ranking, Somalia had the unenviable rank of 1. The top ten failed states include Sudan, Zimbabwe, Chad, Iraq, Democratic Republic of Congo, Afghanistan, Ivory Coast, Pakistan and the Central African Republic (*Foreign Policy,* July/August 2008).

While some states are failing, others are prospering both as economic powers and as political hegemons. Yet several writers have raised the question of whether nation-states are becoming powerless in the face of globalization. We examine this question critically in this chapter. We need to discuss the nation-state for a number of reasons. Although globalization is the main process that we are considering, the actual process obviously takes place in time and space. In terms of the temporal dimension, we need to look at the historical process; for the spatial aspect, we need to consider global processes in terms of regions and countries (Therborn and Khondker, 2006).

A world-wide survey of attitudes revealed that, while a large majority of respondents were in favour of open trade, they were also against migration (Pew Global Attitudes Project, 2007). Nationalism features prominently in anti-globalization discourse. Nationalism remains one of the key forces of globalization today, which is of course geographically rooted. Any understanding of processes such as nationalism, racism, chauvinism, cosmopolitanism and multiculturalism is impossible without reference to nation-states which are the containers or locales of such processes. Issues of migration and the resultant consequences of integration or ethnic conflicts, which are some of the most important events of the day, must be situated in local and national contexts. Rather than opposing the nation-state and the global, it is imperative to see the nation-state as a consequence of globalization as Robertson (1992) avers: "The process of globalization – certainly since the mid-eighteenth century – has definitely involved, contrary to some conventional wisdom, the ongoing but changing crystallization of the nation state." There has been long-standing debate over homogeneity versus heterogeneity which seeks to examine whether globalization will create a homogeneous, standardized, flat world or create a more heterogeneous, multinational and multicultural global society. While George Ritzer has coined the term "McDonaldization" to refer to the process of homogenization, others such as Robertson, through the concept of "glocalization", argued that heterogeneity, instead of disappearing, becomes the hallmark of a globalized society. Nation-states in the contemporary world illustrate the phenomenon of glocalization most clearly. Nations are made from linkages to the past as much as by linkages to the globe at large. Through empirical cases, this chapter will consider how local cultural features in China, India and other developing societies can coexist with global economic and technological structures. Nation-states, despite their claims of uniqueness, follow a pre-packaged set of institutions and strategies. A newly born nation-state such as East Timor illustrates the processes of nation-making in clear terms.

Wars and conflicts still dominate the global agenda, and these are often fought between nation-states. There are of course so-called "new wars" which may involve drug barons and warlords who do not represent nations or nation-states, but nevertheless states still play an important part in military conflicts. Rivalries between nations continue to be one of the fundamental processes of globalization. Ignoring states as actors will severely impair our discussion of globalization. Some of the greatest challenges of the present day are peace, social justice and the maintenance of social order based on economic development. These desirable goals are all contingent on political stability. Democracy plays an important role in providing legitimate political authority. As far as the future of globalization is concerned, democratization will be a key, albeit contested, process. Democracy is grown and nurtured within the parameters of the nation-states and such developments can be a step towards achieving global democracy. Any discussion of democracy will necessarily take us into a consideration of the nation-state.

No matter how often the phrase "global development" is used, national development continues to be a dominant challenge. Nation-states stand at different levels or circles of development. At the end of the so-called Cold War, some writers wished to eliminate the category of the Third World. Whether we do away with this condescending title or not is one issue, but the fact that in terms of socio-economic characteristics some nation-states are different or share certain common indices of national development, whether measured in terms of per capita income, access to schools or medical care, fertility rates or levels of corruption, forces us to accept such categories as "the Third World" or "developing society". The Transparency International 2007 ranking of the corrupt countries put Singapore as one of the least corrupt societies. Burma and Somalia were joint "winners" of the accolade of the most corrupt country. It is not surprising, then, that the popular unrest led by monks in Burma is a protest against repression and corruption. Some writers in their euphoria have underplayed the significance of the nation-state and declared its demise, a pronouncement which has been falsified by the turn of events. We will explore the relationship between nation-state and globalization.

ROLE OF THE DEVELOPMENTAL STATE

In this chapter, as we discuss the relationship between the state and globalization, we need to recount the global developments of the last two or three decades to give our discussion a context. The last decades of the twentieth century witnessed two significant events with regard to social transformation: first, in the very last decade of the century, the socialist experiment ran its course; and secondly, in the last three decades or so, high economic growth characterized some of the East and Southeast Asian economies, which were presented as, putatively, shining examples of successful capitalist development. The instabilities leading to the collapse of the socialist system were attributed, *inter alia*, to the unbearable heaviness of the state. Paradoxically, the rise of the newly industrializing economies in East and Southeast Asia was credited to the active role of strong states. A new term was added to the development lexicon: the developmental state, which was proactive, took charge of the economy, but, unlike the socialist state, did not supplant the market. Rather the developmental state forged an interactive relationship with the market to pursue the role of economic growth. A precondition for the state to play such a role was autonomy. State effectiveness, state capacity and finally governance became the bywords in the development debate. The socialist state too enjoyed full autonomy, yet produced a different outcome. In the "really existing" socialist systems the autonomous state was not always the source of failure. In the early stage of socialist development, autonomous states did manage to achieve their goal of massive industrialization, as in the Soviet Union, though at a great human cost. It may be hypothesized that the socialist states could not sustain their developmental role, one reason being that they were too autonomous and became disconnected from their domestic and global social contexts.

The relatively autonomous developmental states in East Asia and elsewhere were embedded in thick social relationships with various institutions of society. Developmental states did not seek to transform the entire society; rather, they worked closely with the existing social institutions. These states did not want to replace the markets but instead worked closely with them. The developmental states varied in the density of their relationships with various social institutions. In other words, developmental states themselves varied in the strength or weakness of their ties with various social groups. Those states that maintained weak ties were able to act more autonomously than those that maintained strong ties. We argue that this approach to state–society relationships helps us to see the so-called institutional approach to development which was made popular in the 1990s as a variation of the developmental state model. This also helps us avoid formulating the new developmental state theory as suggested by writers such as Polidano (2001). The argument that the institutionalist approach emerged as a critique of the developmental state loses its force if we develop a more nuanced understanding of the developmental state. The abstract model of the autonomous state that emerged in the theories of writers such as Nicos Poulantzas (1969, 1973) bore little relationship with the complex web of the state–society relationships that existed in concrete reality. State autonomy in this sense is an "embedded autonomy", to use the felicitous term of Peter Evans (1995).

The conventional state–society model of discussion has come under renewed scrutiny in recent years with added complexities created by the forces of globalization impacting the processes of social and economic transformation. It has been argued that the conventional role of the liberal state, which is expressed in the acronym TRUDI (territorial, rule-of-law, democratic welfare interventionist), began to be circumscribed by the forces of globalization, but not uniformly so (Leibfried and Wolf, 2005: 484–5). The interface between globalization and state autonomy in the context of the developmental state needs to be situated in both spatial and historical contexts. The main focus of this chapter is to revisit the issue of state autonomy in the state–society dichotomous model under the new framework of globalization. The main argument is that we need to embed the autonomous state in local institutions and norms as much as in the nexus of globalized institutional and normative structures.

Rather than subscribing to the mistaken view that globalization started only in the 1990s or at the dawn of the new millennium (Friedman, 2005), or that it is another name for neo-liberalism, we need to advance a deeper and more sophisticated notion of globalization (Robertson, 1992; Hannerz, 1996; Robertson and Khondker, 1998; Tomlinson, 1999; Scholte, 2000; Therborn and Khondker, 2006). For example, Goran Therborn (2000b: 154) views globalization as "tendencies to a worldwide reach, impact, or connectedness of social phenomena or to a world-encompassing awareness among social actors". These two aspects of globalization involving a world-wide process and a new consciousness have been emphasized by various writers (Held et al., 1999; James, 2005). These global processes and institutions provide both opportunities and challenges for individual and state actors. Globalization, even if defined narrowly in economic terms, is to some extent an old process with a new name. However, what has been added to the new features of globalization is velocity. The East and Southeast Asian financial crisis of 1997–8 was a milestone in rethinking the subject of the autonomy of the state and its autonomous role in steering economic development. These changes are actually indicated by some of the new challenges and vulnerabilities that are being created by the global financial system. The 2008 crisis has also illustrated in concrete terms the instabilities in the economic system driven by neo-liberal globalization. However, when the 1997–8 crisis was successfully tackled and the challenges were overcome, depending on which country one chooses to examine, an equally plausible argument could be made either in favour of neo-liberal economic policies as the reason for their success, or the opposite, that the continued role of the state in governing the market was proof of the limitations of the neo-liberal model.

The economic crisis of 2008, which was triggered by the collapse of the American investment bank Lehman Brothers in mid-September 2008, brought the issue of the role and capacity of state institutions to the fore. These discussions highlighted the importance of an efficient state. The attack on the state by the neo-liberal ideologues and politicians since Ronald Reagan and Margaret Thatcher undermined the capacity of states to regulate the market. One could in retrospect argue that the antipathy towards a regulatory state had deeper political roots, being connected in fact to the legacy of the Cold War mentality.

CONTINUED RELEVANCE OF THE STATE

According to one author, "the claim that globalization is undermining sovereignty [of the state] is exaggerated and historically myopic" (Krasner, 1999: 34). It is also ideological. It is not surprising that those who frequently write the obituary of the state are also the most fervent advocates of neo-liberal globalization. In examining the issue of state autonomy, we need to ask whether the state is able and free to make decisions to protect and advance its own interests. It is possible to suggest that the state as an institution has been self-serving and its main role has been to uphold its own interests at the expense of the public interest. However, we would argue that modern democratic states are entrusted with the responsibility of protecting and improving the public interest.

The role of the state has varied across time and space. A simple model of states based on their degree of autonomy can now be proposed. First there was the colonial state, which simply had to carry out and implement decisions made at the colonial centres. Such a state had no autonomy at all to take the public interest into account. The colonial state represented the interests of the colonial power, not the people of the colony. It championed not the public interest of the people located in the colonial space but the interests of the colonizers in far-away places. It was completely independent from the people – various classes – in the colony and it was consequently disembedded. The opposite of autonomy is control. If the state's power to make decisions is controlled by groups, structures, or ideas outside of the state, then one could conclude that the state is lacking in autonomy. Hence, the colonial state was both independent from the ruled and at the same time controlled by the colonial rulers. Although now defunct, various shades of this model are extant in the contemporary world.

Secondly there is the pariah state that is fully autonomous and in a defiant mood to the extent that it fails to sustain itself. This type of state is not interested in the protection of the interests of any public, except a narrow ruling clique. North Korea would be an example of this type. In the discussion of autonomous states, we may find the state was independent from the ruled society, such as North Korea and a number of Central Asian Republics. Turkmenistan, especially between 1991 and 2006 under the rule of Saparmurat Niyazov, presents such an example (Theroux, 2007: 54–65). At the other end of the spectrum, we have societies without states where state functions are completely subsumed by the society. Somalia comes to mind. But, such extreme and negative examples aside, the capitalist market economies of the OECD also present examples of states subordinated by society. The autonomy of these states is circumscribed by the interests of the dominant classes in society.

Thirdly one can also think of a captured state where the state is captured by a narrow segment of society, the military or some powerful families or groups. The state's autonomy in this instance is controlled by a small group as in the case of countries such as Burma. Countries under military rule or authoritarian rule in general display a great deal of state autonomy. These states are able to act either in self-interest or in the greater public interest or both, being unencumbered by pressure or influences from groups or NGOs that make up civil society or public opinion. Corporatist states also exercise a great deal of autonomy. The fascist state was the epitome of state autonomy. A democratic country too may be ruled operationally by a small group of people. However, for the democratic state the support base of the rulers is broader and the state is controlled or influenced by a variety of groups representing a cross-section of interests. Most states would occupy a place in between these two polar types. State autonomy would vary not just over space but also over time. In this regard, it is important to recall the idea of J.P. Nettl (1968) who viewed the state as a variable, a view echoed by Evans (1995: 11; 1997): "States are not generic. They vary dramatically in their internal structures and relations to society."

The question of state autonomy, which in some ways relates to the literature on state and economy, has its roots in the Marxist and neo-liberal economic position that denied the state any autonomy and made it subservient to economic interests. The only autonomous force worth its salt was the economy. Neo-Marxists debated the question of state's role as the management committee of the bourgeoisie versus the relative autonomy of the state. They introduced the dimension of the post-colonial state, bringing the issue of class fractions and their interests into the analysis. Poulantzas (1969, 1973), Alavi (1972) and Miliband (1970, 1973) debated the basis of relative autonomy, for which they turned to alternative texts of Marx. Poulantzas's and Alavi's views were closer to the so-called Marxist structuralist view that granted relative autonomy of the state for maintaining a bourgeois order which would ultimately benefit the bourgeoisie and its various factions. Miliband stressed a view of the state serving the interests of the bourgeoisie – an instrumentalist view for which he relied on the more abstract texts of Marx. Alavi's theory of the post-colonial state was rooted in the historical arguments of Marx. In these discussions the global actors that are the metropolitan bourgeoisie played a part.

If one regards Marx-inspired discussion as smacking of economic determinism, one could turn to Max Weber (1948) and J.M. Keynes (1967) as the two other proponents of state autonomy. Weber sought to correct the excesses of economic determinism by highlighting the autonomous role of the state. The state was an actor unto itself, not a shadow of the economic interests. Rather, the state was defined as having a monopoly of force in a given territory, that is, Weber connected the issue of the state's autonomy to sovereignty over territory. In the context of post-war depression and high unemployment, Keynes advocated remedial economic policies such as employment generation or fiscal policies of deficit financing to shore up a flagging economy, and in these instances the role of the state was crucial. Writers such as Theda Skocpol (1985) and Robert Wade (1990) sought to bring the state back into the discussion, emphasizing the relationship between state and class. Joel Migdal (1988; Migdal et al., 1994) and Atul Kohli (1988) also made important contributions to the discussion of the relationship between state and society but without giving much attention to the external forces of globalization. For Migdal (1988: 4), strong states are states with capacities to penetrate society, regulate social relationships, and extract and appropriate resources. For Skocpol (1985: 9), state autonomy entails the notion that the state "may formulate and pursue goals that are not simply reflective of the demands or interests of social groups, classes or society". Although many of these arguments still have some bearing on our discussion, the condition of globalization has changed and added new dimensions to the discussion of state autonomy.

The state autonomy model was a useful paradigm in the face of the ideologically charged celebration of neo-liberal, market-driven development cases around the world for which the illustrations were few and far between. The rise of Japan – not just from the post-World War II period but since the Meiji restoration – illustrated dramatically the role of an active state in economic and social development. It was the overt hand of the state – to quote and transform the view of Adam Smith – rather than the hidden hand of the market that steered the economic development of Japan. The often spectacular economic growth of other Asian societies such as South Korea, Taiwan, Hong Kong and Singapore has also demonstrated the important role of the state. All these social science discussions have brought the state back to the centre of the development debate.

Several writers proposed a more nuanced argument about the role of social institutions and their constellations which enabled a society to take off into the development phase. Writers who refused to give up the state autonomy thesis because it still looked rather plausible as a mode of explanation in terms of the dominant class and other class fractions improved the paradigm by incorporating some of the institutionalist arguments. For example, the configuration argument has a great deal of validity. If we do not want to see the state in terms of a collection of inert structures, as posited by the French Marxists, and by contrast populate it with men and women who breathe, live and interact with other aspects of society, then we are compelled to take the institutionalist argument seriously. The state autonomy thesis looked more complicated upon closer examination, calling for the refinement of this paradigm by the embedded autonomy thesis which was based on an amalgamation of these two theories.

It has been suggested that the neo-statist model of Linda Weiss and others was a reaction to the overemphasis of the institutionalist model on the configuration of institutions (Polidano, 2001). Sound as this may be, it tends to dilute the role of the state – hence it is called the neo-statist model – in being a driver of society. Linda Weiss (2000: 13) in fact makes it clear that "globalization and state power are not locked in a negative-sum relationship whereby the advance of the former can only occur at the expense of the latter". This takes us to a consideration of the role of the state in the process of globalization. It would be naïve to ignore the role of the state in market-driven economic reforms in China and India. In China, the state continues to play a central role in managing the business of business (Pearson, 2005). The most important economic reforms were introduced when China was still highly centralized (Cai and Treisman, 2006: 512). In India, too, policies and plans for economic liberalization were developed and implemented by a relatively autonomous and democratic state. Contrary to the claims of much globalization theory, the forces of globalization have not undermined the autonomy of the Indian state (Nayar, 2003).

In the earlier discussion, influenced by the euphoria of globalization and borderlessness, writers such as Kenichi Ohmae (1994) approvingly, or Susan Strange (1996) critically, argued that state was either in retreat or losing its efficacy in the face of globalization. A more dispassionate examination reveals that the state is a functional requirement for steering the processes of globalization. In metaphorical terms, states are the navigational systems of the ship that is globalization. You can put the ship on autopilot for a while, but prudence would suggest that a human captain rather than an intelligent system is actually put in charge. How should, and to what extent would, the state act independently or at the behest of the management? These issues have now returned to theories of the state in the context of globalization. The key issue is the autonomy of the state, to which we turn below.

The helplessness of the so-called developing states in the face of global speculators also pointed to the vulnerability and the absence of autonomy on the part of states. As some of the states were forced to turn to the IMF for a bailout, some of the in-built problems of the IMF became manifest. According to George Soros (2002: 120),

[t]he crisis of 1997–1999 revealed a fundamental flaw in the architecture of the international financial system. The countries at the center of the system are in a position to apply countercyclical policies. For

instance, in the current downturn, the United States has aggressively reduced interest rates and cut taxes. But the conditions imposed by the IMF are pro-cyclical. They push countries into recessions by forcing them to raise interest rates and cut budgetary expenditures – exactly the opposite of what the United States is doing in similar circumstances.

The main strategy for tackling the financial crisis in the United States in 2008 was to launch a bailout package of $787 billion, a veritable lifeline for these ailing financial institutions. Soros recommended a stimulus package that went beyond the $787 billion bailout arrangement, and the plans of President Obama also appear to support a trillion-dollar infrastructure development plan in line with a Keynesian employment-creation strategy to overcome the economic crisis. These strategies have been labelled "depression economics" by the economist, Paul Krugman (2008).

The discourse of relatively autonomous developmental states may provide some lessons in rethinking the role of the state in the face of economic globalization. Here we set out eight propositions to encapsulate this interface between state and the forces of globalization:

1   Economic globalization – transborder investments, exchange of commodities, the reign of neo-liberal capitalism dominated by the MNCs – which is supposed to make the state irrelevant, in fact requires an autonomous state. The logic of the market will not be the ultimate solution for differences and the arbiter of disagreements. Even the neo-liberal ideologues need a minimalist state, but the minimalism itself is a matter of contention. The neo-liberals, according to Immanuel Wallerstein (1999: 23),

> want a night watchman state. Now what does a night watchman do? He sits in relative darkness, twiddling his thumbs in boredom, occasionally twirling his baton or revolver when not asleep, and waiting. His function is to ward off intruders who intend to pilfer property. He does this primarily just by being there. So here we are at basics, the universally noted demand for securing property rights. There's no point in accumulating capital if you can't hold on to it.

Furthermore, according to Wallerstein (1999: 27), "a liberal state is one in which the amount of force is reduced and the amount of deception and concessions increased". In the globalized world, "capitalists depend on the intervention of the states in such a multitude of ways that any true weakening of state authority is disastrous" (Wallerstein, 1999: 32).

The old adage "what is good for GM is good for America" was still valid, especially after the $17.4 billion bailout of the three big car makers in December 2008. Now the adage may be modified to "what is good for Citibank is good for America". Yet, on 1 June 2009, GM filed for bankruptcy and virtually ended up in government hands. The US government's multi-billion bailout plan for its big corporations and automobile industries in late 2008 reinforced the role of the state in the economy. The link between corporate class interests and the state remains as functional as it is relevant today, perhaps more so than at any other time in the past. There are, however, different categories of states – capitalist states, comprador states or fragile states and so on – which reflect the power and dominance of the classes in charge of these states.

2   In a similar vein, Peter Evans (1997) argues that "high stateness" and globalization go hand in hand. Drawing upon Rodrik and others who showed a strong correlation between the expansion of government expenditure and exposure to trade, Evans argued that high stateness (that is, an effective state) is a source of competitive advantage in a globalizing economy. The rise of the regulatory state in China provides an important lesson. The transition from a socialist economy to a market economy in China entailed extensive market reforms in the last quarter of the twentieth century, giving rise to a host of regulatory agencies and institutions to the extent that the Chinese state has become a regulatory state (Pearson, 2005). Even economic deregulation involves creating a new role for the state rather than diminishing its influence (Rodrik, 1997).

Global economic domination is aided by a reconstituted state. The Westphalian state gives way to a denationalized or supranational state (Jessop, 2002:195) where the state embarks on a new role in assisting the MNCs or state-linked corporations in the accumulation process.

3   State autonomy needs to be understood in the context of a global inter-state system. As we have noted, there have been for some time two registers of powerful nation-states. Some states, such as the USA, are powerful both economically and politically. For example, the US invasion of Iraq in 2003 was an example of US unilateralism and can be seen as an example of state autonomy in the face of global forces. Here the US state acted independently to pursue its own interests in defiance of international and multilateral institutions and global public opinion as well as global norms. Other states are either economically or politically powerful. Military power is an aspect of political power. The European Union, Japan, and even China are becoming economically, if not politically, powerful. Here we need to understand the concept of power with regard to state power. "Power is not bombast and it is not a theoretically (that is, legally) unlimited authority. Power is measured by results; power is about getting one's way. The truly powerful can be (and usually are) soft-spoken, respectful, and quietly manipulative; the truly powerful succeed" (Wallerstein, 1999: 23). The militarism of the USA can be seen as a sign of its declining power in a relative sense. But decline is not absence. In the present inter-state system, a superstate such as the USA will exert enormous power to the detriment of the state power of other states. But it is unlikely that this situation can be sustained indefinitely. In the post-Second World War world, the

superpowers divided power and influence and their client states enjoyed varied degrees of autonomy depending on their alignments. The rise of China as
a third force altered the power equations to some extent and played into the
hands of the USA until the eventual decline of the "Socialist system", which
some regard as "state capitalism". The historic lesson here is that even a dominant state like the USSR can collapse. Although the capitalist superstates are
not in any imminent threat of collapse, they may well face a longer-term crisis resulting from their misadventures rooted in a false sense of hyperpower.

4   The relative autonomy of the state gains a universalistic dimension as all
    states are increasingly faced with a set of common domestic issues such as
    multiculturalism and democratic pluralism. The growing concern with human
    rights as a global discourse, albeit eclipsed by the so-called "war on terror",
    is an issue that confronts most modern states. These issues have generated a
    common discourse of rights, cultural community and identity. Although there
    are significant national variations in dealing with these issues, a common
    thread runs across cultures and geographical spaces. In the twenty-first cen-
    tury, it is almost impossible for states to ignore such issues as the cultural
    rights of minorities or to retract rights enjoyed by the labouring classes or
    women or other groups on the margins of society. All states need, and in many
    cases have, developed institutions to deal with these issues largely because of
    their global currency. In the Gulf region, states are sensitive to the criticisms
    of their policies by international organizations. Whenever New York based
    Human Rights Watch or the US Department of State criticizes the Gulf states
    for denying the rights of workers, these states initiate inquiries or take actions
    to ameliorate the deficiencies of their standards so that they are not judged
    adversely by international bodies.

5   The state's autonomy is now gaining a new dimension in the face of global tech-
    nology such as information technology, biotechnology and so on. The impor-
    tance of universalized patent laws, standardized legal protection and regulations
    has added a new dimension to the issue of state autonomy. The state is affected
    by the contradiction between its new capacity for surveillance and the expan-
    sion of democratic spaces to the advantage of ordinary people. States are
    obliged to pay attention to the global ethical regime when it comes to the reg-
    ulation of biosciences and biotechnology. The growth of new sciences and
    technology forces the state to enhance its capacity to deal with these new
    conditions. Such capacity building is predicated upon the state's collabora-
    tion and conformity with the global institutions as much as independence
    from local vested interests.

6   State autonomy is also under scrutiny in view of the development and renewed
    relevance of international non-governmental organizations and suprastatal
    organizations such as the UN, ILO, and the International Atomic Energy
    Organization. Here again, the question of autonomy cannot be separated from
    the issue of the power of the state and the location of the state in the

inter-state system. For example, UN sanctions against Iraq had devastating consequences for both state and society, but such sanctions would not even be contemplated against Israel or Pakistan. State autonomy *vis-à-vis* local civil society still remains an important dimension of state autonomy, but with globalization the global civil society has come to be more vocal and strident, influencing – either curtailing or empowering – state autonomy.

7 The global media's role in the question of state autonomy has also become more pronounced with the availability of satellite television and the Internet. These developments are also influential in shaping and in reconstituting the relationships between local media, state and society. In some states, there are strict censorship rules and guidelines, while in others we see more subtle approaches. In Japan a section of the media tried to smear the Japanese hostages in Iraq in 2007 in order to prevent the Japanese public, primarily young Japanese, making them into heroes. Various states are confronted with this global media regime, which encourages them to develop strategies to take advantage of these channels to promote their own national interests, thereby enhancing their autonomy.

8 Global security threats, which have become more pronounced since 9/11, have also added a new dimension to the issue of state autonomy. Many states have little choice but to forge global alliances to combat such security threats from international networks of narco-terrorists (as in Latin America) or religiously fanatical networks elsewhere. These new alliances empower states and reduce the space of civil society, thereby tilting the balance of power towards the state. "Globalization involves both openings and closings. On the one hand globalization is in large part defined by its linking of one society to another, whereas, on the other, it intensifies the need for protection for security, against others ... the global complexity of globalization demands transparency, but also much surveillance" (Robertson, 2007: 400).

The contradiction of the developmental state is that its role is contingent upon the exercise of a great deal of autonomy, albeit embedded. However, the autonomous role of the state undermines the growth of democratic culture, an environment conducive to creativity and innovation. In the end, the main issue in the pursuit of peace or prosperity is not just whether the state is able to pursue an autonomous role or not. The key political question is autonomy for what? What are the goals the state seeks to pursue? Surely embeddedness is a precondition, which democracy may guarantee, but one has to move beyond this requirement and ask questions about the quality of development and democracy. One needs to turn to an analysis of the ethical framework within which developmental goals and democratic values ought to be nurtured.

5 GLOBALIZATION, CULTURE AND COSMOPOLITANISM

INTRODUCTION

While teaching an undergraduate class in an all-female university in the Gulf region, one of the authors wrote on the whiteboard, "Man is a social animal." The students, otherwise polite and well mannered, reacted sharply. They did not take issue with the sociability of man or with the sexist connotation, but with the use of the phrase "animal". "We are not *animals*", they protested. The lecturer saw not only a shadow of disbelief but also a sense of hurt in the eyes of the students. In a bid to save face, the lecturer joked, "I said *men* are social animals, women are social beings." The students were not impressed. The author then went on a full-scale offensive, arguing that comparing human with animals is not right because such a comparison is an insult to the animals. Animals do not commit genocide. They do not kill each other just for the sake of killing; they do not indulge in drive-by shooting, nor go to a classroom full of children and open fire, nor drop bombs and kill and maim their fellow animals – babies and the elderly – indiscriminately.

It may be a truism, but it nevertheless needs reiteration that some of the cultural differences that mark off one group from another are not just superficial; they are deeply rooted in their respective traditions, social practices and in their collective memories. Islam as a religion provides a compelling image of the human. Following their religious traditions, the majority of Muslims believe that humans are the best of Allah's creations. The Christian notion of the fall of Adam and original sin paints an image of *man* that is fallible and in need of forgiveness. Religions such as Islam, Hinduism and Buddhism do not share this view of primary sin, although they do recognize that human beings are vulnerable. The students who grew up in the Islamic tradition obviously found the use of the word "animal" as a descriptor of humans offensive.

They had a valid reason for being hurt and offended. The lecturer shared with the students their Islamic heritage but also had inherited other traditions such as Bengali culture which is deeply multi-layered, as well as a liberal education and exposure to the globalized capitalist world. In his capacity as a lecturer, he was in a privileged position of being listened to, since respect for authority figures such as teachers is part of the Islam-influenced culture. In the Indian cultural tradition, the idea of the "guru" goes well beyond that of the teacher. The fact that teachers are accorded different levels of respect in different societies illustrates the point about cultural difference quite convincingly.

From this transcultural encounter a number of points can be made. First, there are differences in cultural values which coexist with the commonality of popular cultures. The spread of so-called McDonaldization and the culture of Starbucks should not be seen as erasure of differences. Second, similarities or commonalities at the superficial level are often accompanied by divisions in deeper structures and vice versa; that is, differences at the superficial level coexist with deeper commonalities. Third, these differences and divisions can sometimes be understood, negotiated, and overcome through reasoned conversation. Finally, in order to have such a conversation there is a need for a space (such as a university) that enjoys sufficient freedom of discussion with an attitude of openness. Creating a common globalized culture is a worthy goal for some; others value and cherish the coexistence of multiple cultures and dream of a multicultural, cosmopolitan global culture.

The encounter itself is an instance of globalization. The Gulf region contains some of the most prosperous countries of the world. Some of the smaller countries in the Gulf – predominantly Muslim – are emphasizing higher education, especially women's education, resulting in the outnumbering of men by women in higher education, which is likely to have a profound impact on these societies in the long term. The spread of higher education as illustrated by the mushrooming growth of universities in the Gulf, as in other prosperous regions of the world, is in itself a phenomenon of globalization. Another example is from Singapore where the government has lavished money on its National University to make it a global university to compete within the global system of universities.

This chapter analyses the cultural dimension of globalization by examining the impact of globalization on local or national cultures, the modes of resistance to cultural globalization, and the ensuing fusion of transnational and local traditions, resulting in what Roland Robertson has called "glocalization" and other scholars have called cultural "hybridity", producing a creative tension, a hallmark of cosmopolitanization. Political leaders often position themselves as custodians of national culture, thereby raising the spectre of cultural imperialism. In the ferment of nationalist struggle, the vigorous defence of a culture contributes to the consolidation of nations, but in other contexts such political posturing can be self-serving.

What is commonly known as religious fundamentalism or religious extremism is often viewed as a reaction of the local or traditional culture against the consequences of globalization. In the next chapter we examine the relationship between globalization and religion. Yet it is important to ask whether fundamentalist religion is the main source of opposition to consumer globalization. In the famous book by Benjamin Barber on *McWorld versus Jihad*, he explores the shrinking of democratic cultures in the face of two opposite streams that are drawn from narrow economism and consumerism on the one hand and traditionalism on the other. There are two important aspects of global religion: the rise of popular religions that spread via the Internet in youth cultures or spiritual markets (for example, some of the videos of Madonna presenting her as a religious figure); and fundamentalism which is in part a response to popular/commercial aspects of the religious market. It is of course very difficult to disentangle religion and culture. In Thailand, for example, where do Buddhism, national culture and popular religious practice begin and end? In the Philippines, is it possible to separate Catholicism from Filipino identity? Religions and national cultures interact and influence each other. Yet, for analytical reasons at least, it is often important to make a distinction between culture and religion in order to consider them as separate spheres or domains.

Concepts such as glocalization (Robertson, 1995), "*mélange*" (Pieterse, 1995), "creolization" (Hannerz, 1992), disjuncture (Appadurai, 1996) and hybridity have been used to describe the complex cultures of the world in order to indicate the spread of globalization. Fusions in food, dress, music, language and art are part of our everyday life in modern societies. These fusions and cultural adaptations have given rise to fears about the dilution or disappearance of local or traditional culture. Global culture presents a picture of artificial or multiple cultures, which are a *mélange* of diverse elements. The coexistence of multiple cultures does not mean that these cultures are free of tensions and conflicts. Secular or liberal political cultures can offend religious sensibilities. For example, Salman Rushdie's controversial book or his award of a knighthood captures the headlines, and we see protests erupting in various Muslim-dominated countries. This observation is not a recommendation to accept Samuel Huntington's exaggerated view of the "clash of the civilizations", but to deny real or potential cultural conflicts is simply wishful thinking. For cultural traditions to survive and thrive, rules of exclusion provide the very *raison d'être* while neglecting inclusiveness in a world riven by cultural, religious and ethnic divisions may often have dangerous consequences.

At the present stage of globalization, various national societies are preoccupied with cultural imperialism, Westernization and the domination of the rest of the world by American culture. For example, France has raised many issues of national culture which are seen to be under threat of erosion by American culture. French academics have demanded that French language, cinema and culinary heritage must be protected against this global onslaught and the fact that the anti-McDonaldization movement started with José Bové, a French peasant farmer, points to the fact that this French resistance is not simply an East versus West issue.

Perhaps one of the best illustrations of the consequences of global economic change has been the spread of McDonald's as both a method of management in the fast-food industry and in consumer lifestyles (Ritzer, 2000). Although McDonald's has maintained a common service ethos (speed, cleanliness, cost and predictability), its adjustment to local cultural norms is perhaps a perfect example of glocalization. In Russia, McDonald's no-frills ethos perfectly matches the preference for no trappings in the service industry and the contempt for luxury of the "New Russians". In many Muslim societies, despite hostility to American culture, Muslim parents like McDonald's because their children are safe (from alcohol). In Indonesia, McDonald's has adjusted to local requirements during Ramadan. In South Korea, students like to take their homework and their own food to local McDonald's restaurants where they hang out, thereby compromising the idea of "fast food place". In Asia generally, McDonald's serves rice and green tea (Turner, 2003a). In his work on McDonaldization, Ritzer accepted the evidence for glocalization in which the process of rationalization is both modified and delayed.

RESISTING CULTURAL GLOBALIZATION

There seems to be a global concern with resisting cultural homogenization in the face of a rapid globalized modernization. For example, Chinese modernization appears to involve the wholesale destruction of its cultural past – a sort of second Cultural Revolution. In Beijing, in particular, beautiful old urban communities (*huton*) are being destroyed by high-rise flats, hotels and municipal buildings, leaving almost no trace of the past. Building Olympic facilities involved the rapid destruction of local dwellings, partly because the inhabitants have no property rights. The arguments in favour of such total urban development are that people need better housing and it is cheaper and more efficient to provide it in the form of flats in high-rise dwellings. Apart from the inconvenience that these developments cause (forcing people to live in suburbs a long way from the city centre), this type of development produces a standardized environment without any cultural distinction. There is simultaneously a loss of cultural heritage and a loss of distinctiveness. From an economic point of view, this is short-sighted since tourists will not want to be confronted with high-rise hotels and shopping complexes that no longer have any cultural authenticity.

The result is that Beijing, Shanghai and Nanjing will look like any other modernized city throughout Asia. It has often been said of European cities that they were destroyed twice – first by bombing in the Second World War and then by urban development and town planning in the 1950s. Chinese developers sometimes argue that, when Chicago and New York were building skyscrapers in the "roaring twenties", Europeans criticized these examples of modern architecture, but now the West generally admires the forward-looking radical architecture of these blocks. However, the construction of the modern city of Chicago did not involve the destruction of centuries of previous architecture. In China's principal cities, these new buildings often involve the indiscriminate destruction of their own national heritage. Throughout the world, the surge in inner-city rental values has meant that there has been a very strong economic incentive to knock down old buildings which have low rental value. Therefore one economic tool for conservation is to pressure governments to keep inner-city rentals low, thereby cutting off any significant economic incentive to construct high-rise buildings. In some cities in Malaysia, this strategy of controlling rental values has prevented the destruction of the old centre of Penang.

In Southeast Asia, Singapore experienced the most spectacular modernization by engaging with globalization. In the 1960s and 1970s there was massive clearance of old Singapore to make way for a modern and advanced inner-city business community. Much of old Chinatown along the river was destroyed. However, as a result of lobbying from heritage groups – in particular from the Singapore Heritage Society – some old shop-houses have been preserved, for example in Blair Road. The modern Boat Quay along the river is an area where traditional housing has been preserved and it is a favourite destination of tourists. A large collection of so-called black and white houses, built by the British for their army officers, have also been preserved. However, there are a large number of colonial buildings in need of repair and conservation, such as the Malayan Railway Station and the Majestic Theatre. The preservation of heritage sites has been the outcome of lobbying by architects, historians and academics, but little of old Singapore is intact and, given the huge increase in rental values in the first half of 2007, there is now considerable pressure to pull down older properties and to keep on building higher.

Japan has obviously been committed to a process of state-driven modernization since at least the time of the Meiji Restoration in 1868. Japan's involvement in the industrialization of warfare has been a significant aspect of its emergence as a modern nation, and the American occupation in the 1950s gave Japan a distinctively American orientation to politics, but Japanese consumerism was already well established in the 1930s through the development of shopping malls. Today Japan dominates the global car industry and electronics manufacturing. In the major cities, the destruction wrought by the Second World War meant that very little of their traditional architecture remained. Tokyo is in many respects a wholly modern city with very little that, on the outside, looks Japanese. Apart from cities such as Kyoto, many cities were completely destroyed by bombing – Nagasaki, Hiroshima, Osaka and Tokyo. Like the Singaporeans, the Japanese appear to be fascinated by modern technological solutions to transportation, housing and communications. Even Japanese toilets are highly computerized! Nevertheless Japan has retained much of its cultural past – sumo wrestling, a (re-emerging) emperor system, Shinto shrines, its system of status hierarchy, and a Buddhist monastic culture. Japanese culture – despite the presence of McDonald's and Starbucks on every street – has retained its own dietary culture. Japan is very reluctant to import rice from outside, and it tries to sustain whale hunting despite international protests. Its own cuisine appears to be very strong. Interpersonal behaviour appears also to be strongly promoted and controlled by traditional norms of hierarchy and politeness. Gender relations are still very hierarchal and clearly defined. Japan appears to be able to embrace, to copy and then to redesign external commodities. Japan has a very clear and coherent aesthetic style – for example, the way in which purchases in shops are carefully wrapped and packaged.

In short, Japan appears to be a good example of cultural resistance to globalization based upon retaining its own sense of aesthetics and a strong state. Its language and island status may also contribute to this distinctiveness. The main threat to Japan's culture would appear to be the ageing of its population and hence the need to depend on labour migration from South America, South Korea and elsewhere. The relative decline of its economy in relation to China may result in a decline of Japanese cultural influence in Asia and may also result in conflict over control of the South China Sea.

CULTURAL GLOBALIZATION AND HYBRIDITY: RELIGION

We have attempted implicitly to put forward a view of globalization as having deep historical roots, as being multidimensional, and as being constituted by both social-cultural and political economic causes. We have criticized mainstream globalization theory for its neglect of religion. However, if there is one dominant cultural viewpoint, it is the theory of hybridization, namely, the growth of cultural diversity in which there is also borrowing, simulation and syncretization. We can see this aspect in religious globalization (Beyer, 1994). While the world religions have been involved in inter-civilizational interaction (ecumenicalism) for centuries, modern communication and transport have made the "worldness" of the world religions a practical and realistic goal. The Islamic pilgrimage (*haj*) is a good illustration. It is possible to argue that prior to the modern period, religions existed as religious cultures that were heavily intermixed with local beliefs, magic and superstition. Globalization has meant that the world religions have emerged as more coherent and institutionalized "religious systems" rather than merely "religious cultures". This global institutionalization has meant increasing demands for adherence to orthodox belief and practice. Orthodoxy in the Abrahamic religions underpins the demands of global fundamentalist movements. But these movements are not confined to the Abrahamic religions. The Moonies (Sun Myung Moon's Unification Church) have a specific mission to become completely global. The Baha'i faith and the Buddhist Soka Gakkai International have an explicitly global ideology. Increasing interaction between religions has converted them into religious systems involved in struggles to differentiate and define themselves more precisely and exclusively against their rivals.

While Jewish communities have for centuries been subject to violence and exclusion, being ejected from Spain for example in 1290 and 1492, religio-ethnic conflict is more likely in the modern period where identity politics has become dominant. Globalization has increased conflicts over cultural identity by converting localized religious cultures into self-reflexive religious systems whose identity exists by virtue of its difference from other traditions. In 1893 the World Parliament of Religions met in Chicago, and one consequence was the growth of Hindu nationalism as an attack on the creation of a secular Indian state (Juergensmeyer, 2003). This systematization of religious cultures is in part a consequence of the export of Western Latin Christianity – a process that Derrida calls 'globalatinisation' (Derrida, 1998). This intensification of religious identity has been further enhanced by the spread of global fundamentalism (primarily Christian and Muslim) which has involved an attack on traditional "religious cultures" such as Sufism. Religious fundamentalism employs modern technologies such as television, video cassettes and the Internet to spread its message that returning to fundamentals (for example, fundamental or selected texts) modernizes traditional cultures. This process of radical self-reflexivity involves not only a struggle between Christianity, Judaism and Islam, but also within Islam between Sunni and

Shi'ite traditions, and within Christianity between Catholic and Protestant. The politics of (religious) identity are the basis of claims by writers such as Samuel Huntington (1997) that religion has become the fault-line between West and East. The clash of civilizations is primarily between Christianity (which allegedly separates religion and politics) and Islam (which allegedly does not). These arguments are problematic because they fail to consider the fundamentalist movements in Christianity and Judaism as well as in Islam, they underplay the heterogeneity of Islam, and they equate fundamentalism with anti-modernism (Turner, 2002). Religious fundamentalism is a threat to Western secularism, but it is equally problematic for Palestinian secularism or modernist Islamic movements in Indonesia. In short, the notion of an elementary division between liberal democracies in the West and militant Islam in the East is simplistic.

Religious globalization is inherently paradoxical. While the dominant trend is to create tensions between religious systems in which identity politics, at its worst, requires ethnic cleansing, there is considerable religious hybridity in Western religious markets where New Age groups and other "quest cultures" seek spiritual enlightenment through a playful hybridization of everything (Roof, 1999). Globalization forces religions to compete in a global market place and hence compels them to differentiate themselves; fundamentalization reinforces this process. At the same time, especially in North America, the religious market places allow individuals "to do their own thing". The implications of individualism in the religious market in the West are that religion, at least popular religion, will become a component in the entertainment industry. The pop star Madonna is the most spectacular illustration of this process.

Western economic globalization has to be analysed initially in terms of nineteenth-century imperialism and the nationalist and reformist movements that were engendered by Western cultural imperialism. Both nationalism and fundamentalism developed responses to Western hegemony, and contemporary cultural politics can be regarded as a manifestation of earlier struggles.

CONDITIONS OF CULTURAL RESISTANCE

There are two general conditions of resistance to negative globalization. One is cultural, and will be referred to as the strong aesthetic condition of (national) resistance. This dimension involves a form of cultural conservatism. A strong aesthetic acts as the carrier of national and local traditions that defines the 'distinctive substance' of a community. The second condition is political, namely a viable and robust civil society that provides the basis for decisive (cultural) leadership. This dimension involves strong politics, and it is a largely progressive element. These two dimensions give us conceptually a property space consisting of four sub-types. Societies that combine a strong aesthetic of cultural conservatism with a strong politics (civil society plus leadership) can resist negative globalization, because they can either resist cultural standardization or appropriate external values and practices through the mediation of their own traditions and political structures without destroying their own aesthetic. Those societies that lack both a strong aesthetic and an effective political leadership can offer relatively little resistance to negative globalization and their local traditions are quickly destroyed.

By a strong aesthetic we mean a (national) culture that is coherent to such an extent that its architecture, domestic spaces, musical idiom, poetic traditions and national mythologies give expression to a more or less distinctive and integrated cultural form. In the language of a traditional anthropology, we might refer to this aesthetic as an organic culture. A strong politics is equivalent conceptually to a dynamic and responsive civil society that makes possible a positive sense of public space and public opinion. A strong politics presupposes a public culture in which debate and disagreement are respected and promoted. A (national) society can resist negative globalization if it has a strong aesthetic that can absorb, appropriate and reinterpret global cultures, and if it has a strong politics in which the undesirable aspects of global values and institutions (McDonald's) can be analysed and selectively rejected or incorporated. Effective resistance to negative globalization does necessarily involve reactive parochialism; effective resistance has elements of glocalization, but a glocalism in which the host culture remains hegemonic. The determinants of a strong aesthetic are: a national religion; a viable and dynamic language and possibly a distinctive script; museums and a national university system; a national broadcasting system and independent newspapers and media of communication; public and domestic principles of design and representation; and a national mythology. A strong aesthetic is the idiom or underlying principle(s) giving a culture some degree of coherence and integration. A weak aesthetic means that there is no underlying idiom or theme, and globalization produces an exhaustion of idiom and its eventual demise.

We might identify two rather separate conditions for strong politics. There is a top–down form of political leadership in which the state attempts to exercise hegemonic control of cultural development and leadership. This statist form of political leadership was characteristic of both nationalist and fascist politics (in the 1920s and 1930s). There is also a bottom-up or democratic form of cultural politics in which civil society is critical in maintaining a way of life that can resist standardization. The determinants of strong democratic politics that are capable of exercising cultural leadership are: national systems of representation; a history of voluntary associations and intermediary institutions; a national church or religious tradition; regional representations; collective ownership of national media and communications; and robust citizen institutions. A strong democratic politics can be conceptualized in terms of Alexis de Tocqueville's communal democratic institutions. The most effective forms of cultural resistance take place when the state orchestrates and articulates both national culture and civil society to express a national or collective aesthetic that is relatively coherent and expressive. A strong aesthetic is a (national) habitus of taken-for-granted practices and beliefs that infuse everyday life, architectural norms, national dance, museums and other modes of collective memory.

We can conceptualize these national or societal dimensions within the framework of a theory of cultural and social capital. Societies can resist negative globalization if they possess cultural capital and can strategically resist the standardization that is implicit in McDonaldization or other forms of cultural imperialism. They can also resist these processes if they have an effective associational basis to social life or social capital to act as social glue and provide a protective social shell. When we use the phrase "cultural resistance", we do not necessarily imply that this resistance involves conscious, self-reflexive opposition to negative globalization. The fascist or nationalist politics of cultural representation involves a deliberate attempt to impose an aesthetic, if necessary by forceful and authoritarian leadership.

For example, in the 1920s and 1930s, there were strong statist attempts to impose various forms of public art in order to counteract liberal decadence. In Italy there were significant struggles to impose fascist standards on both the functions and contents of public art. This fascist art embraced an aesthetic that combined avant-garde aspects with populist and monumental ones, and the Novecento painters developed the use of murals and mosaics to depict pre-Renaissance Italian traditions (Stone, 1998: 115).

In the modernization of Turkey, Atatürk borrowed ideas from Germany to develop monumental art, gymnastics, architecture and dress to create a powerful aesthetic. The caliphate was abolished in 1924 and the modernization of Turkey assumed a secular direction. A new bureaucratic middle class adopted Western dress, secular education and Western legal traditions. In recent times, Turkey has been heavily exposed to Western popular culture and the political ambition to join the European Union has forced it to adopt a pro-Western political agenda. Alongside the new consumer shopping centres, monumental statues of Atatürk look anachronistic. Old men still crowd into the traditional coffee houses and tea rooms (Meeker, 2002: 342), but students are more likely to patronize McDonald's and Western bars. However, Turkey has a rich popular and folk culture that is resistant to globalization. For example, there has been an important revival of the folk dance tradition. This revival is associated with Selim Tarcan (1875–1953) who had observed the growth of folk dancing in Sweden in the 1890s which he realized was important for the growth of Swedish national identity. Tarcan's choreography of the *zeybek* dances was important in the growth of Turkish national dance, which eventually found support from Atatürk who witnessed a performance in Izmir in 1925. In the same period, folk dancing as a national expression was promoted by the People's Houses which were republican institutions that also encouraged research in and practice of folk culture. By the 1980s folk dancing spread through the urban middle classes because it was taken up seriously by university students who formed clubs to cultivate this national genre.

In general, it is possible to argue that dance has played a major role in establishing a nationalist aesthetic that is highly resistant to hegemonic globalization. Russia provides another example. Russian classical ballet emerged out of a series of artistic experiments with music, dance and drama in the 1890s in St Petersburg. The imperial school of ballet was important in fostering the high culture of ballet, which explored the Russian fairy tale and folk traditions as a source of artistic inspiration (Lieven, 1936). Russian ballet became influential in Paris as a result of the creative work of Sergei Diaghilev, who brought *Boris Godunov* to a French audience in 1908. European audiences wanted to see Russian national idioms and rejected the cosmopolitanism of Diaghilev's repertoire. Russian ballet constructed a strong national aesthetic that expressed integration between high culture and Russian peasant themes, and was influential in literature, music and art (Figes, 2002). High classical ballet has remained important as an aesthetic of Russian national culture, despite the commercial globalization of ballet through figures such as Rudolf Nureyev.

India provides an important example of resistance to and incorporation of a globalized culture at the same time. The nationalist movement against the hegemonic British colonial culture in the early twentieth century incorporated the so-called Western ideas of liberalism and nationalism to fight against the local orthodoxies and parochialism and to forge nationhood in the struggle against colonial domination. While the politics of Mahatma Gandhi represented this unique fusion of simultaneous

resistance to the Western consumer culture and incorporation of cosmopolitan ideals of peace and tolerance, the aesthetic resurgence of
Indian literature as manifested in the writings of Rabindranath Thakur
(known as Tagore) provided another example of simultaneous resistance and incorporation. Tagore maintained a clear distinction between
"Western imperialism" and "Western civilization", and rejected the former (Sen, 2005: 107). As India in the twenty-first century is poised
to assume a dominant role in the world it continues to maintain this
distinction.

While Italy, Turkey, Russia and India present instructive historical
illustrations, it is probably in the case of Japan that we see the most significant attempt to protect a national aesthetic tradition and culture
against Westernization and globalization. The Meiji Restoration of 1868
represented a determined effort to avoid economic and cultural domination by the Western powers. The reform of traditional Japan involved
dismantling its feudal past and borrowing institutions and ideas extensively from foreign powers. The new constitution was Prusso-German,
British traditions were used to modernize the navy, and Western dress
was encouraged. The Japanese state sought modernization on the principle "rich country, with strong army" (Kennedy, 1990: 207). After its
defeat in the Second World War, Japan was forced to adopt further
Western reforms (of labour law, political institutions and educational
institutions), and yet remarkably Japan has remained distinctive
(Benedict, 1946). Japan has experienced profound globalization, but it
has remained a country steeped in local traditions. How has this
occurred? Japan has remained a highly disciplined and coherent society
with strong religious traditions, especially Buddhist and neo-Confucian.
Japanese culture has successfully absorbed and embraced Western consumerism   without   undermining   its   indigenous   traditions.
Commentators such as Karel van Wolferen (1989) in *The Enigma of
Japanese Power* have argued that Japan succeeds because it has sustained
a myth of national homogeneity that legitimizes an authoritarian and
hierarchical system, masking its real heterogeneity. While Japanese institutions impose and require loyalty and discipline, Japan successfully
avoids globalism by protecting its cultural aesthetic and by exercising
political leadership to counteract any dilution of its heritage. This religio-
cultural ethic is probably most manifest in its tea culture and diet, but its
technological products, especially cars, exhibit the clean-cut and precise
sense of design that pervades objects in the Japanese cultural field.
Although McDonald's is a prevalent feature of Japanese popular culture,
it appears to have little significant impact on traditional diet, tea drink-
ing, the presentation of food, or consumption of *sake*. Preparation and

consumption of tea remain essential features of Japanese everyday life; tea is not simply an aspect of high culture or Zen Buddhism (Okakura, 2001).

These examples provide us with an understanding of hierarchical and (often) authoritarian strategies to resist cultural imperialism. Nationalistic movements in the 1920s and 1930s resisted the global spread of (American) consumer cultures by harnessing national and folk idioms to strategies of nation building. We might argue that these were top-down authoritarian strategies to construct cultural citizenship as frameworks for the nation-state. By contrast with these nationalist strategies, the Scandinavian societies combined a strong aesthetic sense of difference with social democratic politics. Music played an important role in romantic nationalism in Norway through the works of Edvard Grieg (1843–1907) and in Finland through Jean Sibelius (1865–1957) who used the Finnish national epic (the *Kalevala*) in his vocal works. Although in the twentieth century the Scandinavian countries have been heavily influenced by economic globalization and by the European Union, a strong sense of Scandinavian design plays an important role in protecting their cultures from rapid nullification. Because English has become the global language of the world economic system, language maintenance is very important in protecting a local or national aesthetic. Small language communities such as Finland are particularly exposed to the homogenizing influences of globalization, which partly explains the determination of French governments to protect their own language.

Paradoxically, societies that are most exposed to multiculturalism, migration, cultural fragmentation and hybridity are more open to cultural conflicts than societies at the periphery of the global market. The liberal justification of the free market in economic commodities also embraces a free market in cultures and aesthetics, and hence it has relatively little resistance to cultural marketization. America is too diverse to possess a dominant aesthetic, and its popular culture is an essential feature of its economy. Standardized products (Pepsi, McDonald's, Ford motor cars and Starbucks) are an essential feature of American consumerism. We could argue that England developed a strong aesthetic around the music of Edward Elgar (1857–1934) and the arts and crafts movement that was inspired by William Morris who was a major influence on British art and design until his death in 1896. In the contemporary period, it is by contrast difficult to argue that Britain has a national aesthetic and its 'special relationship' with America means that it is culturally as well as politically increasingly subordinate to the American cultural market. One consequence of this process, which we can call the erosion of idiom, is that the liberal democracies are under political pressure from the Right to restore traditional, local or national cultures and to avoid the cosmopolitan societies that appear to be associated with cultural hybridity.

Fundamentalism has been important as a social movement or movements challenging the loss of distinctiveness that follows globalization. The veil has become an important symbol of opposition to Westernization, but it is difficult to generalize too dogmatically about the significance of veiling. In Palestine it was associated with nationalism and resistance as much as it was an expression of Islamic identity (Hammami, 1997). In contemporary Egypt, the veil is often associated with upper-class chic fashion. Although the veil has multiple meanings, a theory of globalized culture needs to address the variety of conservative, traditional and fundamentalist movements that reject cultural inclusion in the global village. Japanese society appears to have successfully accepted and promoted modernization, but it has imposed its own aesthetic brand on global products and ideas. Islamic fundamentalism represents a political and cultural attempt to resist incorporation into Western consumerism. In America, while there are radical movements such as the House of Islam, there are also many ways in which the practice of Islam does not accept standardization. Because Islam requires certain daily dietary and religious practices, there is an Islamic economy that produces religious commodities such as prayer timepieces, but we do not have to regard these as a reduction in distinctiveness (Smith, 1999: 143).

CONCLUSION: HYBRIDITY AND MULTICULTURALISM

Cultural hybridity, complexity and diversity have been important consequences of globalization. Hybridity involves both movements to define separateness through cultural differentiation (such as religious fundamentalism), and the emergence of spiritual market places in Western youth cultures that collapse the distinctiveness of different traditions into a popular melting pot. The rise of identity politics and religious nationalism is also a consequence of globalization. The politics of ethnic identity are further complicated by the growth of multiculturalism and multinational societies. Although white-settler societies were a product of Western colonialism in the eighteenth and nineteenth centuries, contemporary multicultural societies are a product of post-war economic growth, the demand for migrant labour and the deregulation of labour markets.

Cultural hybridity is associated with the decline of cultural distinctiveness. We have seen that the sociology of consumerism has argued that modern societies are subject to strong pressures towards cultural standardization and hence the loss of local or national distinction. We argue against this analysis, because it neglects cultural resistance to cultural anni-hilation. We have identified two dimensions that are important in cultural resistance (aesthetics and politics). By taking a range of historical exam-ples, we have examined both authoritarian and democratic responses to globalization. Many responses to cultural standardization are conserva-tive and authoritarian. Nationalist movements in the 1920s developed a strong aesthetic rejection of cultural modernization. In contemporary societies, fundamentalism (in Judaism, Christianity and Islam) is cultur-ally conservative (but it also uses modern technology and communication systems to oppose modernity). Social movements to create distinctive aesthetic principles are not inevitably conservative. William Morris's arts and crafts movement was closely associated with socialism, and the intellectuals associated with the Ballets Russes were progressive. The problem facing secular and democratic elites today is how to mobilize social forces against global consumer co-optation without embracing reactionary cultural politics or religious fundamentalism. This challenge leaves open the question as to whether a strong cultural aesthetic can be promoted by a democratic mass movement in order to avoid the pres-sures of homogenization and the flattening of the world.

6 WORLD RELIGIONS AND FUNDAMENTALISM

INTRODUCTION

Religion has been one of the earliest globalizing forces in history. In the contemporary phase of globalization religion remains a potent force, often creating rifts between social groups, and yet sometimes offering a glimmer of hope for global peace. It remains a means of both personal salvation and social mobilization. Opinion polls continue to show that an overwhelming majority of people believe in God and divinity. As of the first decade of the twenty-first century, 16.7 per cent (1.1 billion) of world's 6.6 billion people (2007) do not believe in God. The remaining 84 per cent or 5.7 billion people adhere to one or the other form of religion.

Major religions and their adherents

Christianity	2.1 b	30.8%
Islam	1.5 b	22%
Secular	1.1 b	16.1%
Hindu	900 m	13.2%
Non-traditional religions, and others	394 m	5.7%
Buddhism	376 m	5.5%
Chinese traditional religion	430 m	6.3%
Total population	6.8 b	100%

Source: www.adherents.com/Religions_By_Adherents.html (accessed on 5 March 2008).

The continued popularity of religion debunks the secularization thesis which predicted the decline of religion with the onset of modernity. Religion also has the interesting feature of being both very locally embedded in everyday practices and beliefs, and global in its reach and significance.

During the nineteenth century, in the comparative study of religion, the idea of major "world religions" became firmly established. The reference here to "world" has many connotations, but at least one of these is that certain religions are universalistic and think of themselves as culturally relevant to all of humanity. This self-definition in global terms was especially prevalent among evangelical religions which did not treat religious identity as equivalent to ethnic identity. Along with trade and technology, therefore, these evangelical religions – especially Christianity and Islam – became widely dispersed globally. One would be impressed by seeing mosques in remote Xian in China or an old Armenian Church in Bangladesh or a Hindu temple in Bali, Indonesia. These are some of the standing proofs of religious globalization that pre-dates economic globalization by several centuries.

How does religion fit into contemporary processes of globalization? Is religion compatible with the high modernity that globalization represents? What are the various ways religion remains a part of the cultural mosaic? How do several "world religions" coexist in harmony (more or less) in a globalized world? We also wish to consider, following the demise of organized Soviet-style socialism, whether religion can offer or assume a cosmopolitan vision in the modern world. In particular, can religious revivalism (for which we use the convenient short-hand term "fundamentalism") assume a cosmopolitan framework outside the narrow group of converts? These questions need to be addressed in the context of an understanding about secularization as a process and secularism as a set of institutions and assumptions about the relationship between politics and religion.

Religion and state are entangled in an intricate and complicated relationship. The basic framework of Western secularization was established by the Treaty of Westphalia in 1648 which brought to an end the Thirty Years War, when religious differences had contributed to the devastation of European societies. The Treaty ended religious war and created modern states. It demanded that religion was to be a matter of private conscience, not of public identity; the Church was ultimately subordinate to the state; and each prince was to decide which private religion was permissible within civil society. We can see the Treaty of Westphalia as an implementation of Thomas Hobbes's theory of the state in which sovereignty was necessary for the establishment of civil peace on the basis of a secular contract.

The separation of religion and state was often more symbolic than real, and in most European societies the definition of citizenship was politically defined by membership of the state but culturally defined by religion. Until the twentieth century at least, national identity tended to be founded on religious membership. France and Spain might be classical examples, but in a less obvious way Englishness was closely tied to Anglicanism as the national religion. With the rise of fascism, religion went into retreat in Europe, despite the fact that both Hitler and Mussolini periodically mobilized the churches to define National Socialism as different from communism. Through much of the post-war period, nationalism came to be based more on ethnic than on religious principles, and the great era of communism and nationalism saw the suppression of religion in favour of secular nationalism. This movement happened throughout the Middle East – in Nasser's socialism and the Ba'ath Party, in Iran with the Shah and in Indonesia with Sukarno. Communism under Stalin and Mao was clearly hostile to all forms of religion, which they saw as an underground attack on secularism as a principle of solidarity. Communist parties were typically suspicious of all forms of religious association, which they saw as a threat to their monopoly of power.

Although the final collapse of Soviet communism in 1992 ushered in a new era of freedom of religion in civil society, the great turning point was the Iranian Revolution of 1979 which began the process of Islamic reform and the rise of various types of Muslim fundamentalism. In global terms, there has been, mainly through private religious educational systems, a great revival of religious fundamentalism. However, this movement is not a restoration of tradition, but a genuine movement of modernization based on ascetic principles for the self, and a demand for religious values to be upheld in the public sphere. It is a reversal of Westphalia; it has made religious identity a critical matter of politics. The illustration for this movement is obviously Islamic neo-fundamentalism with its demand that Sharia, or religious law, play a large role in civil law. But similar changes have occurred in Christianity, Judaism and Hinduism.

The implication of these changes is that religious revival can be compatible with modernization, but it may also mean that modernity can be a religious culture. Neo-fundamentalism attempts to destroy traditional folk religion and to provide people who are new to urban living with self-identity. These developments are obvious in India, Malaysia, Indonesia and much of Africa. But there are alternative forms of religion in modern society that are closely connected to what Talcott Parsons called the "expressive revolution". Popular religion in the "spiritual market" of modern society is typically syncretic and borrows from a variety of traditions. It is often magical, in the sense that it offers healing rituals and protection against contingency. The difference between neo-fundamentalism and popular religion is related to the anthropological distinction between great and little traditions. Neo-fundamentalism is literate and ascetic; it is concerned with salvation. Popular religion is magical and hedonistic; it is concerned with everyday problems of health, marriage and birth.

Historically the processes of globalization and secularization undermined the legacy of literary hierarchical religion, and the media have made popular religion accessible on a world market. The literate ascetic virtuoso or saint is being replaced by the religious celebrity.

DEFINING RELIGION

"Religion" (*religio*) has two distinctive etymological roots (Derrida, 1998). First, *relegere*, from *legere*, means to bring together, to harvest or to gather. Secondly, *religare*, from *ligare*, means to tie or to bind together (Benveniste, 1973). The first meaning recognizes the religious foundations of any social group that is gathered together. The second indicates the discipline or morality that is necessary for controlling and regulating human beings. The first meaning attends to the role of the cult in forming human membership, while the second meaning points to the regulatory practices of religion in the discipline of the passions. This distinction formed the basis of Kant's philosophical analysis of religion and morality.

Our discussion so far has made implicit assumptions about the nature of religion, and to develop this discussion about religion and globalization we need to consider in more detail what sociologists have to say about religion as a set of social institutions. Émile Durkheim defined religion as a system of beliefs and rituals that unites people into communities or churches (in the case of Christianity). In pre-industrial society religion was social glue, a source of social solidarity and cohesion, according to Durkheim. At the beginning of the Enlightenment in Europe, Immanuel Kant distinguished between religion as cult in which people seek favours from God through prayer and offerings to bring healing and wealth, and religion as moral action that commands human beings to change their lives. Kant further defined religion as a "reflecting faith" or "moralizing faith" that compels humans to strive for salvation through faith alone. The Kantian distinction was fundamental to Max Weber's view of the relationship between asceticism and mysticism.

Weber developed two separate and distinct arguments about religion. There is the Protestant ethic thesis which examined the cultural consequences (or "elective affinity") of inner-worldly asceticism on economic behaviour. The second argument concerned the separation of Church and state (or religion and politics). The so-called "Asiatic religions" failed to foster modernization, because they were world-accepting not world-rejecting religious systems, but they were also more likely, especially in the case of Islam, to develop caesaro-papist tendencies in which the political and the religious were fused (undifferentiated). Democratic capitalist cultures developed when both conditions (asceticism and differentiation) were satisfied. In general, Weber was inclined to regard Asian religions such as Mahayana Buddhism and Hinduism as cultic religions of the masses, while radical Calvinism was clearly a moralizing faith of action. In short, Calvinistic rationalism was the universal benchmark of a modernizing ethic. Weber's attempts to locate rabbinical Judaism and prophetic Islam in this model proved to be especially unsatisfactory. However, Robert Bellah in *Tokugawa Religion* (1957) showed how the modernization of Japan had involved changes in its religious system that supported Weber's argument about the emphasis on this-worldly asceticism.

Between the publication of the Protestant ethic essays and his death in 1920, Weber published a series of studies on the economic ethics of the world religions that in effect constituted what we now know as the sociology of religion. Weber's studies in comparative religion, which included ancient Judaism, the religions of India and China, and various scattered commentaries on Islam, the Protestant sects and Catholicism, formed a monumental contribution to sociological and historical scholarship. Weber created an assembly of rich concepts to understand religious institutions that continue to shape contemporary research – virtuoso and mass religion, rationalization of life orders, disenchantment, inner-worldly asceticism, salvation paths, charisma and so forth.

In Weber's comparative sociology of world religions, the Protestant sects were reflecting or moralizing faiths that exercised leverage over society. In the *Sociology of Religion*, Weber distinguished between the religion of the masses and the religion of the virtuosi. While masses seek comfort from religion, especially healing and good fortune, the virtuosi fulfil the ethical demands of religion in search of spiritual salvation or enlightenment. The religion of the masses requires saints and holy men to satisfy their needs, and hence charisma is corrupted by the demand for miracles and spectacles. More importantly, Weber distinguished between those religions that reject the world by challenging its traditions (such as inner-worldly asceticism) and religions that seek to escape from the world through mystical flight (such as other-worldly mysticism). The former religions (primarily the Calvinistic radical sects) have had revolutionary consequences for human society in the formation of rational capitalism. The implication of this tradition is paradoxical. First, Christianity (or at least Puritanism) is the only true religion (as a reflecting faith); and second, Christianity gives rise to a process of secularization that spells out its own self-overcoming (*Aufhebung*).

In the 1960s the secularization thesis, particularly in the work of the English sociologist Bryan Wilson, supported Kant and Weber in arguing that the early phase of asceticism in the growth of capitalism would be followed by secularism in which Christianity became a self-destructive form of religiosity. Protestant enlightenment paved the way for the death of God debate, because it placed so much emphasis on individual belief in the literal truth of the Bible. As criticism of the Bible developed in the late nineteenth century, such absolute confidence in the unique truth of "biblical religion" declined. Two modern philosophers – Richard Rorty and Gianni Vattimo – argue that we are in the "age of interpretation" where there are no hard facts, only shared agreements about how to use language, and hence religious beliefs are also only interpretations of our world, not God-given revelations (Zabala, 2005).

Against this philosophical scepticism, it is clear that religions are enjoying a remarkable revival globally. The lecture of the Archbishop of Canterbury, Dr Rowan Williams, in February 2008 in which he raised the possibility that Sharia law might operate in Britain in the domestic affairs of Muslims, and the controversy that followed, illustrated the problem of secularism and the apparent retreat from multiculturalism in Europe. The tensions between religion and politics characterize modern Israel and India on the one hand and Vietnam and China on the other. Of course, religion and politics are not inevitably in a oppositional relationship. Politics often embraces religious motives and narratives to give expression to a nationalist agenda, especially the nationalist revival which appears to be essential to contemporary Russian politics, where there has been a dramatic recovery of Russian Orthodoxy.

Even in a secular age, religion often appears to produce the vitality and substance of successful political movements. Perhaps the most telling illustration of the strange political marriage of religion and politics would be the Polish Solidarity movement in which Polish trade unionists and political activists used religious sites and symbols to pursue distinctive political objectives.

The Islamic revival of the last twenty years in Asia has depended on the social role of religious educational institutions (or *madrasas*) in instilling moral regulation on youth, or "technologies of the self" that demand a high degree of discipline and asceticism. This religious training is seen to offer protection to young people from the temptations of Western consumerism and to be a process of excluding popular religious traditions such as Sufism. Secondly, there is also a revival of local religious traditions with the collapse of secular nationalism and communism in the region in which the Internet has been important in transmitting magical beliefs and popular practices to a mass audience, for example in Thailand. In the West, religious subjectivity finds an outlet in romantic individualism. In the East, there is a revival of both religious asceticism and religious consumerism that offers comfort to the laity. Kant's distinction between popular cultic religion and religious rationalism continues to be useful as a conceptual framework for the complex processes of religious change.

THE SECULARIZATION THESIS RE-EXAMINED

With the dominance of modernization theory, it was assumed that religion would not play a large part in social organization. At best it would be confined to the private sphere. Secularization, which was assumed to be a necessary component of modernization, proved to be enormously difficult to define. Following James Beckford's discussion in *Social Theory and Religion* (2003), we suggest that the secularization thesis entailed a number of critical dimensions.

First, there is the social differentiation of society into specialized spheres in which religion becomes simply one institution to provide various services to its followers or to the community; secularization is the decline of the scope of authority structures. Fundamentalism is the attempt to halt this differentiation.

Secondly, rationalization involves the corrosion of the power of religious beliefs and the authority of religious specialists (such as priests). This argument is associated with Weber's notion of "disenchantment". While this argument acknowledges the impact of science on public explanations of phenomena and the conduct of public life, social survey research shows that belief in magic and superstition remains very high in advanced societies. Eschatology can also have a potent role in secular society. In the United States, Christian fictional literature depicting the return of Christ in the publishing series *Left Behind* has sold over 70 million copies. These stories are loosely based on the book of Revelation and this literary genre gives expression to what evangelicals call "the Rapture", which is the contemporary account of the disappearance of Christians from the earth and their entry into heaven, leaving behind sinners and unbelievers. The series combines a traditional apocalyptic religion with conservative political attitudes. For example, in the struggle with evil forces, the United Nations appears as the Antichrist on earth. Around 8 million American Christians believe that the Rapture is coming soon, and this transformation of the world is indicated by, for example, the crisis in the Middle East. In popular culture, Mel Gibson's film *The Passion of the Christ* illustrated the capacity of religion to capture public interest and to ignite traditional forms of anti-Semitism.

Thirdly, modernization (often a combination of differentiation and rationalization) is a cluster of processes emphasizing individualism, democratic politics, liberal values, and norms of efficiency and economic growth. Because modernization undermines tradition, it cuts off the communal and social foundations that supported religion as a traditional institution. However, religion continues to play a role in supporting national, regional or class identities in industrial capitalism, for example in Northern Ireland, Catholic France, the Solidarity movement in Poland, and the Orthodox revival in Russia. Nationalism often appears to trade off or require the traditional symbolic support of religion.

Fourthly, secularization may simply be the transformation or metamorphosis of religion as it adjusts to new conditions. There are many versions of this argument. Sociologists have argued that the social is essentially religious, and what counts as "religion" does not decline; it just keeps transforming. Thomas Luckmann (1967) has argued that modern societies have an "invisible religion" that characterizes the transcendence of the everyday world. There is an "implicit religion" of beliefs about spiritual phenomena that are not necessarily Christian or components of formal religion. In modern societies there is "believing without belonging", because religious membership and attendance decline, but belief in the Christian faith is still prevalent.

Over the last two centuries, secularization in the narrow sense (decline in church membership and attendance, marginalization of the Church from public life, and the dominance of scientific explanations of the world) has been characteristic of Europe (especially northern, Protestant Europe) and its former colonies (Australia, New Zealand, and Canada), but not characteristic of the United States, where religion remains powerful, or in many Catholic societies, especially in Latin America and Africa. In these societies, Pentecostalism and charismatic movements have been growing. In Islam, Christianity, Judaism and Hinduism there have been powerful movements of fundamentalist revival. In many societies, youth culture and popular culture more generally have given rise to hybrid forms of religiosity, often employing the Internet to disseminate their services and beliefs. In post-communist societies, there is clear evidence of a revival of Orthodoxy (Russia and eastern Europe) and Islam (in China and Indonesia), and Buddhist movements and "schools" have millions of followers in Japan.

Sociologists such as Kingsley Davis and Bryan Wilson, who confi-
dently predicted the erosion of religion with the spread of secularism
and scientific cultures, would find it difficult to explain adequately the great
post-communism resurgence of religion. Parsons, who did not accept
the secularization thesis, saw the secular success of post-war America
in the 1950s and 1960s as the triumph of liberal Protestantism. The
history of America – with its separation of religion and politics, and its
pluralism, and individualism – was the fulfilment of religious individualism and Protestant piety. The Cold War tended to reinforce this picture
of the triumph of American culture against secular totalitarianism and
atheist communism. In this period liberal politics was heavily influenced
by theologians such as Reinhold Niebuhr who sought to steer a course
between the political Left that was blind to the excesses of communism
and the political Right that instituted a witch hunt against reds in
Hollywood and Harvard (Mattson, 2005). In this context, Parsons could
see liberal Protestantism as an illustration of the adaptive upgrading of
American society. This view of America was eventually shattered by the
Vietnam War, against which the expressive revolution was a political and
aesthetic response of youth.

In the concept of the "expressive revolution", Parsons followed
Durkheim in studying individualism as a major transformation of society.
There is, however, a contradiction between individualism as either the
legacy of Protestant pietism or the product of modern consumerism.
The student protests of the 1960s were harbingers of a new expressive
subjectivity that, in its celebration of love, has a religious dimension.

The Rise of Modern Fundamentalism: An Expressive Revolution?

While there is much to support the secularization thesis as a description
of modern European history, it is important not to confuse the decline
of Christian institutions with the decline of religion. In other words, we
must not equate "de-Christianization" with the decline of religious
world-views. The importance of values of intimacy (individual emotional attachment and loyalty in intimate relationships) in a secular age
can be taken as an indication of the continuity of religion in Western societies. From Protestantism, Western societies have acquired an emphasis
on the individual and individualism through such phenomena as conversion, a personal relationship to Jesus, private devotion and Bible study.
Conversion experiences emphasized the importance of experiencing a

loving relationship with Jesus, where emotional intensity became a measure of spiritual intensity.

A major feature of many fundamentalist movements is the desire to restore family values, improve Christian education and protect children from lifestyles that are simultaneously anti-American and anti-Christian. We can see the development of the Christian Right as a delayed response to the failure of the Vietnam War and a critique of the values of the radical student movements of the 1960s. This perception of the erosion of American values was at the heart of the Moral Majority that was formed in 1979 under the leadership of Jerry Falwell. The original inspiration for this movement came from political groups that were frustrated with the Republican Party, and it included Protestants, Catholics, Mormons and Pentecostalists. American domestic and foreign policy had to be based on the Bible, and in order to restore America to its true mission it was necessary to struggle against the "moral minority" that exercised power over the government. The New Christian Right, as they came to be known, were against abortion, against gay rights and against drug liberalization. In fact, there was a significant emphasis on problems relating to sexuality (Armstrong, 2001: 311). More recently they have led campaigns against gay marriage and the ordination of gay clergy. Fundamentalists regarded feminism as a "disease" and equated homosexuality with pederasty. It was "secular humanism", a catch-all phrase that included feminism and liberalism, that had emasculated American men. In this respect, fundamentalism was able to address a range of popular anxieties about male impotence, high divorce rates, female self-assertion and low birth rates.

American fundamentalism responded to this cultural and political crisis in a number of ways. From the late 1980s, there were aggressive, and occasionally violent, campaigns against abortion clinics by so-called moral "rescuers". On the educational system, Christian creationists led an attack on evolutionary science and Darwinism in an effort to assert the literal truth of Genesis. In terms of family life, fundamentalists reasserted what they thought to be the biblical view of marriage, namely the importance of male headship. For example, the Southern Baptist Convention meeting in 1988 amended its Baptist Faith and Message Statement to declare that a woman should "submit herself graciously" to the leadership of her husband. The result of the amendment by the largest American Protestant denomination was to jettison the principle of an egalitarian family. This assertion of male leadership was seen to be a necessary step in restoring the family that is seen to be fundamental to the continuity of Christianity and to the health of the nation. In practice, Christian interpretations of what leadership actually means in day-to-day terms are variable and pragmatic, but the influence of these fundamentalist ideas has been significant, as illustrated by former President Clinton's eventual confession of sinfulness to a breakfast meeting of Christian leaders.

While American fundamentalism has been predominantly a Protestant religious movement of the southern states, there has also been a remarkable convergence of opinion between fundamentalism, the political Right, Catholic conservatives and, ironically, components of the women's movement around pro-natalism. These diverse movements have in various ways rejected liberal America in favour of the regulation of pornography, anti-abortion legislation, the criminalization of homosexuality and the virtues of faithfulness and loyalty in permanent sexual partnerships. In short, these values confirmed a religious view of sexual and marital relationships that transcended denominational affiliation. Fundamentalism can be interpreted in this respect as a sustained struggle against the expressive revolution; it is a struggle between two conceptions of the self – the Kantian ascetic and disciplined self, and the expressive-affective mobile self. The first is the direct descendant of Protestant asceticism and the second is a distortion of the expressive self of the conversionist sects of the eighteenth and nineteenth centuries.

Who are the fundamentalists? In terms of their core membership and leadership, they are recruited from the educated but alienated urban social classes. They are frustrated science teachers, unpaid civil servants, disillusioned doctors, and underemployed engineers. In short, fundamentalists are recruited from social groups that have failed to benefit from secular nationalist governments and aborted modernization projects. This pattern of recruitment suggests that fundamentalism is not necessarily a traditional protest against modernity, but rather what Antoun (2008) calls "selective modernization and controlled acculturation". The first approach refers to the process whereby certain technological and organizational innovations of modern society are accepted and others are rejected. The second approach is the process whereby an individual accepts a practice or belief from another culture (the secular world) and integrates it into their value system (the religious world). One illustration of the process of selective modernization is the use of television and radio by fundamentalist Christian groups in the United States. For example, Pat Robertson's Christian Broadcasting Network (CBN) is now the third largest cable network in America, and funds the CBN University offering courses on media production techniques. Another example is James Dobson's radio program, *Focus on the Family*, which offers psychological advice and counselling services. This program has evolved into the equivalent of a Christian call centre and receives 1,200 daily calls on a toll-free number. Among Islamic radical groups, modern technology is also avidly embraced. The militant Hezbollah group has an information network in Beirut with mobile phones, computers and a multiple-version website. Antoun also considers various forms of controlled acculturation for Jewish and Muslim fundamentalists that involve various forms of physical separation. In Israel, Jewish fundamentalists who have to take university courses in academic settings that are secular and liberal have negotiated special arrangements – for example, to be taught by men. In Saudi Arabia, fundamentalists have used distance learning techniques to avoid contact with women who are "immodestly dressed". Fundamentalist groups are not wholly opposed to modernity, and have adapted various modern technologies to improve their organizational and communications effectiveness. We would argue that fundamentalists are specifically hostile to traditional religion which in their view has compromised the fundamental tenets of faith, and that by embracing modern technology and organizational forms fundamentalist movements are, often as an unintended consequence, ushering in radical modernity. This view is of course perfectly compatible with the Weber thesis in which the Protestant sects were the reluctant midwives of modernization. Political Islam, with its emphasis on discipline, asceticism, hard work and literacy, and its hostility to traditional Islam in the shape of the Sufi lodges, may also have similar cultural consequences.

Latin Christianity created a common religious and political culture in medieval Europe. This dominant culture was broken by the Reformation and the division of Europe into competing states with distinctive national religions. The growth of nationalism in Europe had very diverse consequences for the churches, but religious symbols, often combined with epic literature and folk culture, have been indispensable for the creation of nations as "imagined communities" (Anderson 1983). This vitality of religious symbols in nation formation has been constructed on the basis of conservative hostility to both secularism and communism. The dominant transformations of religion in the twentieth century were brought about by the secularization of Europe and the decline of communism as a significant atheist alternative to theological belief systems. In the twenty-first century, the religious map of Europe is changing once more as globalization has created the hybridization of religious culture.

Broadly speaking, we can identify four periods of Islamic political action in response to the social and cultural crises resulting from foreign domination and internal haemorrhaging. These movements have critically attacked contemporary political and military weakness in the name of the pristine Islam of the early community of the Prophet, and hence they have been labelled "fundamentalist". In the nineteenth century, these reformist movements, which were hostile to both traditional folk religion such as the Sufi lodges and the external Western threat, included Wahhabism in Arabia, the Mahdi in the Sudan, the Sanusis in North Africa, and Islamic reform movements in Egypt. The second wave of activism occurred in the 1940s with the development of the Muslim Brotherhood in Egypt, and the third movement began in the aftermath of the Arab defeat in the 1967 war with Israel and reached a crescendo with the Iranian Revolution in 1978–9 and with opposition to the Russian incursion into Afghanistan. The contemporary fourth wave of resistance opened with the Gulf War in 1990, when the entry of American troops into Saudi Arabia led to the formation of the Al-Qaeda network, September 11 and the war on terrorism. Reformist Islam had its roots in the "puritanical" Wahhabi movement (Muhammad al-Wahhab 1703–92), but in the reformism of the nineteenth century Islam was no longer the traditional religion of the Ottoman period, it was connected with nationalism, and it sought to make Islam once more independent of the West. Several Islamic intellectuals and leaders became crucial to Islamic modernity: Jamal al-Din al-Afghani (1839–97), Muhammad Abduh (1849–1905), Rashid Rida in Syria, Hasan al-Banna (1900–49), Sayyid Qutb (1903–66) and Sayyid Abul Ala Maududi (1903–79) in Egypt. These intellectuals and activists had much in common: they saw Islam as weak because it had accumulated accretions that have obscured its radical and modern ideas; they attacked folk religiosity, especially the legacy of Sufism; they embraced many of the technological ideas of Western modernity; they and especially al-Banna, the founder of the Muslim Brotherhood, refashioned the spiritual idea of *jihad* to make it a more obviously political notion; and they reinterpreted a range of traditional theological concepts to give them a more modern relevance – communal consensus was treated as an Islamic idea of democracy and legal interpretation was made a legitimate principle of Sharia. There was in the twentieth century tension and often open hostility between reformist Islam and emerging anti-colonial and post-colonial versions of secular nationalism (often funded and supported by Soviet communism), and Pan-Arabism, namely Nasserism, the Ba'ath Party in Syria and Iraq, the legacy of Atatürk's Young Turk movement, the Persian nationalism of Risa Shah, and Sukarno's leadership in Indonesia. The Six Day War (1967), the collapse of the United Arab Republic, and the economic failures of the region contributed to a sense of the failure of secular politics – reinforced eventually by the Gulf War and in the wake of 9/11.

THE CRISIS OF LIBERAL TOLERANCE

The growth of fundamentalism and the radicalization of many Islamic communities have brought many Western observers to the conclusion that there is a deep crisis in secular liberalism, and this development in turn brings into question the validity of the Westphalian system that we briefly discussed at the beginning of this chapter. Civil society, the rule of law and the enjoyment of rights are important in providing a minimal security for our condition of vulnerability. There must be some level of social order and trust if our vulnerability is to be protected from the vagaries of life. Human vulnerability and the precarious nature of social existence have been severely questioned over the last two decades by a rising tide of terrorism, communal violence, civil strife and warfare. Cosmopolitanism, democracy and multiculturalism have become standard responses to the current crisis. However, this debate has often taken place at a macro-sociological level in terms of "the clash of civilizations" (Huntington, 1993), "the law of peoples" (Rawls, 1999) or the Westphalian "privatisation of religion" (Turner, 2003b). John Rawls in *The Law of Peoples* (1999) provides a classic example of such generalizations when he argues that 'the fact of reasonable pluralism' in a liberal democracy requires tolerance between religious groups, in which no one group imposes its hegemonic beliefs on any other group.

These very general assertions about the separation of religion and politics, the secularization of the public sphere and political tolerance tell us very little about how people in religiously diverse societies, within which there may be significant religious revivalism, actually go about the task of managing their everyday lives. To express this somewhat in the language of ethnomethodology, how do people do "being religious"?

In societies that are being transformed by global migration and the emergence of large diasporic communities, people in their everyday lives find that they may be forced to interact with, eat next to, or talk with strangers, that is, people with very different religious commitments, customs and lifestyles. How do ordinary people manage the complexity of everyday life in terms of selecting friends, choosing restaurants, managing domestic servants or sending their children to school? How does the global transformation of religious identities work out at the everyday level of managing situations which may be perceived as embarrassing, contaminating or even dangerous? To take a mundane example from contemporary Singapore, the Singaporean government supports racial harmony through such events as "Racial Harmony Month", but this official project is somewhat undermined by the compartmentalization of daily life around racial groups – the Chinese, Malays, Indians and others. At a daily level, tensions often emerge in customary practices (Chin and Vasu, 2006). While Chinese middle-class housewives like to keep dogs as pets, increasingly devout Muslim neighbours embracing customary Muslim norms regard dogs as religiously polluting. How does one behave towards neighbours when faced with the threat of religious pollution? There are of course studies of similar situations in the West such as Kathryn Spellman's (2004) *Religion and Nation: Iranian Local and Transnational Networks in Britain.* She explores the domestic lives of Iranian women in London in terms of how they manage "private" religious identities within a diaspora that exists within a secular capital city. But there is relatively little comparative work on religious diversity and growing pressures towards the public adoption of religious identities. How does the private domestic world interact and interconnect with broad changes in global religious identities, especially where these emerging religious cultures have such significant consequences? Islamic fundamentalism, Christian evangelism, Hindu revivalism and Jewish ultra-orthodoxy are, in socially and religiously diverse societies, posing the question: how do I behave as a "good Muslim" (or "good Christian" or "good Jew" and so forth)? Traditional standards of religious behaviour are being both redefined and intensified by such processes, and these changes make the achievement of liberal tolerance, cosmopolitan virtue and multiculturalism deeply problematic.

There has been a world-wide growth of religious fundamentalism (Armstrong, 2001; Berger, 1999; Juergensmeyer, 2003). There are consequently important political questions about how plural societies can survive, and about the role of urban cosmopolitanism, and the possibility of a normative commitment to pluralism (Holton, 2009; Turner, 2002). What policies might support a commitment to ensuring civil harmony in societies that are necessarily more complex and heterogeneous because of international migration and involvement in the global economy? What policies might be relevant in societies with religious groups that are being transformed by fundamentalism, conservative orthodoxy and revivalism? One argument from John Rawls, a political philosopher, has been to suggest that what he calls a "decent liberal society" will require "an overlapping consensus".

Rawls, in attempting to provide the classical liberal defence of freedom of speech and individual conscience, struggles with the problem that religious fundamentalists do not necessarily accept the liberal version of a decent society. Their "comprehensive doctrines" appear to rule out any easy tolerance of difference, and they do not wholly welcome people leaving the group, for example as a result of marriage into another religious tradition or by converting as a result of evangelism to some other comprehensive doctrine. Rawls provides no real practical solution to these problems. Historically liberalism had attempted to solve religious conflict by making religion a matter of private belief, separating church and state, excluding religious instruction from schools, and making "hate speech" a criminal offence. By and large, many religious groups outside liberal Protestantism do not fit into and consequently have not accepted this Westphalian framework (Spinner-Halev, 2005).

If we consider the most basic and traditional sociological perspectives on the social group, then we would have to conclude that the dynamics of group life tend in plural societies to work against Rawlsian reciprocity (Shibutani, 1961). Sustaining group loyalty through revivalism and exclusionary religious norms is important for maintaining group cohesion, but they are not compatible with the idea of cosmopolitan societies emerging with social pluralism. In particular, marital homogamy ("like marries like") has long been recognized by sociologists as a fundamental feature of courtship and marriage. The trend towards marital homogamy in Southeast Asia has increased with religious norms prescribing intra-faith marriage as a religious duty. A series of *fatwas* from the Indonesian Council of Ulemas in July 2005 proclaimed that inter-faith marriages were against Sharia law, and condemned ecumenical activities between different faiths. These pronouncements are not automatically underwritten by the state but they significantly impact on daily practice. For example, Indonesians of Chinese descent and Indonesians whose religion falls outside the official list of recognized religions have difficulty getting their marriages registered, and very few officials will participate in weddings of couples from different religions. In Malaysia the Parti Islam Se-Malaysia has advocated the creation of a strong Islamic state that would enforce customary *hudud* penalties on women, requiring severe limitations on their rights to divorce, and permitting men to have numerous wives (Anwar, 2001).

The emphasis on conversion and the dangers of apostasy make the achievement of social harmony within cultural diversity highly problematic. Several cases have recently appeared in the international media. The most spectacular was the attempt in March 2006 by Muslim clerics to put to death Abdul Rahman, an Afghan man who had converted to Christianity. The apostasy rule goes back to the foundations of Islam when tribal leaders joined in a social contract with the Prophet that was the basis of the Constitution of Medina, creating the original Muslim *umma*. When the Prophet died, some of these tribes attempted to leave the community, resulting in the War of the *Ridda* or Apostasy War. The apostasy rule states that any Muslim leaving the *umma* and who maligns or abuses the community shall be severely punished. The apostasy rule has been criticized by some Muslims, including the former Indonesian president who pointed out in the *Washington Post* that the teaching of the Qur'an states "Let there be no compulsion in religion" (Wahid, 2006). Nevertheless there is considerable customary pressure not to quit the community.

One can usefully apply concepts from Albert Hirschman (1970) to argue that, with religious fundamentalism and the role of religion in defining political identities, religious groups emphasize "loyalty" (being a "good Muslim" or "good Christian" with high commitments), remain suspicious about the exercise of "voice" (being critical of religious leadership), and impose heavy costs for "exit" (apostasy). In recent years, rational choice theories have become popular in the sociology of religion (Young, 1997). We might argue in these terms that the apostasy rule invokes a set of elementary sanctions against the act of "whistle-blowing", while fundamentalist norms of commitment attack any proclivity towards becoming a "free rider".

Revivalism and an emphasis on strong religious identities mean in practice that women, or more specifically mothers, are very important in the construction of religious identities because women are responsible for domestic arrangements such as managing the children's religious education, making choices about food and diet, and organizing private space. Group cohesion is enhanced by in-marriage, by ensuring the effective transmission of culture across generations, and punishing all attempts to exit the group. Group cohesion requires the domestic and public regulation of women, and hence patriarchal religious norms are typically invoked when social groups are under threat, or perceived to be under threat. In Aceh, Indonesia, newly enforced religious rules prevent local women from serving alcohol to Western visitors, and in May 2006 Syarifah Binti Jauhari was sentenced to 10 months in jail for breaking this rule. Similarly, attempts to impose rules against pornography in Indonesia will prevent women having bare arms in public spaces (Tedjasukama and Cangkring, 2006). Muslim militant groups or vigilantes are now common in cities in Indonesia since the fall of Suharto in 1998 to enforce restrictive sexual norms, typically against single women in public.

These group norms are more likely to be invoked when a community is a minority, or where the majority feels it is under threat by a minority which, for example, is economically dominant. These everyday norms that are important for defining religious differences, sustaining group identities and maintaining the continuity of the group may be called "rituals of intimacy". These rituals are part of the drama of representing the religious self in contexts that may be ambiguous, contradictory or dangerous. They are guides to good action – for example: can I serve alcohol to strangers and maintain my identity as a "good woman"? These rituals or codes of conduct provide a series of answers to questions about how to behave towards strangers who are not co-religionists and how to maintain religious purity in societies that are secular.

Norms regulating correct everyday behaviour have of course been present in all traditional religious systems. In traditional Muslim cultures, there are well-established customary guides. These guides to action were often fashioned along social class lines, and what applied to court administrators would not apply to peasants (Hodgson, 1974). What, then, is new in the contemporary situation? One can argue that Islamic norms were originally constructed for the guidance of behaviour in societies which were wholly or predominantly Muslim. With the growth of the world-wide Muslim diaspora, there is a new need to define correct behaviour and to expunge "foreign elements", whether these are Western or indigenous folk components. For example, Al-Qaysi's *Morals and Manners in Islam* (1986) warns of the need to Islamize customary behaviour and ensure that children are raised according to correct norms. The second issue is that with fundamentalism there is, as it were, an inflationary pressure to increase the scope and depth of these norms. As Muslim imams compete for lay followers, there is a tendency to increase the strictness of norms that are seen to be required by Sharia. One interesting example is that while halal food such as the prohibition of pork is well known, in an inflationary religious setting these norms also come to include the idea of halal water. The pornography bill before the Indonesian Parliament will inflate the range of activities and circumstances that can be defined as pornographic, from kissing in the street to revealing "sensual" body parts. Thirdly, the growth of the Internet has greatly increased this sense of the global *umma*, and the importance of strict adherence to norms (Mandaville, 2001). Finally, there is a series of contingent circumstances that have enhanced the perceived need to defend Islamic practice. In particular, 9/11, the notion of a clash of civilizations and the war on terror have all conspired to enhance the norms of group identity (Roy, 1994, 2004).

COSMOPOLITANISM AND CIVIL HARMONY

The argument about the growing disjunction between the state and the public realm, on the one hand, and the everyday world, on the other, can be rendered more precise by drawing a distinction between popular religion, official or institutional religion, and spirituality. The dichotomy between the great and the little tradition or between official and popular religion has been a fundamental idea of both anthropology and sociology (Spiro, 1970; Turner, 1998; Weber, 1996). Indeed, this distinction was fundamental to the whole legacy of Kantian philosophy that shaped the sociology of religion of Durkheim and Weber (Kant, 1960). The presence of popular forms of religion has in part articulated this cultural gap between the everyday world of peasants and the official culture of the literate, urban classes. The development of modern fundamentalism can be seen as yet another attempt to cleanse or to eradicate popular religion by inculcating norms that essentially rationalize everyday life in the name of a stricter, more ethical code.

This development is close to the original meaning of jihad as an ethical struggle to purify religious practice. In modern Islam there is a widespread "peaceful jihad" involving a negotiation of identity against a background of secular modernity (Lukens-Bull, 2005). There is good reason therefore to regard fundamentalism as a global version of Weber's Protestant ethic that brings everyday behaviour under the control of discipline, which attacks magical or mystical practices and which enforces literacy through the study of sacred texts and discourses (Weber, 2002). Fundamentalism is simply the modern version of an attack on popular religion that has been under way, for example in Islam, since at least the rise of Wahhabism in the late eighteenth century under the leadership of Muhammad al-Wahhab. But the difference is that these fundamentalist reforms are genuinely global, and they are no longer confined to specific regions or religious groups.

CONCLUSION: SPIRITUALITY VERSUS FUNDAMENTALISM

We can, however, argue that the globalization of religion takes two forms (Cox, 2003). In addition to global fundamentalism, there is the spread of global popular religion. These religious developments are no longer local popular cults, but burgeoning global popular religions. These have been called "new religious movements" (Beckford, 2003) or "spiritual market places" (Roof, 1993). Such forms of religion tend to be highly individualistic, they are unorthodox in the sense that they follow no official creed, they tend to be syncretic, and they have little or no connection with institutions such as churches, mosques or temples. They are post-institutional and they can be called "post-modern" religions. If global fundamentalism involves modernization, the global post-institutional religions could be said to involve "post-modernization".

In order to describe these new developments, some sociologists have usefully called them new forms of spirituality in contrast to religion and religiosity. Globalization thus involves the spread of spirituality, on the one hand, and fundamentalist religion, on the other. Spiritualities typically offer to involve not so much guidance in the everyday world, but subjective, personalized meaning often combined with therapeutic or healing services, or the promise of personal enhancement through, for example, meditation (Hunt, 2005). One could argue that fundamentalist norms of rationalization appeal most to social groups that are upwardly socially mobile, such as lower middle-class, newly educated couples. Spirituality is more closely associated with middle-class singles who have been most significantly influenced by Western consumer values.

Religion and spirituality can be seen to be in a state of mutual conflict and antagonism. The spiritual individualism of the upwardly mobile, cosmopolitan, middle-class habitus is incompatible with the rationalized norms of fundamentalism. We can assume that this explains the intellectual hostility of fundamentalist religious leaders to the consumerist individualism of the new spirituality.

7 MIGRATION AND TRANSNATIONALISM

INTRODUCTION

Migration, which is simply the physical movement of people from one place to another, has become the most visible face of globalization today. Even those who are sceptical about the notion of globalization and consider it to be an exaggerated claim cannot ignore the fact that in almost every society – that is, nation-state – there are a large number of residents who were born outside the country. This chapter discusses both historical and contemporary migrations as well as voluntary and involuntary migrations which are related to the global cultural and politico-economic processes. It will also deal with the "new slavery" migration of the working class, human trafficking, and forced prostitution, which reveal some of the darker sides of globalization. Migrants cover the whole spectrum of the occupational structure from high-tech professionals who move to places like Silicon Valley, California, the information technology hub in the United States, to low-end workers in risky jobs.

If all the migrants formed a state of their own, with a population of 200 million it would be the fifth largest country in the world, eclipsing Brazil, and following China, India, the USA and Indonesia. What is worth rethinking is the dynamics of the global–national interface that such a huge flow of people has posed.

Obviously one could argue that the movement of people from one place to another is nothing new, and historically there has been a natural flow of people, for example during harvests. Indeed our ancestors moved from place to place in groups, in search of a better life. And at least in theory, people could move more freely across geographical boundaries until the invention of the passport and the monopolization of the control of the means of movement by the state in the nineteenth century. In Europe, until the First World War, the movement of people took place quite freely. During and after the First World War, as mass travel expanded and borders became more rigorously guarded, the regulation and monitoring of human movement by the state became more determined (Torpey, 1998: 254).

What does it mean to say that migration is being globalized? Stephen Castles and Mark Miller provide the following evidence for the globalization of migration.

1   More and more countries are being involved in migration.
2   A large number of people are being caught up in migration.
3   There are now varieties of migration, such as seasonal, permanent and semi-permanent, and thus migration has become highly differentiated.
4   Migration is becoming feminized as more and more women are drawn into the migration circuit.
5   There are growing political controversies over migration.

To this we would add:

6   More people are on the move from one destination to other destination countries. Migration in the old days implied a change of place, from one country of origin to a country of destination; now that destination country has become a moving target. In international migration, some countries play the role of a platform for further migration. For professionals, the Gulf countries in general and the United Arab Emirates in particular play the role of a launch pad for further migration to North America and Australia.
7   The globalization of migration also brings to the fore the interface of the national and the global. Although different classes deal with this interface differently, sometimes trying to reconcile their national belonging with global imperatives, sometimes drawing the line between them sharply, no one can escape this duality.

Aristide Zolberg questions "the popular notion that the late twentieth century was 'the age of migration' (Castles and Miller, 1993), suggesting that the proportion foreign-born remained at the same level between 1965 and 2000, approximately 2.3 per cent, indicating that international migration grew slightly faster than world population" (Zolberg, 2006: 232). In terms of the percentage of population in the circuit of migration there has not been a major shift, yet the volume or the aggregate number has its own force. What is unique about migration in the age of globalization is that, as more and more people are moving to and from more and more countries, their movements are being closely documented and surveyed. Controversies over the undocumented movement of people are an affirmation of the importance of documentation and surveillance.

Migration is a result of a complex set of social, economic, political and cultural processes. There are several types of migration: voluntary, involuntary or forced, and economic or political. Often a combination of factors drives people to migrate.

CAUSES OF MIGRATION

John Maynard Keynes, the famous English economist, said half a century ago that "migration is the first act against poverty". According to a report prepared by the United Nations, much migration is accounted for by demography, development and democracy. People tend to move out of so-called overpopulated countries to less populated countries, from less developed to more developed countries, and from authoritarian to democratic countries. Less populated rich countries such as Canada and Australia remain popular destinations for migrants. While some migrants move permanently, the oil-rich Gulf countries remain destinations for temporary migrant workers. There are international migrants and refugees as well as internally displaced persons. The latter group is often a product of civil war or social unrest.

Migrants can be temporary or permanent, professionals or working class, male or female, and from various parts of the world. Millions of people now live in places where they were not born. According to the UN Department of Economic and Social Affairs, 191 million persons, representing 3 per cent of the world population, lived outside their country of birth in 2005. The equivalent figure in 1960 amounted to 75 million persons or 2.5 per cent of the world population. Almost one in every 10 persons living in more developed regions is a migrant.

In the United Arab Emirates, 8 out of 10 people are migrants. Although the main reason for such a high proportion of migrants is economic, it has various political consequences. The discussion of citizenship rights, labour rights and democracy takes on a different meaning in such a context. In Singapore 20 per cent of the population are migrants. In some contexts, for example in the UAE or Singapore, the migration of labourers takes place strictly on a temporary contractual basis. In the Gulf countries, temporary migrant workers are under contractual obligations to return to their countries of origin after the end of their contract period. This policy is uniformly applied to both working-class migrants and white-collar professionals. In European countries such as Germany, there was a well-developed program for accepting guest workers, but such "guests" rarely acquired citizenship rights through naturalization. In Europe and the USA, the issue of migration is closely tied to citizenship issues.

In the USA, for example, migration has been a contested political issue. Since the USA has historically been a society of migrants, the issue of migration is a sensitive one. Should the USA allow undocumented migrants to gain a legal status, thereby undermining the existing queue of migrants waiting for legal recognition through a formal process? It is well known that illegal migration without proper documentation is heavily exploited, and occasionally undocumented migrants turn to petty crime simply to support themselves and their families. One solution is to give them citizenship or at least accelerated access, but to do so is to undermine the official procedures. This dilemma was a major political issue during the presidency of George W. Bush (2001–9). Of course, migration is not simply a modern problem of globalization.

Historically, migration has been the normal condition. People migrated in large numbers from Africa to the rest of the world. Asian migrants populated the Arctic and reached North America well before the continental drift. Similarly, in Europe there was seasonal migration, for example as workers followed the herring season along the coasts of northern Europe. The modern world is different because, with the invention of national citizenship, the passport and worker permits, workers cannot freely move around in search of employment, because nation-state boundaries cannot be crossed without formal identification and permission. In this sense, "guests" have become "aliens" (Sassen, 1999b).

According to Adam McKeown (2004), world migration reached new peaks in the 1920s, and the immigration restrictions of the 1920s were also part of a much longer trend of regulation, border control, and nationalism that had grown concurrently with migration since the middle of the nineteenth century. There were three main circuits of long-distance migration from 1846 to 1940. During this century of migration, 55–58 million Europeans and 2.5 million from India, China, Japan and Africa migrated or were taken to the Americas. During the same period the other main destination was Southeast Asia, the Indian Ocean Rim and the South Pacific where 48–52 million people from China and Indians moved.

In the twentieth century, alongside forced involuntary migration caused by war, voluntary migration grew enormously. At the beginning of the twenty-first century, owing to a combination of factors such as relatively cheap air travel, the expansion of job opportunities, falling birth rates in some countries and the availability of surplus populations in other countries, more and more people are becoming increasingly mobile. Asked where she lived, the Columbia University professor and well-known scholar of globalization and migration, Saskia Sassen, replied "while not on a plane, usually in the United States". An enhanced mobility has become a central feature of contemporary globalization. At the end of the twentieth century, close to 2.6 billion people travelled by the world's airlines per year (Hobsbawm, 2007: 86). Unlike the historical migrations in the past, migrants are now able to maintain closer links with their family members back home and are also able to maintain multi-local residences. In Hong Kong, many family men became "Astronaut fathers" because of their frequent shuttling between Hong Kong and Canada or Australia, two of their favourite migration destinations. In Europe, too, migration and migrant communities are the subject of great political and social debate. The USA, which remains the most popular destination of migrants from various parts of the world, has an estimated 12 million illegal or undocumented workers. Migration in the past had the connotation of people leaving their places of origin for good. Recent migration has seen so much flexibility and frequency of people moving from place to place and country to country that the word "migration" is no longer an accurate descriptor. The new and more accurate notion is "mobility". Interestingly, Pitrim Sorokin, a Harvard sociologist and an immigrant from what was then the Soviet Union, used the term about half a century ago to differentiate between horizontal and vertical mobility. The former implied migration and the later social mobility or class mobility.

REFUGEES AND MIGRANT LABOUR

During the war of liberation waged by Bangladesh against Pakistani forces in 1971, between 9 and 10 million refugees crossed over into bordering Indian provinces. After the end of the war, as Bangladesh became independent, a large number of refugees returned to Bangladesh, creating a major humanitarian challenge for the government attempting to put in place policies for rehabilitation and the rebuilding of a war-ravaged economy. Wars are often the main cause of large-scale population displacement. In the first decade of the twenty-first century, when American forces occupied Iraq and engaged in a war to defeat the resistance forces, 2 million or 10 per cent of the Iraqi population took refuge in Jordan, Syria and Iran, the three bordering countries.

About 60 per cent of all migrants are now found in the world's most prosperous countries and around 40 per cent in the developing regions (Global Commission on International Migration, 2005). Migrants to industrially developed countries often seek permanent status and citizenship. Because of the high mobility of people across nations, many countries now accept dual citizenship. Professionals in certain specialized fields are very much in demand and some countries offer incentives to attract these specialists. Indian software engineers can be seen in many different countries. Some countries have taken a proactive attitude towards the export of labour, as in the case of the Philippines since the mid-1970s under President Marcos. In the first decade of the twenty-first century, Filipino workers are employed as domestic workers in over 130 countries of the world (Parrenas, 2001: 1). It is estimated that there are 8 million Filipino workers – both domestic workers and in other trades – who are known as Overseas Foreign Workers and play a vital role in the economy of the country.

The issue of the rights of migrant workers has become a key question in many labour-receiving countries. Here international organizations such as the International Labour Organization (ILO), which is an institution of, but pre-dates, the United Nations, the International Organization of Migration and Human Rights Watch, a New York based human rights organization, keep a close watch on the condition of migrant workers. The US State Department, which annually publishes a country-specific report on the situation of human trafficking around the world, ranks countries on the basis of their human rights record. In a globalized world, nation-states, regardless of their wealth and influence, can hardly ignore such external evaluations. Migration generates a whole host of issues related to the politico-economic realities of the present world. For example, historically the Gulf countries never had to deal with organized labour movements but are now faced with demands – albeit disorganized – by foreign workers and are under the scrutiny of international human rights organizations.

It can be argued that politico-economic globalization began with the slave trade in the sixteenth century with the forced movement of African slave labour to the Caribbean and North American plantations, and such forced and exploitative labour movements still exist in various parts of the world. Colonialism and the European land-grab led to difficult economic conditions in which the poor of many colonies were marginalized and eventually driven by economic necessity to become indentured labourers. In the nineteenth century, the migration of Europeans to various parts of the world created white-settler societies such as in Australia, New Zealand and South Africa. Here the migration issue was connected with racism and the marginalization of various indigenous communities. Many of those problems still remain, especially around the status of aboriginal people and their relationship to the land.

Some people choose to leave home in search of better jobs and security elsewhere, and such economic migration is often in response to the push and pull of the forces of globalization. They leave their homes to avoid poverty and repression, while others are attracted by the prospect of a better life in other places. Some people make choices on their own, but others are forced to migrate because of a host of factors ranging from economic deprivation to political repression and outright expulsions (or so-called compulsory repatriation). An extreme form of forced migration is human trafficking; children and women are often kidnapped, stolen and sold into slavery. In 1833 slavery was officially abolished in the British Empire, in 1863 in the USA by Abraham Lincoln's Emancipation Proclamation and in 1886 in Cuba, but the practice goes on in our society under a different name. Human trafficking is the twenty-first-century version of slavery. The extent of slavery in the contemporary world is extensively documented, for example, in Kevin Bales's *Understanding Global Slavery* (2005). According to Bales, since its general abolition in the late nineteenth century, slavery has slipped easily into the shadow economy. Slavery may be defined as the complete control of a person for economic exploitation by violence or the threat of violence (Bales, 1999: 461). With slavery, the person becomes a mere commodity or thing.

According to Skinner (2008: 64):

Slavery exists today on an unprecedented scale. In Africa, tens of thousands are chattel slaves, seized in war or tucked away for generations. Across Europe, Asia, and the Americas, traffickers have forced as many as 2 million into prostitution or labour. In South Asia, which has the highest concentration of slaves on the planet, nearly 10 million languish in bondage, unable to leave their captors until they pay off "debts".

Bales estimates that there are 27 million slaves in the world today, of whom 15–20 million are in India, Pakistan and Nepal. The positive view of the free movement of labour in a global economy will not want to deal with these issues and instead attempts to focus on the material improvement of people in a deregulated global economy, where people have in principle the freedom to cross borders with ease. In general terms, the science of economics does not deal effectively with black markets and criminal activity in the market place, concentrating instead on the formal market in which goods and services are transacted according to formal, public rules. As a consequence, academic economics dealing with formal and legal exchanges does not normally include criminal activity, which may keep a large section of the community in employment, in the gross domestic product. Slavery, trafficking and the informal, undocumented movement of people often remain unnoticed and unaccounted for. These people remain permanently marginalized.

Migration raises interesting issues about the relationship between market forces and the authority of the state. It is the classic law of supply and demand that dictates movement of people across national boundaries.

However, the state in the receiving countries, in providing assistance to market forces, usually complies with the dominant economic forces, but the state is also responsible to its own citizens. The sending states also play a role in sometimes promoting the interests of the migrants workers by providing all kinds of assistance, or alternatively blocking their movement in the event that there are possibilities of workers falling into exploitative situations overseas.

Exploitation is rife with regard to labourers. This problem is exacerbated by the absence of definite and decisive political rights. At the very best, migrant workers are only quasi-citizens with limited rights, despite the fact that they have to pay taxes to the host society. In some countries even the local or national workers are deprived of their basic rights, making the issue of the rights of the foreign or guest workers even more tenuous. When it comes to understanding the plight of foreign workers, Marxist interpretations of the exploitation of labour provide a useful frame of analysis. If market forces were given free rein, workers would remain exposed to high levels of exploitation. Employers would like to pay them wages as low as possible to ensure maximum profits for themselves. The wages paid to involuntary labour are often only sufficient to keep the worker alive. Foreign workers rarely have adequate insurance cover against industrial accidents, and probably only limited medical care. Here the role of the state becomes crucial. The state, which at least formally has the responsibility of protecting all classes of people in a society, is bound to take into account the interests of the workers. In labour-exporting countries where there is some democracy, as in the Philippines, the government takes many legal measures to secure and protect the interests of its migrant workers. Moreover, there is an economic interest, since remittances from overseas workers represent a substantial aspect of the Filipino economy. As a Roman Catholic society with a very high birth rate, the Philippines has a surplus workforce which cannot find local employment because of limited investment opportunities and a weak economy, and the export of its own workers provides one economic solution – however paradoxical – to its demographic problems. In fact the Philippines has one of the highest birth rates in the world and hence economic migration is one response to this demographic conundrum. Birth control through contraception is opposed by the Catholic Church and it is likely that the Philippines will continue to export its own working class.

In 2006, the World Bank estimated that remittances from world-wide reached US$268 billion, India topping the list with US$23.5 billion, and China and Mexico following closely with US$22.4 billion and US$21.7 billion respectively. By November 2008 the World Bank estimated the total remittances to the developing world at US$283 billion. For many small economies remittances from foreign workers were significant and substantial:

46 per cent of GDP for Tajikistan, 38 per cent for Moldova and 24 per cent
for Lebanon in 2007 (*The Economist*, 17 January 2009, p. 52). For the
Philippines, remittance income has also been a large proportion of income
from export revenues – about 8 million migrant workers contributed nearly
US$ 14 billion to the economy of the Philippines in 2007. In Bangladesh,
the migrant workers remitted $8 billion in 2008 which is the highest source
of foreign currency income. Yet there are all kinds of middle-men and
exploiting classes standing between the foreign workers and the families that
depend on such remittance payments. The issue touches on the broader
question of governance. Countries with failing states such as Burma are
cases where workers remain most vulnerable and where local people turn
to migration (to Thailand and Malaysia) as a solution to the problems of
poverty and oppression. It is estimated that there are over 30,000 Burmese
sex workers in Thailand, many of them brought in by the lure of employment in hotels and other more reputable services. In the shadowy world
of illegal border-crossing, people do desperate things, often resulting in
personal tragedies. Fifty-four Burmese migrants – 37 women and 17 men –
suffocated to death in a cold-storage container while being smuggled to
Thailand to escape desperate conditions at home. According to the Thai police,
121 people had been crammed inside an airtight frozen seafood container 6
metres long and 2.2 metres wide (*Gulf News*, 11 April 2008, p. 26). In January
2009, nearly 300 workers from the southeastern border regions of Bangladesh
on their way to Malaysia perished as their boat was intercepted and turned
away by the Thai police (*The National*, 22 January 2009).

In addition to migrants and refugees, there are 24.5 million internally
displaced persons in 52 countries as of December 2005 according to the
Internal Displacement Monitoring Centre, set up by the Norwegian
Refugee Council. Sudan has 5 million, Colombia 3.8 million, Iraq and
Uganda each 1.7 million, and the Democratic Republic of Congo 1.1 million. Most of these countries are undergoing some form of civil war or
internal conflict triggered by external aggression. The war-torn Darfur
region in Sudan produced 1.8 million internally displaced persons by the
end of 2006. Burma has a large number of internally displaced persons
in addition to nearly a million refugees in neighbouring Thailand. Sri
Lanka has huge numbers of internally displaced persons owing to government oppression. Burma is a classic case of a military dictatorship and a
corrupt oligarchy, governing in complete defiance of the will of the people. Often well-qualified foreign workers accept jobs with little or no relation to their training. In labour-receiving countries such as the UAE or
Brunei, it is often found that Burmese and Filipino domestic workers
have university degrees. They take up any work available as a result
of desperate economic conditions. Many Bangladeshi construction
workers and Filipino domestic workers in Singapore have college degrees.

In labour-receiving Gulf states which have experienced a development boom, foreign workers play a key role. In the oil-rich UAE, almost 80 per cent of the population are expatriates. In the construction sector, over 95 per cent of the workforce is drawn from migrant workers. The migrant workers often bring their family and friends with them and try to develop a community of their own. There is a new form of cosmopolitan life to which migrant workers are exposed in high-density urban areas in the Gulf region.

Different countries follow different rules with regard to granting citizenship status. Some countries follow highly restrictive policies. In the Gulf region citizenship is not an option, while countries like Singapore have a selective citizenship policy. Professionals are given permanent resident status, but foreign workers are rarely granted citizenship. Workers with a lower income are not allowed to bring their family members. The Singaporean policy is based on an implicit technocratic ideology which welcomes "talent" but believes that such talent is only concentrated in certain age groups and racial communities. Singapore attempts therefore to avoid or at least delay the problems of an ageing workforce that is increasingly dependent on social benefits. Given the very low birth rate in Singapore, its economic dependence on selective migration will remain a permanent feature of its society.

In the international arena, there are some circumstances where migrants can find local support especially among their own diaspora. For example, a Bangladeshi migrant in London can easily find fellow Bangladeshis for initial support and hospitality. This would not have been the case in New York two decades ago. But not only will a Bangladeshi migrant now be able to meet fellow Bangladeshis in New York, she/he will be able to purchase goods in a Bangladeshi grocery shop, dine in a Bangladeshi restaurant and watch Bengali TV programs, thanks to satellite TV. Cheap telephone calls and the Internet would also enable her/him to maintain close links with the folks back home or in other countries.

RIGHTS DISCOURSE AND MIGRATION

By contrast human rights have been, since their formal proclamation in 1948, promoted as universal rights. The relationship between the social rights of national citizenship and the human rights of the UN Declaration provides a useful case study in which to discover whether sociology can provide concepts and theories that function across conceptual boundaries and territorial borders. Furthermore, the human rights discourse may prove to be the primary candidate for sociology to operate as an effective discourse of global social reality. However, human rights require duties if they are to be binding.

Some of the organizations that work for the protection of the rights of workers are based in Asia. For example, the Asian Migrant Centre is a network based in Hong Kong working to protect the human rights of migrant workers. This organization has become a key player. Their Hong Kong Declaration asserts their support for the Manila Declaration, expressing their solidarity and commitment to "imagine and construct an alternative world based on the fundamental principles respecting human rights and human dignity" (Manila People's Forum on APEC Declaration, 1996) (www.asian-migrants.org/index.php, ILO, 2009). The Asian Migrant Centre has a Migrants Human Rights Program which is an umbrella organization of seven migrant workers' organizations and unions.

By and large, migrant workers operate outside the sphere of trade unions. They have hardly any bargaining power and remain vulnerable to exploitation. Domestic workers in the UAE or Singapore receive differential salaries based on their nationality. In Singapore, newspapers advertise these differential salaries publicly. Domestic workers from the Philippines are paid higher wages than those from Indonesia, who in turn command higher wages than their Sri Lankan counterparts.

In the USA, churches play an important role in defending the rights of migrant workers, alongside the American Civil Liberties Union and many other civil rights organizations. Churches often use the traditional right of sanctuary to protect foreign workers within their walls. The march of over a million migrant workers who were undocumented was an illustration of this complex problem. In the USA this issue receives special attention because that country is made up of migrants and the number of foreign-born workers is on the increase. In the last decade, the number of foreign-born workers has increased from 2 to 5 per cent. The ILO proposed the decent work clause: "Opportunities for all men and women of working age, including migrant workers, to obtain decent and productive work in conditions of freedom, equity, security and human dignity should be promoted." The ILO agenda included the declaration that "The human rights of all migrant workers, regardless of their status, should be promoted and protected."

HUMAN TRAFFICKING

Human trafficking has been identified as a crime against humanity – a new form of slavery – in the present world exposing some of the ill-effects of uncontrolled globalization. The International Organization for Migration calls human trafficking the "most menacing form of irregular migration due to its ever increasing scale and complexity involving, as it does, arms, drugs and prostitution". In this shady world, precise figures are difficult to come by. The ILO estimates that each year between 700,000 and 2 million women and children are trafficked across national borders around the world. In the Middle East, rich countries such as Saudi Arabia have become sites where children from extremely poor countries such as Yemen are traded as involuntary sex workers or domestic servants. An ILO report estimates that some 12.3 million persons are in some form of forced labour or bondage; more than 2.4 million are in forced labour due to human trafficking. The ILO report estimates that annual profits from human trafficking alone may be as much as US$32 billion (ILO, 2009).

Trafficking may be considered a consequence of "the commodification of migration". According to the *Nepal Monitor*, the national online journal, "between 7,000 and 12,000 young girls, aged 9 to 16, are trafficked each year from Nepal, mainly to India. There are more than 200,000 Nepali girls in ... Indian brothels" (Adhikari, 2007). The case of Nepal also points to an interesting and devious nexus between the so-called local tradition and the forces of modern capitalism. Some of the regions of origin of sexual slaves had "traditions" of providing sexual service to the upper castes and the royal palaces.

Some cultural systems have also helped create the atmosphere for forced sex-slavery. The Badi community in [the] western part of [Nepal], especially in Dang district, has made sexual subservience ... a way of life over a long historical period. Young girls from this community serve other groups. This has become a tradition and a means of livelihood. Many girls, even if they are unwilling, are forced to serve as sex slaves. (Adhikari, 2007)

In the Trafficking in Persons Report of 2009, published by the US State Department, Secretary of State Hillary Clinton in a Congressional briefing called it a "modern slavery, a crime that spans the globe, providing ruthless employers with an endless supply of people to abuse for financial gain. Human trafficking is a crime with many victims: not only those who are trafficked, but also the families they leave behind, some of whom never see their loved ones again" (Clinton, 2009a). Human traffickers prey on the most weak, primarily women and children, and lure the victims into involuntary servitude and sexual slavery. The United Nations estimates that there are 12 million people around the world who are victims of trafficking (Clinton, 2009b).

Apart from sexual slavery, human trafficking also perpetuates child labour, making children into a global commodity. Other pernicious aspects of human trafficking are child soldiers and child prostitution.

According to UNICEF, more than 300,000 children under 18 are currently being exploited in more than 30 countries as combatants.
"While the majority of child soldiers are between the ages of 15 and 18,
some are as young as 7 or 8 years" (US Department of State, 2007,
p. 24). Sexual tourism in Thailand in particular has led to the wholesale exploitation of young girls. "Child sex tourism … is a dark side of
globalization, with some two million children exploited in the global commercial sex trade", according to the US Department of State (2007, p. 23).

TRANSNATIONALISM

Not all migrants, however, are poor and exploited. Some migrants feature in the Forbes list of the richest people. One of the richest men in
the world, Eduardo Sim, a Mexican telecom tycoon, is of Lebanese heritage. Another billionaire, Laxmi Mittal, one of the ten richest men in
the world, is of Indian origin but domiciled in London. Mittal made his
fortune in steel, with his operations spanning the entire globe, and he
often portrays himself as the saviour of Europe. These migrant success
stories graphically illustrate the diversity in migrant populations around
the world. Only a handful of migrants are as rich as Sim and Mittal.
However, many migrants are professionals, at least in the USA, a country that draws much of its scientific and engineering talent from overseas. A careful examination of these patterns of migration from refugees
to professionals will give us a valuable insight into some of the key
processes of modern globalization.
    Since the colonial period, a large number of diasporic communities
have emerged in many parts of the globe. It is, for example, possible to
find Chinatowns from Johannesburg to Brazil and from Sydney to
London. Equally, one can find Japanese diasporic communities in Brazil
and Peru. In the early phase of modernization following the Meiji
Restoration of the 1860s, many Japanese began to migrate out of Japan
in search of better economic opportunities. The USA was a favourite destination for these Japanese migrants. The flow was interrupted when a
race-based migration law stemmed Asian migration to the USA in 1924,
and a year earlier in Canada. Countries such as Brazil and Peru in
South America became principal destinations for the Japanese. One of
their descendants is Alberto Fujimori, elected president of Peru in 1990
and, after serving two terms, accused of corruption in 2000, subsequently
receiving temporary asylum in Japan. In 2005 he returned to Peru to face
charges. There are several examples of members of diasporic communities

assuming leadership positions in their adopted countries. For example, the Minister for Climate Change and Water in the Australian cabinet in 2008 is Penny Wong, who was born in Malaysia of Chinese ancestry. The current president of El Salvador, Elias Antonio Saca, and his leftist opponent, Shafik Handal, who was defeated in the 2004 presidential elections, are both from Palestinian immigrant families. In 2007, President Nicolas Sarkozy of France, who has Hungarian ancestry, appointed three Muslim women in his cabinet, two of whom were born in North Africa and one in Senegal. President Barack Obama, who took office as the 44th President of the United States of America in January 2009, is the son of a Kenyan man who studied in the USA. The Prime Minister of Thailand, Abhisit Vejjajiva, who took office in December 2008, was born in Newcastle upon Tyne, England.

Diasporic communities rarely sever their links with the country of their origin, although in many instances these links may stretch over several generations. The close community bonds of the diasporic groups sometimes have negative or unfavourable consequences. The radicalization of young people often takes place in the diasporic environment of alienation and strangeness. Modern technology has played an important role in maintaining links between families and communities in the world of the diaspora. Unlike the diasporic situation of the past, migrants maintain a close link with their home countries, thus rendering the meaning of home tenuous. Many transnational groups actively support various radical (even separatist) activities back home. For example, the diasporic Tamil community has provided material support to Tamil radical groups in Sri Lanka. Similarly, diasporic Sikhs have provided support for the cause of the Punjab in India. Diasporic Islamic groups often show a heightened sense of religiosity bordering on radicalism. Recent research has shown how some diasporic communities come under the influence of radicalized religion, thereby becoming the source of religious extremism in their countries of origin (Kibria, 2008).

Following trade liberalization and the opening up of the economy to investment from outside, China has received huge funds and expertise from overseas Chinese communities. In fact, China maintained an ethnicity-based immigration policy to attract people of Chinese origin. In the rush to capitalist development, this economic stimulus was timely and important. In India, small school children were once asked what they would like to be when they grew up. Many of them replied that they would like to become NRIs, which means "non-resident Indians". In 1995 the Indian government convened a gathering of persons of Indian origin, including Nobel laureate, V.S. Naipaul, and a former prime minister of Fiji, Mahendra Singh. Such a gesture implied a great deal of respect for the lost and prodigal sons and daughters of India. With the collapse of communism, and as many Eastern European countries embarked successfully on the road to capitalist development and democratic political culture, many successful émigrés returned home. For example, Thomas Bata, whose father founded the famous shoe company which he had to relocate from Czechoslovakia to Canada in 1939, enjoyed dual Czech and Canada citizenship. The status of dual citizenship allows many professionals and entrepreneurs to continue to contribute to the socio-economic development of their ancestral homeland.

In the 1970s, "brain-drain" was a popular slogan and it was often regarded as one cause of the poor economic performance of those countries that were exporting their most talented doctors, engineers and scientists to the rich, developed countries. Indeed, many talented young men and women migrated from the periphery to the core of the world economy for better educational and career opportunities. The universities in the rich countries, for example the United States, were magnets for foreign-born talent. This process was reversed in the 1990s and in the first decade of the twenty-first century; "brain-drain" gave way to "brain-gain". Analee Saxsenian, an expert on the migration of scientists, provided a new idea, namely that of "brain in circulation". A commentator in India once said that brain-drain is better than brain in the drain. Countries such as India produced a large number of talented men and women in various scientific and engineering fields to be absorbed by the sluggish Indian economy of the 1960s, 1970s, and 1980s, which led to a serious outpouring of the Indian creative class to North America and elsewhere. In the 1990s and especially in the first decade of the twenty-first century, many such talented Indians experienced in high-tech industries began to return to their own countries, which by then had created conditions that would allow them to pursue their professional careers.

The idea that national borders had became more porous for the creative class was popularized by Richard Florida (2002). The footloose nature of the creative classes and frequent movement of professionals have led some writers to develop the notion of "flexible citizenship" (Ong, 1999). Although she developed the notion to describe the global flexibility of the Chinese business class, the phrase has become popular in the literature on global migration. While it may apply to a small number of skilled professionals who move around at ease, often having more than one passport, for the vast majority of working-class migrants, national boundaries remain a hard reality.

Some countries, such as Taiwan and Israel, have had effective incentive policies to reverse the outward trend of migration of talented people.

A reverse brain-drain ensued. In the case of Taiwan, many Chinese from overseas – mainly from the USA – returned not only with plenty of cash, but also with valuable scientific and technological knowledge which assisted Taiwan's remarkable economic development. India has also been successful in capitalizing on these trends and many Indians with years of overseas experience are now returning to India. A number of Indian professionals in the information and technology industries have left Silicon Valley to return to Bangalore, the Indian information hub, bringing with them rich experience in technology, education and finance. This rapid economic growth has also given India a prominent international status. It is no longer seen as a country crippled by backwardness, overpopulation and poverty. India is the largest democracy in the world which has set new standards of tolerance and pluralism by electing a woman president, a Muslim vice-president, a Sikh prime minister and an Italian-born woman as the president of India's and world's largest democratic party, the Indian Congress. Yet despite this shining image, India is home to 300 million poor people. Poverty and wealth coexist in India in striking contrasts. In 2007 desperate poverty and the rising costs of fertilizers and seeds drove many poor Indian farmers to commit suicide. At the same time, *Fortune* magazine's 2008 list of the world's ten richest people included three Indians.

Social inequality compounds the problems of ethnic integration resulting from migration. For example, France in 2007 saw an eruption of ethnic violence where the economically disadvantaged migrants of North African origin fought pitched battles with the police. In a comparative study, it was found that the French are more tolerant of local poor people who share their democratic and liberal (or Republican) values than with the North African migrants who are primarily Muslim. In the USA, working-class respondents are more receptive to migrants as long as they share the same work ethic, but they are less tolerant of their own poor who are thought to be lazy and not in tune with the work ethic. Contemporary migration in the globalized world has many facets which provide rich illustrations of the perils and opportunities of globalization.

CONCLUSION

The principal conclusion of our discussion is that the economy and the state are driven by very different interests or logics. Modern economies require a flexible labour market in which workers can move rapidly and easily between different work sites depending on the local demand for labour inputs. For example, local labour markets may not have enough young workers if the society as a whole has had a low fertility rate for many decades. Or there may be a shortage of skilled workers or technicians. In such situations, local capitalist firms need to draw on fresh inputs of labour. However, large-scale migration can often create racial conflicts. For example, in the post-war period Britain recruited large numbers of Caribbean and Indian workers to support its demand for unskilled workers. The result was often racial conflict, and politicians like Enoch Powell called for an aggressive policy of repatriation. More recently, attacks on the Twin Towers, the Madrid railway and London's underground have led to Islamophobia, attacks on mosques and condemnation of liberal traditions associated with freedom of speech. In this context of the demand for greater political security, the state becomes involved in more stringent control over borders. These controls inevitably involve the greater management of migration and the result is the interruption of labour mobility. The state's need for sovereignty and security outweighs the economic needs of labour mobility.

While liberal politicians and cosmopolitan intellectuals may wish to celebrate the cultural diversity that comes with open borders and boundaries, modern states appear to be committed to limiting multi-culturalism and containing difference. From the perspective of political pragmatism, it is easier to rule in a social context that is homogeneous rather than heterogeneous. However, this struggle over difference is by no means over and there was global enthusiasm over the election of President Obama, whose new foreign policy promises, to keep the door open.

8

MEDICAL GLOBALIZATION

INTRODUCTION: THE END OF THE GOLDEN AGE OF MEDICINE

From 1910 to 1970 scientific medicine enjoyed a golden age of increasing influence, status and wealth. Research hospitals were models of scientific excellence, acute diseases that had ravaged Western societies were being eliminated, and the medical profession enjoyed the trust and respect of middle-class society. The Flexner Report (1910) laid the foundation for the medical model of illness, established the social conditions for medical dominance, and produced the professional circumstances that simultaneously created the passive patient role. The American Medical Association and the British Medical Association were powerful professional lobbies that exercised significant political power on behalf of medical science through Congress and Parliament. The professions had considerable success in claiming that the collectivist principles behind social medicine and public health would undermine individualism, self-help and self-reliance, upon which Western medicine had been built. This pattern of scientific medical education became the dominant global model for training doctors. The end of the 'golden age of doctoring' was indicated by Richard Nixon's 1970 speech announcing the crisis in health care in the United States. The health crisis was also an economic crisis brought about by a greying population, increasing problems with chronic illness, rising insurance costs, the corporatization of medicine and the mounting expense of medical technology. It was a professional crisis, as the traditional authority and autonomy of doctors was eroded by corporate control of doctoring, declining trust in doctors, and growing demand for different types of medicine such as complementary and alternative medicine.

The social and political conditions that produced professional medicine have changed for a variety of reasons. While allopathic medicine provided spectacular cures for acute illness, chronic illness that is related to lifestyle, sedentary occupations and an ageing population cannot be easily cured or effectively treated. Medical science appears to have reached a number of limitations in the effective treatment of cancer, heart disease, diabetes, and other degenerative conditions where the germ theory that was the basis of the medical model does not offer easy or efficient solutions. A public that has become increasingly sophisticated and conscious of its rights as health consumers has flocked to acupuncture, aromatherapy, yoga, homeopathy, and chiropractic. The slow but significant growth of health-care insurance for alternative medicine in the United States such as chiropractic and the growing number of young doctors who do not join the American Medical Association have been regarded by some sociologists as an erosion of medical dominance. Recent corporate developments to capture the commercial potential of health and illness constitute the global emergence of the medical economy. These global changes are transforming the traditional doctor–patient relationship, but they are also opening up new possibilities, the future directions of which are unclear.

Professional medicine has long been concerned to regulate, largely unsuccessfully, self-medication and "folk medicine", but in a high-risk environment it is also important to control scientific medicine. In order to gain the full benefits of medical innovation, there has to be some regulation of the social and cultural risks associated with contemporary medical sciences in relation to cloning, new reproductive technologies, organ transplants, surgical intervention for fetal abnormalities, cosmetic surgery, the prescription of antidepressants, sex selection of children and, more recently, cryonically frozen patients.

HEALTH, RISK AND GLOBALIZATION

We can no longer study the treatment of disease in an exclusively national framework because the character of disease and its treatment is increasingly global. Medical institutions and professions are subject to global pressures, especially from insurance and funding arrangements. To take one obvious illustration, the ownership and current development of the pharmaceutical industry are global. We are also on the verge of health-care systems that will depend on global electronic communications and information systems. One remarkable example is "telesurgery", which involves the use of robot-assisted distance surgery. Such operations have to overcome a variety of problems, including long-distance transmission delays. Surgery has historically evolved through its association with the military. The development of surgery, for example by Ambroise Paré in his treatment of gunshot wounds in the sixteenth century, has been driven historically by military conflict and the need to treat traumatic injuries sustained in combat. Telesurgery will make it possible to provide rapid surgical support in future global military campaigns. The consumer demand for health products is also increasingly organized through global economies. The healthy body is being promoted globally through fitness clubs and sports associations. For example, Fitness Holdings is one of the world's largest health club companies, with outlets in 11 countries including Hong Kong, Sweden and South Korea. In the UK, Fitness First, a fitness chain, has also expanded with the growth of global and domestic demand for healthy lifestyles.

However, health-care systems have often been slow to adopt innovations in information technology, because the hardware and software are often insufficiently advanced to make a useful contribution to care. The value of "telemedicine" will vary considerably by medical speciality. For example, because clinical work in pulmonary medicine, neurology and cardiology is still based on a physical examination and questioning of the patient, telecommunication is not seen to be important. However, in the future, patients and doctors will be able to use broadband technologies to deliver health-care packages to homes and hospitals. The growth of "e-health" will create virtual hospitals, transform health education, and deliver health services to elderly or disabled patients who have limited mobility. E-health could also improve health delivery to remote rural communities. The technology and delivery systems for such innovations will be necessarily global, and they will be organized and owned by global health corporations.

In a period of global communication and transport, disease does not recognize national borders. The 2003 outbreak of SARS that spread rapidly from Beijing to Toronto is a good example. The spread of infectious disease is also closely associated with the global conduct of war. The deadly disease Ebola is often carried in central Africa by guerrilla troops, for example by the Lord's Resistance Army, a messianic rebel army that blends Christianity and Islam, passing between southern Sudan and Uganda in 2003. The global spread of narcotics also has an important impact on national health statistics through their negative effect on individual health behaviours. The domestic politics of Colombia have a major outcome on health behaviour in New York, because the supply of drugs can be disrupted by domestic conflicts in South America. For the same economic and political reasons, the collection of the opium crop in Afghanistan and central Asia has a direct impact on health and lifestyle in London and Sydney. The rapid spread of crack cocaine as a lifestyle drug among young people, sex workers and ethnic minority groups in inner-city areas in the last fifteen years has had detrimental consequences for health, especially in terms of enhanced HIV risk (Green et al., 2000). Crack use has given rise to new forms of prostitution (sex for crack) among young women, who become socially stigmatized as "crack whores". These global markets shape the health risks of Western urban cultures, but there is a still darker side to this discussion of medical globalization. Bioterrorism is now a major threat to modern states. Government concerns about the use of biological weapons have increased as a result of the sarin nerve gas attack by a Japanese religious cult that killed 12 and injured 5,000 on the Tokyo metro in 1995, and the anthrax attack on the United States in 2001. The US army has identified smallpox, anthrax and botulism as organisms that can be easily disseminated in a civilian population. In order to understand the rapidly changing environment of health and illness, we need to look more closely at how social scientists analyse globalization and risk.

Globalization involves both a qualitative and quantitative transformation of risk. As a result, the intensification of risk requires global regulation. Public interest in these global processes has produced an important intellectual paradigm shift in which the boundary between environment ("nature") and society ("culture") is contentious and problematic. Ulrich Beck's *Risk Society* (1992) helped to transform a somewhat tired and stale discussion of modernization and industrialization into a dynamic analysis of "late modernity" where "reflexive modernization" is the key process. In response, many sociologists have argued that the conventional theoretical paradigms of the social sciences have to be abandoned in order to grasp a new social reality based on global flows and networks rather than national societies. This new system of communication requires a "mobile sociology" (Urry, 2000) that can discuss the end of "society" and the rise of a new social order based on networks, flows, complexity and "scapes". If modernization assumed that modern society would be well structured and orderly, then contemporary sociology understands late modernity through the lens of complexity and contingency. Global society in a deregulated global economy is supremely disorderly, as the bombing of the World Trade Center on 11 September 2001 sadly demonstrated.

In mainstream sociology, globalization and risk have been understood primarily in terms of three dimensions – the economic, cultural and political. There has been far less interest in the globalization of medicine and health risks, despite the ongoing HIV/AIDS epidemic. The idea of health risks has been a regular aspect of public health, epidemiology and medical sociology for decades. For example, women with a family history of breast cancer are themselves "at risk". However, the importance of the idea of risk has expanded considerably in the last two decades in relation to the analysis of interpersonal health risks resulting from risky sexual behavior. The HIV/AIDS epidemic produced a wealth of sociological research on the perception and management of risk in casual sexual encounters and needle etiquette among HIV-positive people. Beck's theory of risk and study of modern relations of intimacy in *The Normal Chaos of Love* (Beck and Beck-Gernsheim, 1995) provided insights into risk-taking and risk management. The HIV/AIDS crisis has shown yet again the close connections between the personal and the political, especially how relations of intimacy are bound up with the political processes of the state. The study of HIV-positive people has revealed a basic tension: love and intimacy presuppose interpersonal trust, and any sign of distrust indicates the absence of complete love. By insisting on safe sex (for example, condom use), a cautious lover shows care for his partner, but may paradoxically display distrust (Rhodes and Cusick, 2000). Romantic passion is threatened by questions about the partner's current health status and previous sexual practices.

Early sociological approaches to risk and HIV were dominated by practical public health concerns that concentrated on homosexual behaviour. The principal issue of health education was to encourage gay men to adopt safe sex practices. There was considerable resistance to testing for infection on grounds of civil liberties in a social environment where HIV-positive gay men were stigmatized. However, to a large extent the health education campaign in the Western world has been successful: the incidence of HIV infection was dramatically reduced in the gay community. The spread of HIV/AIDS in the heterosexual community, and specifically the increase in female infection, shows that risk behaviour is not exclusively confined to gay men. In the developing world, the spread of HIV to women has been an alarming development, especially because of the risk of bearing HIV-positive children. While men and women may suspect that their partners are not faithful, it is difficult for them to question their behaviour without undermining trust (Giffin and Lowndes, 1999).

Although risk research in medical sociology has increased, there is little evidence as yet of systematic interest in the globalization of risk and its implications for individual health outcomes or for national aggregate effects. In terms of the sociology of sex, Dennis Altman's *Global Sex* (2001) provides a unique account of the stigmatization of sexual behaviour in the context of the globalization of prostitution, gay politics, AIDS and sex tourism. He demonstrates that countries cannot remain totally isolated from the spread of infectious diseases and viral conditions. The social problems of AIDS education and containment gave rise to a new public health strategy that involves working with local communities and outreach groups.

RISK AND MEDICINE

Many of these changes in medicine can be seen as illustrations of Beck's idea of the risk society. Medical practice has been protected from public scrutiny by the development of professional associations and the organization of the clinic. The clinical institution provides an organizational roof under which medical research training and practice can be securely interrelated. It is within this professional context that medicine operates in what Beck calls an "arena of sub-politics", that is, medicine can bypass and avoid formal political institutions to develop its own professional power base. Medicine within the experimental laboratory operates beyond the immediate scrutiny of the law and the state. Furthermore, given the speed of medical innovation and invention, the general public is typically presented with the results of the problems of medical innovation long after they are relatively well established within the experimental setting. The law and the state are often brought in to regulate medical science after the experiments and discoveries have already been achieved. The negative consequences of these developments include thalidomide babies, mad cow disease (or bovine spongiform encephalopathy, BSE), and Creutzfeldt–Jakob disease (CJD). These medical crises are often a consequence of inadequate health policies, poor coordination of health care, and lack of effective auditing and monitoring of services. For example, the French government has been forced to re-examine its public health policy after a series of scandals concerning contaminated blood, CJD, and growth hormone in the food chain. Post-transfusion blood contamination is almost eight times higher in France than in Germany. These cases indicate the importance of public health regulation in the containment of medical risk.

There is a well-established intellectual tradition of scientific dystopias that envisage science and technology as destructive of the human spirit. This dystopian tradition has been analysed by Francis Fukuyama in *Our Posthuman Future* (2002) and by Leon Kass in *Life, Liberty and the Defense of Dignity* (2002). They endorse Huxley's (1946) biotech dystopia as a compelling vision of contemporary society, where medical sciences are pushing us towards the post-humanization of the species. Both authors agree that the medical benefits of microbiological science are clear and potent, but political interventions to establish a legal framework are necessary if we are to avoid the negative consequences of Huxley's world. According to Kass, the rational assumptions of science, advances in biotechnology, and their applications to improving health are consonant with the liberal and individualistic foundations of American democracy. Kass's argument, which in many ways replicates the assessment of science and values by Weber and Beck, is that science has the unintended consequence of eroding the social meanings that underpin fundamental social relationships. Science can help us solve practical problems, but it cannot tell us what is valuable or important. For example, applications of microbiological sciences to infertility have through new reproductive technologies created "extracorporeal fertilization" or "asexual reproduction", with

far-reaching and unanticipated consequences for fundamental social relations including parenthood. Reproductive technology has cut the natural
connection between sexual intercourse and reproduction and it has
fundamentally challenged traditional meanings of generation and parenthood. Because parenting is an important part of social citizenship, adult-
hood and civic responsibility, the implications of biological technology for
civil society are worrisome. In a risk society, technological advances have
meant that spontaneous reproduction through heterosexual intercourse is
being supplemented by planned reproduction with or without heterosexual intercourse. Lesbian parenthood has evolved through such means as
adoption, surrogacy and sperm donation, and gay parenthood is emerging
through extracorporeal fertility techniques. The obvious benefits of "therapeutic cloning" for inherited disease may well pave the way towards
"designer babies" as a routine aspect of reproduction. For Kass and
Fukuyama, the existential problem with Huxleyan democracy is a paradox: while most of us will be happier and healthier, we will no longer be
human.

Fukuyama is less concerned with ethical arguments about dehumaniza-
tion and more concerned with the social and political implications of the
new genetics. He argues that political and legal regulation is required to
manage scientific innovations and their commercial exploitation. The
biotechnology industry and the community of research scholars are for
obvious reasons against regulation, but Fukuyama supports regulation if it
can prevent replicating past pharmaceutical catastrophes such as sul-
phanilamide elixir and thalidomide, or other regulatory disasters such as
BSE and CJD. Kass supported the Bush administration on research into
stem cells. These are the primordial cells that turn into the differentiated
tissues that produce our vital organs such as the liver, heart and kidney.
Stem-cell technology is a booming industry that promises to provide an
endless source of replacement tissues for ageing bodies. The Bush administration took a prudent and cautious approach that restricted the scope of
such research. While Kass supported this prudent approach in the case of
stem-cell research, he argued that there should not be excessive federal
regulation. Prohibitions are impossible to enforce and dangerous, because
the costs of interference with fundamental scientific research might be
greater than the harm they actually prevent. Legislative regulation is generally ineffective and counter-productive. Therefore, Kass was persuaded
that internal professional guidelines and self-regulation by scientists will
be sufficient to deter the more adventurous from breaking professional
norms.

There are, in general terms, three agencies or institutions that can regulate genetic research and its applications: the market, the professions and
the state. Public opinion may also exercise some degree of regulation, but

it is typically expressed through the market and the state. Markets regulate institutions through the price mechanism, states achieve control by legislation, and the professions monitor their members by training, custom and rules of conduct. Economic mechanisms such as price regulation are indifferent to ethical norms, and may only control scientific development retrospectively. By contrast, state regulation is undermined by non-compliance, deliberate infringement and the research opportunities that are made possible by the globalization of science. Scientists who are unhappy with the legislative constraints of their own societies may simply migrate to other countries that do not exercise regulation over scientific experiment. In the United States, the National Organ Transplantation Act has attempted to impose some regulation on the internal market, but many agencies are pressing for the routine salvage of cadaveric organs, and the American Medical Association has considered proposals to offer funeral expenses to families who donate organs. While legislation in the United States might achieve some control over the supply of organs, the globalization of the organ transplant market has been resistant to legal regulation, thereby creating intense social stratification between poor healthy female donors from India and rich unhealthy male recipients in the developed world (Scheper-Hughes, 2001a, 2001b).

While state regulation is typically compromised by the global demand for science and professional services, professional controls are weak and ineffective. In the United Kingdom, the professional authority of the British Medical Association has been seriously undermined by a series of scandals such as the Bristol organ crisis that involved the removal and storage of organs from autopsies of children without parental consent, and the report in 2003 that over 20,000 brains had been removed and stored without consent. The development of professional ethicists as advisers to regulatory boards does not appear to have achieved significant results. Many problematic developments such as surrogate motherhood, sex selection, the appropriation of dead bodies as a source of organs, and pre-implantation genetic selection have been given ethical endorsement without serious regard to deeper social or moral issues.

Globalization has made the political and legal mechanisms available to individual states ineffective, but there are other reasons for their apparent failure. Consumer demand for healthy children, effective treatment of chronic illness, and the promise of enhanced longevity is compelling. Although many aspects of medical technology often turn out to be merely a "mirage of health" (Dubos, 1960), these consumer demands for health and longevity are not unreasonable, and hence governments are often forced to satisfy these demands as a result of electoral pressure. Furthermore, in the competitive and meritorious world of science, the rewards to scientists for innovation, regardless of the social consequences, are significant. Hence, scientists who want to build reputations in growing and influential fields such as microbiology, biotechnology and nanotechnology will have strong peer pressure to compete. Corporate pressure on research agendas, especially outside the university system, is equally significant in shaping the behaviour of research scientists. Salaries and promotion prospects are far greater in corporate research centres than they are in the majority of universities, especially universities that are heavily dependent on state rather than private funding. Scientists will for obvious material reasons be drawn to the corporate sector, but the consequence is that their research interests and inclinations will be shaped by the need for corporate profitability.

Fukuyama recognizes that regulatory controls will be difficult to enforce, but he points to the success of protests in Europe against the unregulated spread of genetically modified (GM) foods as an example of the impact of public opinion on government and market activity. As a result of environmental protests, agricultural trials of Monsanto crops in the United Kingdom have often been unsuccessful, despite government support for GM crops. In response to public opinion and consumer demand, the promotion of organic food has been commercially successful as an alternative to industrialized agriculture and factory production. Nevertheless, the history of organ transplantation suggests that, without international agreements and determined state regulation, local and national attempts to control biotechnology will fail in a global environment.

Regulatory controls over individual liberties are, in any case, difficult to implement in Western democracies, which champion personal freedoms. This tension between the individual and the state is particularly evident in terms of sexual activity between individuals in private. In the past, states have attempted to control the spread, for example, of sexually transmitted diseases and have waged educational campaigns to promote the use of condoms, but Western democratic states have been reluctant to control the spread of AIDS through the use of criminal law. The idea that governments might seek to regulate sexual practice is seen to be a fulfilment of Huxley's *Brave New World*. The separation of private sex acts from reproduction by technology does complicate the legal issue. Do individuals have an unrestrained right to reproduce by whatever technological means possible, regardless of the future implications for social identities and relationships? The social implications of this pressing question are disturbing because we do not have clear and convincing answers. In the absence of clear social policies and values, biotechnological advance and its associated risks continue without effective control or direction. The majority of Western democratic societies are nervous about implementing anything that looks like eugenics, given its association with the ethnic policies of German fascism.

INFECTIOUS DISEASES

By the 1970s it was assumed that the conquest of disease in Western societies would require the development of drugs which would delay or manage old age, as childhood deaths from infectious diseases became a thing of the past. As medical attention moved from acute to chronic diseases, preventive medicine and health education focused on the containment of such conditions as diabetes and heart disease. This complacency was shattered in the 1980s by the emergence of the epidemic of HIV/AIDS, which was first reported in 1979. HIV spread rapidly among the gay and homosexual communities of North America, Europe and Australia, and subsequently to heterosexual couples and to drug users who shared needles.

In previous centuries, plagues were spread by migration and trade, but diseases generally remained relatively specific to geographical niches. With the growth of world tourism and trade, the global risk of infectious disease has increased rapidly. Influenza epidemics now develop almost instantaneously. There is widespread anxiety about the development of a variety of new conditions that are difficult to diagnose and classify, complex in their function and diffusion, and resistant to rapid or conventional treatments. The list of such conditions includes the eruption of newly discovered diseases such as the hanta virus, the migration of diseases to new areas such as cholera in Latin America, diseases produced by new technologies such as toxic shock syndrome and legionnaires' disease, and diseases which spring from animals to humans such as SARS. The West Nile virus (WNV) arrived in New York in 1999 and the epidemic is growing as it moves westwards. In 20 per cent of cases, victims develop fevers and in the elderly the brain can become infected. In 2002 the virus caused 4,156 confirmed cases and 284 deaths. Between 1999 and 2009 some 29,000 Americans had been infected with the disease and over 1,000 had died. These problems, along with Ebola, Marburg virus, Lassa fever and swine flu, have generated a concern for 'the coming plague' (Garrett, 1995).

The globalization of disease can be usefully illustrated by the outbreak of SARS in January 2003 in the Chinese province of Guangdong. The World Health Organization warned that SARS was moving across the world with "the speed of a jet". By early April 2003 there were 1,268 reported cases and 61 deaths in Hong Kong. SARS is a unique form of pneumonia that is caused by an influenza-type virus rather than bacteria. Having infected hundreds of people in China and Vietnam, the condition spread quickly to the United States and Europe, being carried mainly by air passengers exiting Asia through Singapore and Hong Kong. SARS had a major impact on the Asian economy and led many air carriers in the region such as Qantas to cancel flights as governments warned citizens not to fly. SARS is a clear illustration of the unintended health consequences of globalization. The H1N1 virus, commonly known as "swine flu", was first spotted in Mexico in April 2009. As the virus crossed the border into the United States it quickly attracted world attention. By the beginning of July 2009 the virus had infected nearly 4,000 in the USA and 80,000 world-wide, killing 17 and 337, respectively (*China View*, 3 July 2009). On 12 June 2009 the World Health Organization officially declared the H1N1 virus outbreak a pandemic.

THE GREYING OF MODERN SOCIETIES

While the new infectious diseases associated with globalization are important, governments also face a problem from ageing populations and hence from the economic burden of chronic illness. In the study of ageing societies, the work of Peter Laslett (1915–2001) has been influential. In his historical demography, he shattered many myths about family history and structure, particularly in his *The World We Have Lost* (1965). His empirical research demonstrated that in pre-industrial society families were typically nuclear, composed of married parents and their children; households were small, while three-generation households were rare. His research destroyed the widely held view that the nuclear family was a modern product of industrialization and urbanization. He showed that early modern English society was highly mobile in geographical terms and that, for each new generation, residing in the same parish was uncommon. In his contribution to historical demography, he invented the term "secular shift" to describe rising life expectancy in the century after the 1880s (Kertzer and Laslett, 1995). This secular change was dramatic. Taking life expectancy at birth for men only in England and Wales, the increase was from 44.2 years in 1881 to 70.1 in 1991. Similar results for this period can be reported for other societies. For example, in the United States the increase was from 42.5 to 71.3; in France from 40.8 to 72; in Germany from 35.6 to 71.8; and in Japan from 42.4 to 75.5. The proportion of the population over 60 years of age during the secular shift rose in England and Wales from 7.4 per cent to 17.0 per cent, in the United States from around 5.4 per cent to 15.9 per cent; in France from 12.3 per cent to 16.6 per cent; and in Germany from 7.9 per cent to 16.7 per cent; in Japan there is no figure for the 1880s, but it was 12.9 per cent by the end of the twentieth century.

In the United States the proportion of the population over 65 years is projected to rise from 12.4 per cent in 2000 to 19.6 per cent in 2030. In absolute terms, the number of people over 80 years will rise from 35 million in 2000 to an estimated 71 million in 2030. There are, as in Japan, important regional and state differences. In Florida 19 per cent of the population was over 65 in 2003, a figure projected to rise to 26 per cent by 2035. The percentage of the American population over 85 years was 0.1 per cent in 1900, 1.5 per cent in 2000 and is estimated to rise to 5 per cent by 2050. In England and Wales, in 1948, 7.2 per cent of the population was aged 65–74 years and 2.9 per cent aged 75–84 years. In 2006 these figures were 8.2 per cent and 5.5 per cent. In absolute numbers those over 80 years have increased from 1,572,160 in 1981 to 2,749,507 in 2007. This age group is the fastest growing sector of the population. Much of the gain in life expectancy was achieved in the twentieth century. In 1900 average life expectancy at birth for the whole world was only around 30 years, and in rich countries around 50. The figures in the first decade of the twenty-first century are 67 and 78, respectively (*The Economist*, A Special Report on Ageing Population, 27 June 2009, p. 3).

These raw statistics of life expectancy are one aspect of the demographic transition which describes the historical shift from a period of high fertility and high mortality rates to a period of low fertility and low mortality. The causal factors that bring about this transition are much disputed, but broadly speaking it was a consequence of improvements in the food supply, better public health provisions (clean water and sanitation) and eventually the impact of medical improvements (such as vaccination). The demographic transition also produced an epidemiological transition. Whereas in the past when most people died before they were old the principal causes of death were infectious diseases, in the modern period the principal causes of death – cancer, heart disease and stroke – are among the elderly.

These changes in demography and epidemiology led James Fries (1980) to argue that in contemporary societies there is a compression of morbidity and mortality towards the end of life, that is, that a temporary period of illness precedes death. In the past morbidity – the tendency to fall ill – occurred throughout the life course, whereas in the modern period it is compressed towards the end of life. This change results in "the rectangularization of the survival curve" in which more and more people from a given generation survive into old age, when they die fairly rapidly from the principal degenerative diseases. Although this argument is useful in helping us to think about the characteristics of a greying population, Laslett (1995: 24) has questioned its accuracy by noting that in fact life expectancy shows no sign of faltering or declining. In short, the rectangular may never be actually described.

The ageing of the developed world is regarded by the World Bank as a threat to economic growth, and hence there is much economic excitement about the possibilities of stem cell research as an aspect of regenerative medicine. Companies operating in tourist destinations as far afield as the Caribbean, Thailand and Malaysia are already offering regenerative medicine as components of holiday packages, designed to alleviate the negative consequences of degenerative diseases such as multiple sclerosis or diabetes. Holiday packages will come to include cosmetic and regenerative medicine as part of the world cruise for the super-rich. The idea of gerontological tourism offering rest, cure and rejuvenation might also become an addendum to sexual tourism in the world of advanced biocapitalism. One sign of the times was an academic event hosted by Cambridge University Life Extension and Rejuvenation Society in October 2004 in which Aubrey de Grey announced that human beings could "live forever", by which he meant that within twenty-five years medical science will possess the capacity to repair all known effects of ageing. The average age at death of people born thereafter would exceed 5,000 years!

CONCLUSION: FROM ENVIRONMENTAL TO MEDICAL CITIZENSHIP

Concern for the negative consequences of industrial capitalism on the natural environment has become a dominant issue of global politics. Individual governments have, at various levels of intervention, attempted to protect their national populations from the effects of public and involuntary risks (acid rain, radioactive waste and oil spills). They are also concerned by the unpredictable consequences of the industrialization of agricultural production, carbon dioxide emissions from motor vehicles, and contamination from civil nuclear power. Howard Newby (1996), writing about the development of environmentalism in Britain, identified four stages in the emergence of "environmental citizenship". First, from 1880 to 1900 there was a concern for preservation as epitomized by the National Trust. Second, in the inter-war years there was growing middle-class criticism of laissez-faire economics and an emphasis on the need for regulation and the provision of public amenities. Between the early 1960s and the 1970s, environmental anxieties were expressed in a third stage through organizations such as Friends of the Earth and the Ecology Party. Finally, in the late 1990s the parochial British debate was challenged by a political recognition of the universal dimensions of global warming. With a new emphasis on sustainability, the traditional language of amenity was replaced by a discourse of global crisis and catastrophe.

A similar pattern also appeared in the growth of the American environmental lobby where a legal framework was created to regulate industry and protect the environment through the Land and Water Act (1964), the Water Pollution Act and Clean Air Act (1965), and the Clean Water Restoration Act (1966). After the so-called "Conservation Congress" of 1968, there followed a suite of regulatory provisions: the Environmental Protection Act, the Toxic Substances Control Act, and the Occupational Health and Safety Act, and a number of Food and Drug Acts. Beck's concept of risk captures the critical dimension of ecological consciousness as a lack of confidence in expert opinion and lack of trust in government policy. There have been major public debates exposing internal divisions in the academic community and inconsistencies in the scientific evidence. The first case of BSE in Japan in September 2001 confirmed the global interconnectedness of food production and distribution, where there are no closed borders for goods or diseases. The result was an immediate decline in meat imports which in turn had a direct impact on the Australian economy. Against a background of distrust for government reports and expert advice, green politics gives public expression to ecological concerns in terms of the right to a safe and, if possible, "natural" environment.

These emerging rights (to a safe environment, aboriginal culture and land, and ethnic identity) point to and are underpinned by a generic right to ontological security as a parallel to social security. This demand is the foundation of a new medical citizenship that broadly encompasses the right to health. Human beings are characterized by their frailty and vulnerability, and by the precarious character of their social and political arrangements (Turner, 2006). Citizenship is a socio-political system that provides some protection from the particular risks of an advanced society. Where life is nasty, brutish and short, citizenship functions to make the world more secure and civilized. The irony of globalization is that in many respects our world is becoming more risky and precarious, because the dangers of modern technology often outweigh, or at least cast doubt on, its advantages. This basic right of ontological security is closely connected to questions of human embodiment, but it goes beyond reproductive rights and involves entitlement to respect. The right to ontological security underpins other environmental, cultural and identity claims characteristic of modern social movements. In this context, medical citizenship can be deployed as a collective umbrella for this cluster of rights. Ontological security can only be safeguarded by a new set of values that promote stewardship of the environment, concern for precarious human communities, recognition of cultural differences, and respect for human dignity. In short, we need a set of obligations that correspond to the demand for human rights. These rights to ontological security are closely tied to recognition of women's rights and to the risks of unregulated economic development.

These three post-national components of citizenship rights (ecological, aboriginal and cultural) are identified here as analogous to the three stages of the historical development of national citizenship (Marshall, 1950). They form a hierarchy: environment, community and human beings. These new rights are conceptually and historically connected by the risks to human embodiment in a global system. Post-national environmental rights are connected by human frailty and by the fact that the nation-state cannot adequately respond to this vulnerability within an ecological system that is globally disrupted by modern technology. What is less clear is the presence of an institutional structure to which these rights correspond. National citizenship rights were matched by the rise of specific institutional structures, courts of justice, parliamentary institutions and the welfare state. Environmental, aboriginal and cultural rights are all enshrined in some components of the Declaration of Human Rights and more recently in the legal recommendations arising from UN conferences on the environment (Rio), population (Cairo) and human settlements (Istanbul), but as yet there is no decisive set of global governmental arrangements that enforce or match these rights. The notion that there should be global governance has been canvassed by numerous social scientists, but we still need to spell out how a global political community could exist and exercise legitimate power.

9   NEW WARS AND TERRORISM: GLOBALIZATION OF MILITARISM AND VIOLENCE

INTRODUCTION: THE VIOLENT STATE OF THE WORLD

War, as one of the four horsemen of the Apocalypse, has been with us for millennia, in fact ever since humans began to live in settled communities. War and globalization are linked to the extent that one author states that "it is not sufficient to claim that globalization causes war and other violent conflict but rather that war itself is a form of interconnection. War is not only an example of globalization, it is one of the principle [sic] mechanisms of globalization, a globalizing force" (Barkawi, 2006: 92). While the wars between ancient "tribes" and cities and groups of people remain shrouded in various myths and folklore, the first recorded war for which historical evidence can be marshalled took place in 2700 BCE between two peoples "when Mebaragesi, the first king on the Sumerian King List, undertook a war against the Elamities" (Gabriel, 2005: 51). The war between Sumer (part of modern Iraq) and Elam (part of modern Iran) presaged the Iran–Iraq wars several centuries later.

Wars at a time of enhanced global communications have gained a new meaning both objectively and subjectively. Watching the evening news on television or taking a cursory look at a daily newspaper in any part of the world, one has to agree that the level of violence in the world has not diminished and shows no sign of decline. With the remarkable innovation in military technology that followed the industrial revolution and as the new technology – the means of destruction – was globalized, the nature of war, not its causes, has changed. One of the distinctive features of modern war is the increase in the number of civilian casualties. Alongside organized warfare between nation-states, we now see random violence known as terrorism where violence is inflicted not by the state but by groups and networks with or without the patronage of a state. Acts of terrorism – bomb-blasts and other innovative means – kill and maim innocent, unsuspecting civilians almost every day in some part of the world. Defining terrorism is almost impossible because of the political entanglement of this concept. At the normative level, whether one is for or against a cause has a bearing on the evaluation and hence definition of terrorism. Terrorism, notwithstanding the appearance of mindless acts of vandalism, is often politically charged. Hardman (1930: 575) defines it as "the method or theory behind the method whereby an organized group or party seeks to achieve its avowed aims chiefly through the systematic use of violence". Over time, terrorism has gained new notoriety and, by and large, there seems to be a consensus against viewing terrorism as indiscriminate killing of the non-combatants. But this has not been always the case.

Terrorist attack as a method of resistance was well accepted by many nationalist movements, especially when they turned into armed struggle. The origin of modern terrorism was linked to imperialism. For example, during the anti-colonial struggle in India, *santrashis* or terrorists were idolized as folk heroes who targeted civilian administrators with their crude weapons. In Bengal, Khudiram Basu (1889–1908), who went to the gallows following an abortive attempt to kill a British administrator, became a folk hero. He was a popular subject of novels, plays and movies, more so than Mahatma Gandhi, whose method was *satyagraha,* or passive resistance. Like their counterparts today, a high sense of self-sacrifice and deep political commitment motivated their acts. However, unlike in terrorist acts today, the so-called collateral damage involving innocent, non-partisan civilians was rare or accidental. Some people see terrorism as the weapon of the weak. Other writers have spoken about state-initiated terrorism. In defining acts of terrorism, we focus more on the means of inflicting violence than on the goals or underlying causes where one group may not find any other means of registering or solving their grievances but to do something drastic in order to draw global attention to their plight. Terrorism, an organized effort to kill people and destroy property at random and to instil fear or terror into society at large, has been around since the anti-colonial struggles of the early twentieth century. Such acts have become more violent and random in the late twentieth and early twenty-first centuries. The first major terrorist act of the twenty-first century, beamed throughout the world on live television, was the attack of 11 September 2001 which led to catastrophic wars and prolonged cycles of violence in Afghanistan and Iraq.

It is incumbent on social scientists to examine the state of violence in the world by using all their theoretical and methodological resources.

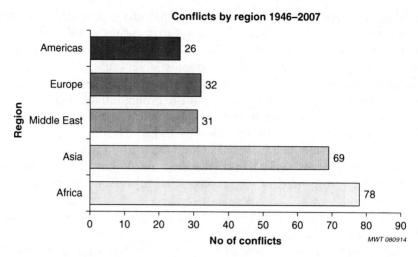

Conflicts by region 1946–2007

Source: Uppsala Conflict Data Program (UCDP) accessed on 20 December 2008, UCDP Database: www.ucdp.uu.se/database Uppsala University. Reprinted with permission.

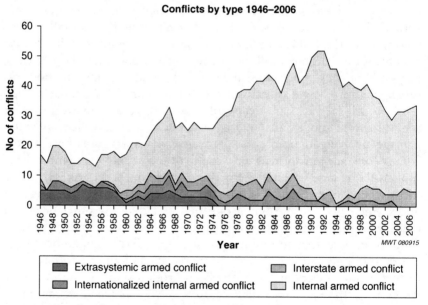

Conflicts by type 1946–2006

Source: Uppsala Conflict Data Program (UCDP) accessed on 20 December 2008, UCDP Database: www.ucdp.uu.se/database Uppsala University. Reprinted with permission.

A multidisciplinary and historical understanding of the problems of war and violence at a time of generalized lawlessness in various parts of the world is an urgent need of the day. It is also crucial for social scientists to examine the forces of globalization that may have contributed to the transformation of the world as a dangerous place, as well as the possibilities, albeit faint at the moment, of changing this permanent state of war into a permanent state of peace. Despite the importance of expert knowledge, academic specialization in social science has not been very helpful with respect to the study of war and violence. These are subjects that are too important to be left to the terrorism or military expert. This chapter will discuss the causes and consequences of global violence and put forward some propositions towards ending or reducing the conditions of violence.

There has been hardly a single year, since the end of the Second World War, when the world has not seen some kind of military action in some part or other of the world. High-intensity wars often coincide with long-drawn-out, low-intensity conflicts.

SOCIAL ORDER AND DISORDER

Sociology, despite its claim to be a scientific study of social order according to the assumptions of Auguste Comte, one of sociology's founding fathers, has been surprisingly reticent in discussing the implications of one of the most disruptive forces in society, namely war. Wars play an important part in the history of social discontinuity. Sociologists now examine social disorder, the breakdown of society, historical discontinuity and crises, but they rarely contribute directly to the study of war. The sociology of disasters studies disasters which are sometimes "natural" like the tsunami of 26 December 2004 or "man-made" crises such as famines. Wars are "man-made" disasters. Both the short-term and long-term consequences of wars are typically disastrous. Yet, the subdiscipline of the sociology of disasters has also ignored war and violent riots. Only a small number of historical sociologists have examined the causes and consequences of revolutions, state breakdown or the consequences of wars.

SOCIAL PROGRESS AND THE END OF WAR

In the eighteenth and nineteenth centuries in the wake of the industrial revolution and emerging democracies, a number of Enlightenment philosophers argued that with human progress wars would become redundant. Rational human beings would be able to negotiate and resolve conflicts, which are often inevitable, in a peaceful manner. With the advancement of rationalization, wars would disappear, they thought. The German philosopher, Immanuel Kant (1724–1804), advanced a theory of perpetual peace.

He laid the basis for the theory that democratic regimes would not go to war against each other. Although his theory has been subject to considerable criticism, especially following the unilateral wars undertaken by the United States during the Bush administration, there are still international relations experts who support this viewpoint. The belligerent posturing of North Korea towards its neighbours might be one example of an authoritarian regime that threatens its more democratic neighbours.

The English sociologist Herbert Spencer (1820–1903), who had many followers in Japan during its period of industrialization, also envisioned the transformation of society from what he called "militaristic" to "industrial". With their focus on business and trade, according to Spencer, trading nations would not fight wars. All these optimistic propositions grounded their evaluation on the rationality of human beings and the social institutions they have created. Although there was relative peace in the nineteenth century, viewed in terms of the absence of large-scale wars between states, the wars of global proportions in the twentieth century gave the lie to such optimism and renewed the idea of human capacity for irrationality or competing rationalities.

Can wars be seen only as expressions of human irrationalities or are there roots of wars in the actual structures of society? In other words, are irresponsible and power-hungry leaders to be blamed for wars or are there politico-economic forces, aiming at the control of resources and political domination, that create the conditions for wars and nationalistic conflicts? Social scientists and historians often debate these competing explanations. A plausible approach is often to take an eclectic view of the causation of wars and conflicts. There are both structural – that is, long-term and deep-rooted – causes as well as situational issues prompting wars. In the discussion below, we will take a long-term and as much as a multidisciplinary view of the causes and consequences of wars by examining the social structural factors that are now inescapably related to the forces of globalization.

GLOBALIZATION AND WARS

With the intensification of globalization, there was an increase in violence in the twentieth century and this violent period appears to have continued into the twenty-first century. Whether globalization has actually increased the frequency or intensity of wars between nations is a matter of some debate. However, what is beyond doubt is that the global media and information technologies have brought war and violence right into our living rooms. The attack on the World Trade Center in New York was not the only terrorist event in the first decade of this century, but definitely the most spectacular one. It was on live television. The image of the American Airlines passenger plane ramming into the Twin Towers will remain etched permanently on the minds of all who saw it around the world. The agony on the faces of New Yorkers, the helplessness, the vulnerability were captured for all to see. The first Gulf war in 1991, when the US-led allied forces drove out the invading Iraqi soldiers to liberate Kuwait, was in fact the first modern war on television. There was an American television crew in Baghdad beaming out live war footage with the camera zooming in on low-flying missiles. It is often said, somewhat cynically, by post-modern critics such as Jean Baudrillard, that all modern wars are simply TV events.

Various radical groups, the so-called "Islamic Jihadists", the Tamil Tigers and narco-terrorists in the jungles of Colombia, have made cynical use of the new media either as a tool of terror by spreading images of atrocities, or as a means of networking around the world, exchanging information with their members. In a number of cases, pictures of hostages appeared on the Internet. Ironically, military technology such as ARPANET paved the way for the Internet and revolutionized communications in the last quarter of the twentieth century. In the first decade of the twenty-first century much of the information communication technology is fully exploited by the radical groups outside the bounds of law, with deadly consequences.

During the terrorist attacks in Mumbai, India, of November 2008, the terrorists used mobile and satellite phones to coordinate their attacks in three locations. Because their calls were monitored, the Indian intelligence authority could determine their nationalities from their accents, and the calls were subsequently traced to their leader in locations in Pakistan. Closed-circuit television cameras captured the image of a young man in a Versace T-shirt and carrying an AK-47 Kalashnikov assault rifle with which he had outgunned the poorly armed Indian policeman at the train station where the attacks had started.

The twentieth century saw two major episodes of war with trails of destruction and human suffering of historic proportions: the so-called Great War (1914–18), followed by the equally disastrous Second World War (1939–45). The Great War was the first truly global war involving nations in far-flung regions of the world with battle fronts in Europe, Africa and Asia. With hindsight it was called the First World War, reflecting the global dimensions of the conflict. The death toll of these two wars – 8 million in the First World War and 50 million in the Second World War – was truly catastrophic. In the aftermath of the Second

The 15 countries with the highest military expenditure in 2007
(in market exchange rate terms: spending figures are at
constant 2005 prices and exchange rates)

Rank	Country	Spending (US$ bn)	World share (%)	Spending per capita	% of GDP in 2006
1	USA	547	45	1,799	4.0
2	UK	59.7	5	995	2.6
3	China	58.3	5	44	2.1
4	France	53.6	4	880	2.4
5	Japan	43.6	3	339	1.0
6	Germany	36.9	3	447	1.3
7	Russia	35.4	3	249	3.6
8	Saudi Arabia	33.8	3	1,310	8.5
9	Italy	33.1	3	568	1.8
10	India	24.2	2	21	2.7
11	South Korea	22.6	2	470	2.5
12	Brazil	15.3	1	80	1.5
13	Canada	15.2	1	461	1.2
14	Australia	15.1	1	733	1.9
15	Spain	14.6	1	336	1.2

Sources: Military expenditure, SIPRI (2008, Appendix 5A)

World War, a different kind of "war" began, which was caused by the rivalry between two ideological systems, namely capitalism and socialism. The rise and fall of socialist state systems, and with it the end of the Cold War, produced a stalemate between the two superpowers – the United States and the Soviet Union. With the end of the Cold War and after the disintegration of the former Soviet Union, it was widely expected that peace would prevail and that reduced military expenditure could be redeployed and used for peaceful purposes, including promoting human welfare.

Such optimism was reflected in talk of the "peace dividend", but the optimism quickly dissolved into a nightmare as new wars and "ethnic cleansing" became a common feature of modern violence. Actual hot wars did not disappear either. The Russian attack on Georgia over Georgia's role in South Ossetia in August 2008, and the US reaction, led some people to talk about a return to regional conflicts as states sought to (re)impose their control over their "own" regions. The nature of the war changed from conflicts between states with high military casualties to the rising casualties of civilians – a process that began in the twentieth century. The historian Eric Hobsbawm showed that the twentieth century was the most violent century in history, with the loss of 167 million lives in these violent confrontations. Wars in which more civilians than combatants are killed have become a predominant feature of the so-called "new wars". According to Michael Mann (2004: 4), "[w]hereas civilians accounted for below 10 per cent of deaths in World War I, they rocketed to over half in World War II, and to somewhere above 80 per cent in wars fought in the 1990s".

The military budget of the world reached over $1 trillion at the beginning of the new century. The US accounted for nearly half of that. The proposed US budget for 2007–8 stood at $481 billion dollars (*International Herald Tribune*, 5 February 2007). It is true that the US military budget declined somewhat from $306 billion in 1990 to $301 billion in 2000, or from 5.3 per cent of gross domestic product (GDP) to 3.1 per cent of GDP, but it shot up again after the attacks on the 9/11 United States. According to the Stockholm International Peace Research Institute, world military expenditure is estimated to have been $1,339 billion in 2007 – in real terms an increase of 6 per cent over 2006 and of 45 per cent since 1998. This corresponded to 2.5 per cent of world GDP or $202 for each person in the world (SIPRI, 2008).

In late September 2007 US Defense Secretary, Robert Gates, urged Congress to approve $190 billion to fund the wars in Afghanistan and Iraq for 2008. The total expenditure for the two wars for the American taxpayers will amount to $800 billion (*Chicago Tribune*, 29 September 2007). The long-term and indirect cost of the war has been estimated at $3 trillion (Stiglitz and Bilmes, 2008).

IMPACT OF WAR AND GENOCIDE IN HISTORICAL PERSPECTIVE

Martin Shaw (2003) in *War & Genocide* has examined the impact of "organized killing" in modern society. His historical narrative opens with the

Armenian genocide in 1915 and concludes with the Rwanda genocide in 1994. It would be useful to push this discussion further back to the violent encounter between colonial settlement and aboriginal people. These early genocidal encounters were features of the "great land rush" that formed the modern world between 1650 and 1900. The first illustration that we might consider was the Wounded Knee massacre of 1890 when between 150 and 300 men, women and children of the Lakota Sioux people were killed by members of the US Seventh Cavalry. This massacre, which involved the use of four Hotchkiss cannons that were capable of firing 50 two-pound explosive shells per minute, has all the hallmarks of what came to characterize twentieth-century violence: the mechanization of organized killing; revenge (for the Battle of the Little Big Horn); ethnic cleansing, whereby the Lakota were characterized in the *Nebraska State Journal* as murderous redskins; and the indiscriminate killing of women and children. Finally, the attempt by the Lakota people to secure an apology from the US government has not been successful (Brown, 1971).

Were men in tribal societies less violent? Violent combat in pre-modern societies and the use of torture have often been regarded as evidence of a lack of moral restraint. Historians and sociologists have often suggested that the "primitive warrior" enjoyed the violence that he inflicted on the enemy. Passionate killing led to a form of collective ecstasy that some historians detect in traditional warrior brotherhoods. Extreme violence towards other human beings can be taken to indicate that outsiders were not in fact regarded as human. Anthropological research suggests that pre-literate societies did not have an expansive or comprehensive notion of humanity, but on the contrary defined themselves exclusively as "the People". Exclusionary rituals that created a decisive and definite sense of otherness often enclosed such traditional communities. This ritualistic notion of an exclusive inside and outside world that separated "the People" from outsiders was often inscribed upon the body in the form of tattoos and body piercing, demarcating an ontologically separate community. Notions of taboo and pollution are also important in describing the boundaries that separate human communities. Ritual cannibalism and head hunting may be regarded as practices that decisively demarcated the inside and the outside world. What and whom we are entitled through ritualized practices to enslave, to hunt or to eat are powerful indicators of the extent of the boundary between the human and the non-human. This notion of the closed boundary of traditional or pre-literate societies raises an interesting question about civilizing processes. Norbert Elias (2000) has argued that modern societies depend on self-regulation rather than physical suppression and that aggression in modern warfare is increasingly

impersonal. The transformation of human emotions is a significant feature of this history. In the discussion "On changes in aggressiveness",
Elias (2000: 161–2) provides an important account of how violent passions in the early feudal period were slowly transformed as the civilized
norms of court society slowly evolved.

There is no doubt that Elias produced one of the most influential
and far-ranging theories of the transformation of violence in human societies in terms of what he called the civilizing process. His argument is well
known. In summary, it states that, with the transformation of feudal society, the rise of bourgeois society and the development of the modern
state, interpersonal violence came to be increasingly regulated by social
norms that emphasized self-restraint, control and personal discipline. Thus
the meaning of "civilization" in Elias's theory refers to the growth of individual moral restraint and the containment of aggression and passionate
emotions in social interaction. The theory can be regarded as a moral pedagogy of the body in which raw passions and emotions are self-regulated
through new disciplinary regimes. The theory shows how developments
in social institutions (such as the court, the state and the bourgeois family) are important for and interact with the emotions and dispositions of
individuals. Personal civility and civilizing institutions are bound together
in a dynamic historical process. As a result, in contemporary societies,
social restraint and social order require the development of self-attention
and self-regard in which through self-reflection (such as imagining what
others think of us) we exercise self-surveillance and control (Barbalet,
1998). In this sense, we can regard the theory as a historical psycho-
analytical study of violent emotions within the sociological paradigm
of the modern state. In pre-modern societies, 'primitive man' was a
more aggressive and emotional social being, but his primitive technology
also meant that killing was a more inefficient and limited activity.

In modern societies, the capacity for killing has been greatly enhanced
by technology, and hence we can kill on a scale that could not be
imagined in earlier societies. For the first time, in Hiroshima and
Nagasaki tens of thousands of people were killed in a matter of few
minutes, with lingering consequences and an increase in deaths from
cancer and similar (wasting) diseases. Modern men and women are also
more likely to have grown up in societies where extreme violence
towards outsiders is not a normal aspect of their experience, social training and development. The professional training of soldiers in a modern
army means that they are socialized to kill without emotion, and in any
case hand-to-hand combat has become somewhat unusual in modern
conflict, at least on the part of professional soldiers. The preferred form
of killing in modern warfare is now through aerial bombing in which

casualties to armed forces are minimal, while damage to an enemy is maximal. Bombing with so-called smart weapons can typically take place without actually seeing the enemy. This technology obviously creates an emotional division between dropping smart bombs on an unknown enemy and the sense of personal, emotional combat as described, for example, in the Icelandic sagas of Erik the Red.

Elias's theory is therefore that, in terms of psychology, modern soldiers, unlike medieval warriors, are not trained to be enthusiastic and passionate killers, but the evidence is in fact very mixed. The rape of Nanjing, the fall of Berlin to Russian forces, the killing fields of Cambodia, the slaughter of women and children in Rwanda, and the killing in Darfur suggest that the "civilizing process" described by Elias may be a fragile constraint on human behaviour. Elias's theory attempts to say that modern man kills dispassionately without emotion. An alternative view is that modern societies, as opposed to modern people, are more violent than pre-modern societies. Technological change has made killing more efficient in modern societies, and wars are won by destroying civilian populations. This growing technological capacity has meant that the growth of the idea of "humanity" is a measure of actual inhumanity. In addition, it is possible to argue that there has been a "re-personalization" of killing in modern warfare. Mass warfare and universal conscription have largely disappeared, and the powerful commercial states – the United States, China, Japan and the European powers – are increasingly integrated economically and diplomatically. At the same time, there has been an increase in local conflicts between rebel forces, warlords, drug barons and states, which often involve ethnic cleansing and genocide. Conflicts such as those in the former Yugoslavia, Chechnya and central Africa frequently involve neighbourhood killing, robbery, organized rape and slavery, and they are characterized by extreme violence against the bodies of women and children. The aim often appears to be to induce as much fear and intimidation of civil populations as possible. The methods involve camp rape, looting, pillage and hacking off of limbs. Indeed, "violation of the body, with maximum pain, has become a common method of slaughter" (Shaw, 2003: 138). It is possible to argue, following Elias, that the Nazi concentration camps involved an impersonal system of mass killing (Bauman, 1989). However, the idea of an evolutionary and unidimensional "civilizing process" is inadequate as a perspective on the personalized violence of combat in contemporary conflict zones. The frequent use of children as child warriors in new wars raises in an acute form a question mark about the civilizing process.

The growth of human rights institutions can be said to be a response both to the mass killings of the Second World War and to the more localized, brutalized and personal killing of contemporary wars. Technological developments with modernization in the twentieth century enhanced the capacity of states and their military to inflict violence on civilian populations. Hiroshima and the Holocaust were both instances of the violent application of modern technology against civilians. In the second half of the twentieth century, however, there were important transformations of warfare. Herfried Münkler (2005) has identified three principal characteristics of "the new wars". First, while old wars were typically between states, new wars are "de-statized", that is, there has been a privatization of warfare, made possible by the reduction in the costs of armaments. For example, the Kalashnikov rifle is a relatively inexpensive but very effective weapon that has become a basic element in "small wars". The effective use of these cheap, portable weapons does not require a lengthy period of training, and they are not associated with traditional forms of drill and discipline. Second, there is typically a significant asymmetry between the competing forces. Unlike the First World War where large armies engaged with each other on a battle front over many years, in new wars small armed forces (guerrillas or terrorists) create localized havoc, usually against civilians. They try to avoid conventional confrontations with trained forces. Finally, Münkler perceives an "autonomization" of forms of violence that were once subordinated to and incorporated in a military system. One indication of this trend is that the division between criminal organization, insurgency and warfare no longer exists. Just as terrorism is a privatization of the military, so the security forces that protect politicians and corporate leaders are themselves private, profitable agencies. Private security forces in Iraq are the obvious example.

There are three consequences of this privatization of warfare that are important for understanding modern conflict situations. The first is that modern warfare is characterized, in Münkler's terms, by short wars between states and long wars within societies. Secondly, there is a very close association between new wars and epidemics and starvation. Thirdly, there is escalating violence against women. Whereas in the Balkan wars up to 50,000 women were raped, in the Rwanda genocide the figure was over a quarter of a million. Rape in new wars is designed to destroy communities by excluding young women from marriage and reproduction when their honour and self-esteem have been symbolically and physically destroyed. These three consequences all point to one conclusion, namely that new wars make everyday life precarious, and human life becomes more vulnerable with social changes that are driven by a new economy of warfare based on the sex trade, drug control and contraband. Child soldiers and cheap armaments have become the symbols of the new wars in which military discipline, a sense of military honour or rules of engagement play no part. While the new wars serve to underscore the argument that human vulnerability is the linking thread in human rights developments in the twentieth century, these new wars are obviously not subject to or regulated by human rights conventions. Whereas wars between states are in principle subject to interventions by courts, the possibility of controlling marauding warriors in Darfur or child soldiers in Burma is remote.

The privatization of war marked a new dimension when, in 2003 during the Iraq war the US government hired a number of mercenaries and used them in selective combat duties. The difference between the official US troops and the mercenaries was not just the high salaries they received. They also had "licence to kill", as they enjoyed immunity from prosecution. Following a blatant massacre of unarmed civilians in September 2007 when 17 Iraqis were killed by the security guards of Blackwater Worldwide, one such outfit, public attention was drawn to them as mounting protests in Iraq exacerbated a difficult political situation. Investigations that followed resulted in the surrender of five Blackwater men, all former US military men, in Utah in December 2008 (*New York Times*, 8 December 2008).

CONCLUSIONS

The study of war is thus an important, if depressing, sociological contribution to the analysis of human rights, but this descriptive account of the historical evolution of private wars in the modern period does not in our view excuse sociologists from their failure to engage in or contribute to normative debates about human rights and the importance of legal regulation of violence. The emphasis on technological and economic changes in warfare does not mean that cultural and social factors have played no part. Indeed, the value of Münkler's approach is that he recognizes the fact that the privatization of warfare also means that the traditional values of military discipline and respect for the conventions of war have collapsed. Indeed, he perceives an important social relationship between the culture of new wars and the glamour with which Hollywood surrounds male violence in a post-modern culture. There is a sad irony in which the West, while condemning the mindless violence of terrorism, produces feature films that celebrate extreme physical violence as the hallmark of masculinity. We might call this "the Schwarzenegger factor". The cultural connections between Hollywood, new wars and terrorism mean that intellectuals should seek to defend a higher order of values rather than pessimistically concluding that the defence of civilized life is a lost cause. The sociological imagination compels us to understand both the empirical social constraints on human behaviour (such as the impact of Kalashnikov rifles on the military organization of child soldiers), and the normative opportunities that are created by the historical rise of global human rights. The task of sociology is to understand the empirical circumstances that make everyday life precarious and the normative possibilities of a shared vulnerability. This analysis of the interface between empirical constraints and normative possibilities requires both comparative historical research and ethical analysis of the human condition.

10 GLOBALIZATION OF DISASTERS AND DISASTER RESPONSE

INTRODUCTION

With their manifold causes and consequences, disasters, defined here as unscheduled events caused by nature or by human interventions, illustrate many aspects of the processes of globalization. This chapter argues that the nature of disasters, their consequences and the responses to them in the contemporary world, reveal not only the interconnectedness of the modern world but also some underlying problems of the governance of disasters. Contemporary disasters include a wide variety of calamities from natural to nuclear disaster, from wars, civil wars, and large-scale human rights violations to terrorist attacks. In November 2008, Mumbai, the commercial capital of India, was brought to a halt for nearly three days while terrorists seized three key places in the tourist district of the city. The consequences of disasters on human societies, the response to post-disaster adjustments, and long-term recovery have a bearing on the global processes.

Disasters as unscheduled events destroy human lives and property and, more importantly, undermine social stability. While a cyclone or earthquake is a visible "natural" disaster, often accompanied by dramatic television footage of ruins in its path, there are creeping disasters – disasters that build slowly and steadily over a period of time. The consequences of these creeping disasters are no less lethal, and the damage and disruptions no less catastrophic. Food shortage and famine are disasters which have also been labelled as "creeping disasters" (Khondker, 1989), because the build-up to such events is typically long-term. The rapid inflation in food prices in 2008 led to a "silent famine" in many parts of the world. Since politicians are loath to use the term "famine", various euphemisms have surfaced to describe the crisis, which in itself is suggestive of the link between politics, media and disasters.

Industrial accidents, such as the near-meltdown at the nuclear plant at Three Mile Island at Harrisburg, Pennsylvania, in 1977, the deadly methyl isocyanine gas leakage at the Union Carbide plant in Bhopal, India, in 1984 and the accident at the Chernobyl nuclear plant in 1986 generated interest in industrial disasters. The Union Carbide disaster in Bhopal raised questions about whether transnational companies maintained the same safety standards in a developing country as they would in their Western home bases.

In December 1987 at its 42nd session, the General Assembly of the United Nations designated the 1990s as the International Decade for Natural Disaster Reduction (IDNDR). The basic idea behind this proclamation was, and remains, the unacceptable and rising levels of human losses which disasters continue to incur, on the one hand, and the existence, on the other hand, of a wealth of scientific and engineering know-how which could be effectively used to reduce the losses resulting from such disasters. As its name implied, the IDNDR officially came to an end in 1999. However, during its ten-year span of activities, it achieved such important successes – especially in forging vital links among the political, scientific and technological communities – that the United Nations created a successor body to carry on its work. This new body of coordinated action programs, with a secretariat in Geneva, is the International Strategy for Disaster Reduction (ISDR).

HOW NATURAL IS A NATURAL DISASTER?

For a long time social scientists and philosophers have questioned the nature-centric view of disasters. The mediating influence of social arrangement on disaster was noted even by Jean-Jacques Rousseau in the eighteenth century. The Lisbon earthquake of 1755, which took a toll of 90,000 lives, became a subject of some philosophical musings by the Enlightenment philosophers, who pondered over the meaning of the earthquake in the contexts of human reason and God's will, and evil. Voltaire, one of the key Enlightenment figures, saw the earthquake as a metaphysical event. In a poem he raised the problem of evil, doubting the Enlightenment view of progress and optimism.

Rousseau's reply to Voltaire outlined a surprisingly modern social science view. Rousseau pointed out that it was not the seismic event itself which was important but the nature of the human community.

"Without departing from your subject of Lisbon, admit, for example, that nature did not construct twenty thousand houses of six to seven stories there, and that, if the inhabitants of this great city had been more equally spread out and more lightly lodged, the damage would have been much less and perhaps of no account." (Rousseau quoted in Dynes, 2000)

Similar discussions took place following the devastating earthquake losses in Pakistan in 2005 with fatalities estimated at 86,000, in Bam, Iran, in 2003 with 31,000, deaths, and in Izmit, Turkey, in 1999 with a death toll of over 17,000.

Human history has experienced a litany of disasters and thus can be seen as the constant struggle of human communities against such crises. One of the measures of social progress is the human ability to tackle disasters by foretelling, preventing, and wherever possible mitigating the losses. Human agency and organized social responses have reduced our collective vulnerability. However, calamities such as the Asian tsunami of December 2004 or the Sichuan earthquake of 2008 in China are reminders of the helplessness of people in the face of the fury of nature. A true measure of social progress is the reduction of vulnerability to disasters caused both by the forces of nature and by society itself. Some countries such as the Philippines and Bangladesh are regularly visited by a whole range of "natural" calamities from cyclones to earthquakes. It would be impossible to deny the role of nature in the causation of disasters, but natural causes are mediated by social and political processes and hence we must insert quotation marks around the word "natural". The Asian tsunami, which affected countries as far afield as Somalia and India, is a case in point. The worst affected countries were Sri Lanka, Thailand and Indonesia. Of the estimated 220,000 fatalities, the majority were from the Indonesian province of Ache. The beaches that bore the brunt of the waves were sites developed for tourists and were consequently denuded of mangroves. Seashores lined with mangroves might have withstood some of the ferocity of the tidal waves. Just as human intervention was visible in the clearing of the mangroves, the other facet was in the administration of disaster relief. Clearly some societies are better able to cope with disasters than others.

China suffered a 7.9 magnitude earthquake in May 2008. It is estimated that 70,000 people perished in the earthquake, with another 18,000 missing. Many of the victims were school children. It appeared that the school buildings were not built to the appropriate safety specifications. Unlike the Tangshan earthquake in China in 1976 with a death toll of 240,000 when the Chinese government was not forthcoming with information about losses, the Chinese authority in 2008 was more open in disclosing information on earthquake damages (*Gulf News*, 16 May 2008).

GLOBALIZATION AND DISASTERS

Disasters in times of globalization have consequences far beyond the location where they strike. The globalization of the consequences of disasters is revealed clearly in epidemiological crises such as avian flu, SARS or tuberculosis. These have become transnational diseases thanks to the movement of people across national borders. There are several examples of epidemics in history which were also results of the movement of people. The plagues in medieval Europe were a consequence of the Crusades as the crusaders brought rats in their ships back to Europe. The European colonialists infected the indigenous people in Central and North America with viruses such as measles and whooping cough against which indigenous people had little or no resistance. In the early part of the twentieth century an influenza virus killed millions of people in Europe – an infection that was taken from Europe to America and Asia. The influenza was incubated in Italy with a detachment of American troops who brought it back to the USA and then later on to parts of Asia. The connection between war and the spread of diseases provides us with many such examples.

The silent disaster of the twenty-first century is hunger, which is caused by the poverty that keeps nearly a quarter of the world population at a level of vulnerability where simple shocks can put their lives at stake. The 2008 crisis in food prices and the threat of global hunger were a surprise to many observers, because for a decade food prices had been stable or falling. Writing in 1987 about futurology in an article called "The world and the United States in 2013", Daniel Bell (1987: 18) made a number of valuable and precise predictions, for example about the growing economic influence of China and India, but he also made a surprising statement about food. He claimed that "almost every country in the world is just about self-sufficient in food, and seeking export markets. ... Until the twentieth century, a famine was recorded almost every year somewhere in the world. Today famines are rare ... the problems of food production are *political*." Bell was obviously too optimistic about the disappearance of famine, but he was surely correct in arguing that the principal causes of famine arise from political conflict, mismanagement and violence. Many of the causes of malnutrition and famine in Africa – Darfur, Ethiopia and Zimbabwe – are political.

In March 2008, a sudden rise in cereal prices caused a great deal of uncertainty in various parts of the world. In Egypt women were out on the streets protesting and fighting the police over the disappearance of bread. There is a certain irony to this protest in that Egypt was not only the cradle of human civilization but also the birthplace of systematic agricultural production based on irrigation. The Cairo-based regional office of the World Food Programme (WFP) identified greater demand for food, with a dwindling supply, in the emerging economies of China and India, the increased use of land for biofuels, climate change and failed harvests, high oil prices and increasing transport costs, as major causes of the surge in food prices. Added to those factors were the lack of liquidity in the financial market and the problems of governance in various developing countries where hoarding of food grains distorted the market. Flooding in the American Midwest also damaged the harvesting of crops such as soya bean and maize in 2008, thereby further driving up the price of grain. A concern for improved ecology was one of the factors in the demand for ethanol which is thought to be less polluting. But the diversion of crops from human consumption, compounded by drought in Australia, exacerbated the food situation, leading to hunger. Global warming also contributed to the increased frequency of floods and other natural calamities. It is difficult to gauge exactly how much the increase in commodity process was a result of speculation, but these price fluctuations will obviously continue. In response to demand, farmers planted more wheat and by late 2008 it looked as if wheat prices would stabilize following a rise in supply, but the overall trend appears to be inflationary, with unsatisfied demand driving up prices.

Suddenly, countries until recently touted as the breadbaskets of the region covering parts of the Middle East and Africa such as Iraq and Sudan were short of food. Bangladesh, which attained self-sufficiency in food in 1999–2000, faced a serious food crisis in late March and early April 2008. Famines which were a thing of the past, a subject fit for history books, lingered into the last decades of the twentieth century only in Africa and North Korea. The fear of famine in Bangladesh, Sudan and Somalia in 2008 was back on newspaper front pages and television talk shows. Ethiopia, according to one media report, faced a "toxic cocktail" of global inflation, armed conflict, and associated plagues that threaten 14 million people who are in need of food aid. North Korea, largely for political reasons, remains globally isolated and is faced with famine on a more or less constant basis, despite the efforts of South Korea to normalize relationships (*USA Today*, 17 August 2008).

Bangladesh suffered a famine in the mid-1970s as the country was trying to recover from a trail of devastation left behind by a bloody war of liberation in late 1971. Wars and famine are natural allies. Poverty lies at the heart of famine. Amartya Sen reminded us that entitlement failure, often translated into lack of purchasing power, and not the shortage of food, is the real cause of famine. This idea was by no means a new discovery, though the formulation was. But in some famines, failure of entitlement and shortage of food occur simultaneously. More than half a century before Amartya Sen's *Poverty and Famines* (1982), W.H. Moreland (1923) made a distinction between "food famines" and "work famines". In a straightforward manner, he said that some localized famines were caused simply by the shortage of food. Other famines, such as those which characterized the colonial period in India, were caused by the lack of employment: no work and no income, and therefore no food. At the turn of the last century, such explanations were presaged by J.T. Sunderland who, in an article entitled "The cause of Indian famines", attributed famines to "the extreme poverty of the Indian people – poverty so severe that it keeps a majority of all on the verge of suffering, even in the years of plenty" (Sunderland, 1900: 58). Those realities have not changed significantly. In Zimbabwe today, the mismanagement of the economy by a national hero turned dictator, President Mugabe, has led to 80 per cent unemployment and price inflation at unimaginable levels, with the inevitable consequence that Zimbabwe is in the grip of famine.

Famines are extreme disasters, and widespread hunger and starvation often culminate in social collapse. Famines are rarely equal opportunity disasters, unlike a tsunami that sweeps away everybody and everything in its path. Famine and starvation affect a society unevenly. It is the poor who become the first casualties of such disasters. This historical knowledge has driven such programs as feeding the poorest of the poor, the unemployed or, in Sen's terms, those whose entitlement to food cannot be ensured by the play of market forces alone. Hence public action, that is, the role of the state in mitigating hunger, becomes essential. In a globalized world, states are able to mobilize resources, not only from the international food market, but also from food-surplus nations and multilateral agencies.

Unlike the situation in previous centuries, by the middle of the twentieth century international cooperation and global institutions evolved to tackle precisely these sorts of problems. By the late twentieth century, the World Food Programme was feeding the hungry around the world. Although most writers avoid any discussion of the Malthusian apocalyptic vision of population growth outstripping the food supply in view of a dramatic increase in the production of food, population growth, as one of the critical factors in the modern food crisis, cannot be completely ignored. Every year 78.5 million newborn children are added to the world population, which is more than the entire population of Turkey or Egypt. The world population is projected to increase from 6.7 billion in 2008 to 9.3 billion by 2050 (Population Reference Bureau, 2008), which is likely to stretch severely the capacity of global food production.

In the first decade of the twenty-first century, the two countries that vied for world attention for their rapid economic developments, having moved up the ranks from poor to industrializing countries, were China and India. In the historical discussion of famines and disasters, ironically these two countries would often be mentioned for disasters, competing with each other for the title "land of famines". Books were written in the 1960s with titles such as *Famine 1975!* (Paddock and Paddock, 1967) predicting impending famine in India, which was teeming with poor people. The predictions were falsified by India's ability to feed its population. Poverty remained but hunger was no longer an endemic problem. Famine did not strike, nor did it stalk the poor. With socio-economic development, societies have achieved greater capacity to control natural and man-made disasters. Famines, which were common in Europe in the Middle Ages and the early modern period, became mere relics in history with the advancement of social development and industrialization. The only famine in Europe in the twentieth century was the Dutch famine caused by a deliberate strategy of the Nazis during the Second World War.

Famines have been contained in parts of Africa and Asia, and countries well known for famine have overcome this scourge in the late twentieth century. India experienced the last famine during the Second World War which was linked to the war efforts of the British. Post-independence India suffered one panic famine in the Punjab in the late 1960s, but India averted disaster owing to US President Johnson's timely intervention. China suffered a major famine during the so-called Great Leap Forward movement in the heyday of Maoist communism when local officials inflated production figures and hid the real picture from the central authorities. In other words, political and bureaucratic mismanagement was the root cause. The realization that lack of education and political mismanagement play major roles in famines led Amartya Sen to develop his theory that democracy is the main antidote to famine and other similar crises.

Famines were always complex crises. A host of social, economic and political factors often conspired in the past to create famine situations. The march of progress minimized the threats of famine or contained them in the high-poverty regions of the world. As a result of the globalization of information and communication networks, news of such shortages spreads rapidly, and interventions and assistance can be effectively and quickly mobilized. Yet the world is not free of threats from food crises. As we have already noted, in 2008 there was a shortfall of wheat production, causing sharp price increases in various countries and pushing tens of thousands of people to the brink of starvation.

TYRANNY AND FAMINES

In the twentieth century many large famines were caused by oppressive political regimes such as British rule in India, the Nazi occupation of the Netherlands, and communism in the Soviet Union and China in 1930s and 1950s, respectively. With the decline of the bureaucratic and centralized socialist systems and the rise of democracies in the 1990s, it was hoped that famines would disappear. They did not. Globalization introduced a new dimension to famine. As economies became more and more connected and interdependent, an economic crisis in one place spilled over, not only into neighbouring regions, but also into distant places. Food shortages in the first decade of the twenty-first century revealed some of the deep-seated problems of globalization. Financial instability in the credit crunch of 2008 which had severe negative effects from Iceland to Singapore is one rather obvious example of this interconnectivity.

The world-wide shortage of food grains was caused by a complicated set of factors. With rising petroleum prices, the demand for biofuel grew, and with more ethanol coming from corn and other edible food grains, the price of marketed food grains for human consumption sky-rocketed. As China and India became prosperous, the demand for meat and a more sophisticated cuisine grew, putting further strain on food prices. While the rich ate more meat and drove ethanol-powered cars, the poor starved and walked for miles in search of food and water. The international political and economic arrangements of inequality between nations sustain the conditions for global hunger.

Yet the crisis of subsistence is often exacerbated by the local or national political economy. The case of Burma illustrates the problem only too well. In the wake of devastations left by Cyclone Nargis, the military rulers in Burma, rather than mounting all-out relief operations, carried out a national referendum with the aim of legitimizing the constitution sponsored by the military regime in May 2008. The Burmese military regime did not want the presence of foreign aid workers except to give a token amount of foreign aid which went to the supporters of the regime. While Rangoon was cleaned up relatively quickly for both strategic and cosmetic reasons, the hinterland, which was by definition out of sight, languished. It was reported that in the middle of these devastations and acute shortages of food, Burma was exporting rice to Malaysia and Singapore (*International Herald Tribune*, 11 May 2008). The military regime in Burma had usurped political power by denying the results of a democratic process that elected Aung San Suu Kyi to office in 1990. The resulting political crisis in Burma has not only resulted in a stagnant economy, but Burma is also perceived as a pariah state by the international community and a large number of Burmese have crossed into neighbouring Thailand as refugees and migrants, creating a humanitarian crisis there.

Some disasters are routine, structural and anticipated; others are unanticipated; and some are a mixture of these characteristics. For example, natural calamities occur at frequent intervals and have become almost routine annual features in certain countries, yet one cannot predict exactly when they will occur. The USA is regularly visited by tornadoes and flash floods. Yet even with advanced science and technology, it is not possible fully to anticipate the consequence of such disasters. In March 2008, a sudden flash flood in the Midwestern states of the USA killed 18 people and washed away properties worth millions of dollars. Hurricane Katrina in 2005 affected Louisiana and three other southern states, causing hardship and social dislocation of such magnitude that we cannot escape the conclusion that we are all vulnerable. It is the common denominator of the human condition, no matter where human beings live. Cyclone Sidr lashed Bangladesh in November 2007, washing away tens of thousands of human lives, livestock and houses, ruined agricultural land and pushed people into starvation. In 2007 tidal waves resulted in 138,000 fatalities. Fortunately, massive international assistance helped to mitigate the full horror of this crisis. An earlier cyclone-driven tidal wave in November 1970 had an even higher death toll – estimated between 200,000 and half a million – but did not receive the same level of attention from the Pakistani government of the day, triggering resentment and fomenting a nationalist movement in Bangladesh. These national leaders used the lack of response as an instance of the neglect of the geographically isolated eastern part of the country (now Bangladesh) by the military rulers of Pakistan.

HURRICANE KATRINA - A CASE STUDY

It is valuable to examine the disaster of Hurricane Katrina and its consequences in the states of Mississippi, Alabama and Louisiana, especially in New Orleans, and compare this American disaster with that of the Asian tsunami. The comparison, as far as the death toll is concerned, may be preposterous – the Asian tsunami killed about 300,000 human beings, whereas the death toll from Katrina may be less than a thousand, despite initial estimates on the higher side. The Asian tsunami was worse in terms of the loss of human lives, but Hurricane Katrina was costlier in financial terms. This comparison reveals an intriguing aspect of globalization. The US government in both events responded first in a sluggish manner and then – after much media criticism in the New Orleans case – with a huge outpouring of generosity. In a speech delivered from flood-soaked New Orleans on 15 September 2005, President George Bush committed $60 billion in recovery and rehabilitation, promising to rebuild the city to an even higher standard than before disaster struck. In that speech he admitted not only the failures of the federal government but also the social and historical causes that exacerbated the suffering of the victims, a disproportionate number of whom were African Americans. "As we clear away the debris of a hurricane, let us also clear away the legacy of inequality", he declared (*International Herald Tribune*, 16 September 2005).

Apart from the failures of the government, the suddenness of the disaster and magnitude of the losses produced comparisons of a cosmological nature. Reuters reported that "Some evacuees see a religious message in Katrina":

"Natural disaster is caused by the sin in the world," according to Major John Jones, area commander for the Salvation Army ... "The acts of God are what happen afterwards ... all the good that happens."

"God made all this happen for a reason. This city has been going to hell in a handbasket spiritually," Tim Washington, 42, said at New Orleans' Superdome on Saturday as he waited to be evacuated.

"If we can spend billions of dollars chasing after (Osama) bin Laden, can't we get guns and drugs off the street?" he asked. Washington said he stole a boat last Monday and he and a friend, using wooden fence posts as oars, delivered about 200 people to the shelter. "The sheriff's department stood across the street and did nothing," he added.

(Tanner, 2005)

Soon after the Asian tsunami had lashed the coasts of Ache, Indonesia, southern Thailand and parts of India and Sri Lanka, the disaster evoked similar connections between sin and God's wrath. In the Asian case, of course, the discussion was much more pronounced and broadened to include some Gulf nations as well. Following the tsunami, some Muslim commentators in Saudi Arabia and elsewhere suggested that the disaster was a response to wanton behaviour. On an Islamist website, one commentator wrote: "Asia's earthquake, which hit the beaches of prostitution, tourism, immorality and nudity, is a sign that God is warning mankind from persisting in injustice and immorality before he destroys the ground beneath them" (reported in the Lahore *Daily Times*, 6 January 2005).

As regards Hurricane Katrina, apart from right-wing Islamist websites, no one took such alleged connections seriously. But the similarity between the cases of the New Orleans tragedy caused by Hurricane Katrina and the Asian tsunami of 26 December 2004 does not end there.

In both instances the disasters were man-made, but the events – tsunami and hurricane – that caused them were hazards of nature. However, even this "natural hazard" may have been in part brought about by global warming and other human interventions.

The two disasters also reveal certain processes of globalization at work. Disasters often bring to the surface deeper aspects of society that otherwise remain hidden under normal circumstances. As one newspaper put it: "The violence of the storm and his faltering response to it have left to Bush the task not just of physically rebuilding a swath of the United States, but also of addressing issues like poverty and racial inequality that were exposed in such raw form by the storm" (*International Herald Tribune*, 18 September 2005).

Looting, rape and the breakdown of law and order reflected a social collapse in New Orleans that remained hidden from the public view. The real crisis in New Orleans was a social collapse that was manifested in the weakness of governance. New Orleans, despite its reputation as the jazz capital of the world and a tourism hub, was a city in which 27.4 per cent of the people were living below the poverty line, of whom over two-thirds were African Americans (DeParle, 2005). According to an NBC news program, most of the poor did not have insurance. Some 134,000 people could not leave, because they could not afford transportation (Faw, 2005). According to the *New York Times*, 35 per cent of the black households did not have access to a car, compared with just 15 per cent of whites (DeParle, 2005). The ills of New Orleans were a microcosm of the wider social problems of the USA, a nation adrift. The hurricane was merely a fuse for a time bomb created by years of neglect by the Republican agenda of "freedom" of hand-gun ownership, compounded by the neo-liberal strategies of privatization and deregulation of services, resulting in a further erosion of social services. The fact that the sale of guns rose following the hurricane reflects some of the deeper problems of the USA. Former President Clinton said in an ABC interview: "You can't have an emergency plan that works if it only affects middle-class people" (*International Herald Tribune*, 19 September 2005). Clinton pointed out that the tax cuts for the rich and the welfare cuts for the poor in the preceding decade made poorer the poor people who did not have the means to evacuate to safety.

Yet the link between poverty and social collapse may not be automatic. The case of impoverished Bangladesh is illustrative. Bangladesh is no stranger to floods and assorted calamities, yet in 1988 when a massive flood engulfed the elite part of the capital city Dhaka there was an unprecedented response. The government woke up to the realities of flood management that would protect the capital city, whereas the coastal regions of Bangladesh experience flood almost on an annual basis with little consequence and alarm on the part of the government (Khondker, 1992). The aftermath of floods in Bangladesh often produces a high degree of fellow-feeling – an aspect of social capital that otherwise remains hidden in everyday life. Civil society organizations spring to action spontaneously, cross-cutting socio-economic classes. Only on rare occasions do the authorities have to worry about social collapse. A number of commentators in the Bangladeshi press talked about how the lessons of Bangladesh could be used in handling flood-disasters in the USA.

The Asian tsunami of 2004 also revealed a number of interesting social, cultural and political processes. Both Indonesia and Thailand were recently restored democracies that had to encounter this challenge. In Sri Lanka, as in Indonesia, the disaster hit regions that were experiencing civil unrest emanating from years of separatist movements. One of the positive outcomes in Ahce, which was the hardest-hit disaster area, was the arrival of a peaceful settlement in August 2005.

One of the most disturbing allegations is that criminal gangs are befriending children orphaned by the tsunami, and selling them to sex traffickers. The Indonesian government has banned children under the age of 16 from being transferred from the devastated province of Aceh amid fears that trafficking syndicates were moving into the area. The UN children's agency, UNICEF, said it had received several reports of criminals offering kidnapped children from Aceh for sale or adoption: "A spokesman for Unicef in Indonesia, John Budd, said there had been one confirmed case of a child being smuggled from the devastated Indonesian province of Aceh to the nearby city of Medan for trafficking purposes" (McGeown, 2005).

A women's group in Sri Lanka, the Women and Media Collective, reported "incidents of rape, gang rape, molestation and physical abuse of women and girls in the course of unsupervised rescue operations and while resident in temporary shelters". The rapists preyed on homeless survivors. Save the Children warned that youngsters orphaned by the tsunami were vulnerable to sexual exploitation. "The experience of earlier catastrophes is that children are especially exposed," said its Swedish chief, Charlotte Petri Gornitzka. In Thailand thieves disguised as police and rescue workers looted luggage and hotel safes around Khao Lak beach, where the tsunami killed up to 3,000 people. Sweden sent seven police officers there to investigate the reported kidnapping of a Swedish boy of age 12 years whose parents were carried off by the wave, http://uk. news.yahoo.com/050103/325/f9k58.html (Accessed on September, 15 2005)

Incidents of crime and preying on victims are no longer limited to Asian disasters. These crimes reflect social blight and failures of governance which have taken on global proportions. Apart from the failures of everyday

governance, it also touches on the issues of the relationship between state
and its citizens. Jesse Jackson, amongst others, was peeved by reference to
the evacuees in the media as "refugees". He reminded the press that they are
citizens of the United States and not refugees:

> "It is racist to call American citizens refugees," the Rev. Jesse Jackson
> said, visiting the Houston Astrodome on Monday. Members of the
> Congressional Black Caucus have expressed similar sentiments.
>
> Others have countered that the terms "evacuees" or even "displaced"
> are too clinical and not sufficiently dramatic to convey the dire situa-
> tion that confronts many of Katrina's survivors.
>
> President Bush, who spent many days trying to deflect criticism that
> he responded sluggishly to the disaster, came to address the problem.
> "The people we're talking about are not refugees," he said. "They are
> Americans, and they need the help and love and compassion of our
> fellow citizens."
>
> (MSNBC, 2005)

In the aftermath of the Turkish earthquake of 17 August 1999, known as
the Izmit earthquake, it was discovered that the citizens received assistance
only after a prolonged period of negotiations with the authority. Citizenship
is more than a juridical matter; it also entails traditional rights. In many situations, the entitlements of disaster victims cannot be taken for granted. In
the American case, Katrina also exposed the issue of the rights of citizenship and the links between class and citizenship. The poor in New Orleans
were citizens without access to their full citizenship rights, which were
undercut by economic deprivations.

The slowness of the response from the federal government and finger-
pointing by politicians, with the Mayor of New Orleans blaming the State
Governor and both accusing Washington of negligence and mismanagement, created a political crisis in the middle of a humanitarian calamity.
The fact that President Bush was on vacation did not help either.
However, once the barrage of media criticism, international attention and
public outrage pushed the US government into action, it acted decisively.

GLOBALIZATION OF DISASTER RESPONSE

The international response was both generous and widespread, reflecting another aspect of globalization. With the usual Asian alacrity,
Singapore committed its military helicopters, which were usually based

in the USA for training purposes, to disaster relief. Air Canada mounted a massive help line. India, Cuba, Venezuela, Kuwait, Bangladesh and even Afghanistan came up with financial assistance, not so much to provide material aid but to express solidarity with the suffering people in the most powerful nation of the world. Symbolic though it might have been, it was unprecedented.

Such disasters remind us that vulnerability is the basis of common humanity. The collective, global response to such crises also points to the emergence of an incipient global moral system. The disasters befalling New Orleans and coastal regions of Bangladesh are by no means local disasters. Scientists have argued that global warming has contributed to the frequency of tornadoes and cyclones in recent years.

In the USA, Hurricane Katrina also drew attention to the importance of disasters caused by nature but complicated by society. The Asian tsunami affected not only several Asian countries but also hordes of European tourists who were on vacation in Thailand, Sri Lanka and Bali. Western tourists who are not usually familiar with natural disasters such as the surge of the ocean had first-hand experience of a natural calamity. The response to the disaster was global, as the tragedy itself was global, affecting a large number of countries and affecting individuals of diverse nationalities.

The globalization of disaster response has been linked in part to the role of the media in bringing the news of disaster to the living rooms of those lucky to avoid the disaster spots. In the 1980s, when Ethiopia and several other African countries were in the throes of famine, a massive humanitarian appeal was made by Bob Geldof, Midge Ure, Harvey Goldsmith, the Band Aid Trust, a number of musicians, and aid-workers who organized "Live Aid". This was a milestone event, linking people in the affluent West who were ready to help with the plight of the victims of famine.

At one level, it is ironic that people starve in times of global affluence. Yet the response was a sure sign of the recognition of a common exposure to risk and a vindication of what we will call a global morality. The world is not completely devoid of generosity. The idea of a global moral economy (Khondker, 1985) was an elaboration of the ideas of E.P. Thompson and James Scott who found norms of reciprocity in early England and in Southeast Asia, respectively. The norms of reciprocity and its discovery by historians and anthropologists questioned the assumptions of economic rationality and the transactional or exchange model of society. One of the important lessons of globalization is that economies are embedded in societies. At the heart of social organization there lies a moral nexus. However, with modernization and growing individualization, the moral system is transformed, in terms of Émile Durkheim's sociology, from mechanical to organic solidarity. Society is hardly able to survive without a moral framework, and we can assume that a global moral economy will be a viable response to the problems besetting the world.

While it is well known that reckless economic development in China has put China's ecosystem at risk, it is not well known that China is also taking important steps towards containing such ecological damage. In other societies, such counter-measures are often the result of democratic mobilization and the action of civil societies. In this respect, democracies have a natural advantage. The successful resistance of Indian non-governmental organizations to the Narmada project, which threatened the ecosystem as well as the economic livelihood of many local people, illustrates this difference between democratic and authoritarian polities. In China, the resistance against the Three Gorges Dam project was feeble at best and the government was able to go ahead with the project as scheduled. Over the years, an increasing number of musicians and popular figures have joined in the fight against hunger and related disasters. Bob Geldof in the UK launched a crusade against hunger in Africa and his efforts have resulted not only in his personal achievement of an honorary knighthood but also in an enhanced global awareness of poverty and famine in Africa. Globalized mass media and popular culture joined hands in aiding disaster management and raising global awareness of the problems of development in the poorer regions of the world. The rise of world-wide disasters coincided with a global response, indicating the possibility of the emergence of a global moral consciousness.

11 GLOBALIZATION, CITIZENSHIP AND HUMAN RIGHTS

INTRODUCTION: THE EAST–WEST ILLUSION

"The expansion of the right of the individual to behave or misbehave as he pleases has come at the expense of orderly society. In the East the main objective is to have a well-ordered society so that everybody can have maximum enjoyment of his freedoms" (Zakaria, 1994: 111). These words of Singapore's pre-eminent leader, Lee Kuan Yew, allude to a caricature of the East–West divide, whereby issues such as human rights, democracy and individual freedom are characteristics of the so-called West, and social order is the primary concern of the so-called East. Such a view, which Lee thinks can be called the East Asian position on rights has been disputed by the Korean leader, Kim Dae Jung, who argues that "Asia has a rich heritage of democracy-oriented philosophies and traditions." According to Kim, "The ancient Chinese philosophy of *Minben Zhengchi*, or 'people-based politics,' teaches that 'the will of the people is the will of heaven' and that one should 'respect the people as heaven itself'" (Kim, 1994: 191). The Pew global survey amply demonstrates that a large majority of people in countries as disparate as Bangladesh and Egypt have favourable attitudes towards democracy and individual freedom. Such refrains that "human rights is part of an American imperialist agenda to control the rest of the world" or "democracy is a Western value unsuited for the developing world" are without any empirical basis. Yet such views are often heard from authoritarian political leaders. The weakest endorsement of democracy comes from the Russian Republic, where an overwhelming majority prefer a strong leader than democracy to solve their problems (Pew Global Attitudes Project, 2007). Historical research has shown that several innovations in democracy took place not in the heartland of Europe but at the peripheries (Markoff, 1999).

Globalization has expanded the idea of citizenship beyond the historical context that gave rise to its modern form based on entitlements. Modern citizenship is fundamentally a Western political and legal concept; it is also a concept relevant specifically to a democratic polity. The global expansion of the idea of citizenship coincides with the history of the spread of the nation-state as the universal mode of political organization.

The fact that violations of human rights arouse such global protests, whether those violations take place in a Saudi Arabian court or at Guantánamo Bay prison, illustrates the widespread acceptance of human dignity and a minimalist view of human rights. When a 19-year-old woman in Saudi Arabia's provincial town of Qatif was punished along with her rapists in accordance with the strict Wahhabist version of Islamic law, a world-wide protest led to her eventual freedom. In the original sentence she was given 90 lashes, which upon appeal was more than doubled to 200 lashes (*The Economist*, 24 November 2007, p. 52). She was reprieved from the lashing by King Abdullah, but the laws were not reformed. The arguments based on cultural relativism that each state is entitled to its own laws grounded in its own traditions did not hold in the face of global public opinion. The London-based human rights organization, Amnesty International, is as critical of the United States for the torture of the terrorist suspects at Guantánamo Bay as it is of China and Saudi Arabia for their large number of annual executions.

Although the ideas of democracy, accountability and rights have spread globally to become the discourse of modern politics, it is the case that citizenship as we know it had its origins in medieval city-states and then spread from the West with the growth of nation-states and nationalism. The ideas about citizenship and rights were then embraced by intellectual groups in Japan and China in the nineteenth century. To understand modern citizenship, we need to examine briefly its rise in the West.

THE ORIGINS OF CITIZENSHIP

Historically, the citizen was closely connected with the rise of the European city, civility and civilization. The word itself is derived from the Old French and German *citeseyn*, *citezein* or *sithezein*. A citizen was originally a member of a city and, while enjoying certain privileges, was equally burdened with obligations. Service in the city militia and taxation were typical duties of the citizen. A citizen was primarily a denizen of a city as a legal entity. Because the countryside was pagan and uncivilized, pagans were lacking in urbanity. Citizens were part of the *civitas* – the urban culture of the city and church. While we can trace these components of citizenship from the Greek *polis* and the early church, citizenship is most appropriately regarded as a modern concept that first emerged with the creation of autonomous cities in medieval Europe, but came to maturity with modern revolutions.

It is important sociologically to treat citizenship as a product of three political revolutions – the English Civil War, the American War of Independence and the French Revolution. These revolutions are the cradle of modern nationalism, and citizenship came to involve the rights and duties of a person who is a member of a national community. The creation of European nation-states from the seventeenth century necessarily involved the construction of communities which assumed the existence of, and which went a long way to create, homogeneous populations. These national communities were held together, against the divisions of class, culture and ethnicity, by nationalistic ideologies. The Treaty of Westphalia in 1648 was the origin of the modern world system of nation-states, and state formation involved the creation of nationalist identities. This process was the cultural basis for the creation of national forms of citizenship.

The notion of citizenship spread from Europe to Japan and then on to China. Intellectuals in both countries were influenced by a range of political ideas from Europe in the late nineteenth century about civil society and citizenship. Especially in China, citizenship was slow to develop and remained connected to the idea of patrimony, benevolence and kinship. It is a citizenship of blood, or what we might call a "citizenship of kinsmen". Like many other empires, China did not give rise to a notion of citizenship based on a market place of strangers, but there was a distinctive development of ideas about citizenship in the period 1890–1920 in which Chinese intellectuals struggled to find a language appropriate to the public domain that could express the first stirrings of modernization. In Japan, citizenship developed with modernization, but remained tied to the idea of the loyal subject of the emperor. In Meiji Japan, the sociology of Herbert Spencer had become known among both senior government officials and intellectuals associated with the movement of the liberal democratic Right. Spencer was therefore the first sociologist whose works came to be translated into Japanese in Meiji and Taisho Japan from 1877 to the early twentieth century. Japanese academics and civil servants were especially interested in his combination of evolutionary theory, utilitarian individualism and laissez-faire economics. From Spencer, they developed the idea of individual rights within the liberal state. With American occupation, the new Japanese political institutions included aspects of Western citizenship, but this was essentially a top-down or passive citizenship.

In other Asian societies, the growth of citizenship has been associated with post-colonial struggles. For example, Indonesia – as a consequence of the national struggle against the Japanese and Dutch in the period 1944–6 – has developed a notion of national citizenship in the context of an emerging nationalism. Whereas Chinese and Japanese citizenship has often been authoritarian and dominated by the state, Indonesia has evolved with a clear notion of citizenship and a viable civil society. In conclusion, while citizenship emerged in the West, it has been appropriated by Asian political culture.

THE ORIGINS OF HUMAN RIGHTS

The great expansion of human rights legislation and culture over the last century has been a consequence of the mechanization of warfare, the growing number of civilian casualties in both civil and international wars, and the horrors of biological and chemical warfare. In his *Crimes against Humanity*, Geoffrey Robertson (2002) traces the historical origins of human rights back to a decision of the Second Lateran Council in 1139 to prohibit the use of the crossbow in wars between Christians. This historical interpretation is interesting in drawing attention to mechanical instruments of warfare (the crossbow) and its use within a community (of Christians). Failed attempts to ratify a global ban on landmines in the twentieth century can be seen as a modern illustration of the same process.

The encounter between colonial settlement and aboriginal people has been another important setting for the emergence of rights in modern history. These colonial conflicts were features of the great land rush that formed the modern world between 1650 and 1900. One illustration was the Wounded Knee massacre of 1890, described in Chapter 9.

The "juridical revolution" of the twentieth century, involving the international recognition of human rights as formulated in the United Nations Declaration, is a major illustration of the general process of globalization. Human rights may be defined as the entitlements of individuals qua human beings to life, security and well-being. They are said to be universal, incontrovertible and subjective, that is, individuals possess them because of their capacity for rationality, agency and autonomy. Human rights legislation assumes that individuals have certain fundamental powers ("inalienable rights") that no political order can expunge. They are legal instruments by which governments (or more frequently their despotic leaders) can be held criminally responsible in international law and prosecuted in the courts for the ways in which they mistreat their own citizens. Human rights were essentially a twentieth-century legal response to atrocities committed against civilian populations and, as a result, where such atrocities have been witnessed by a world audience with the spread of global communication systems, people began to think and act as global citizens.

CITIZENSHIP VERSUS HUMAN RIGHTS

Political statements about human rights and citizenship, state sovereignty and rights are often contradictory. For example, the National Assembly of France declared in 1789 that "the natural and imprescriptible rights of man" were "liberty, property, security and resistance of oppression", but it went on to assert that "the nation is essentially the source of all sovereignty" and that no "individual or body of men" could be entitled to "any authority which is not expressly derived from it". While human rights are said to be innate and inalienable, social rights are created by states. These two contrasting ideas – the imprescriptible rights of human beings and the exclusive rights of citizens of sovereign nation-states – have remained an important dilemma in any justification of rights. The protection offered by nation-states and national citizenship is declining, and yet the state and citizenship remain important for the enforcement of both social and human rights.

It may be useful to underscore the differences between the social rights of citizens and individual human rights. Social rights are entitlements enjoyed by citizens and are enforced by courts within the national frame-work of a sovereign state. These social rights, which are typically related to corresponding duties, are "contributory rights", because effective claims are associated with contributions that citizens have made to society through work, war (or a similar public duty) or parenting (Turner, 2001). A sys-tem of universal taxation and contributions to social services through income tax are obvious indications of social citizenship. By contrast, human rights are rights enjoyed by individuals by virtue of being human, and as a consequence of their shared vulnerability. Human rights are not necessarily connected to duties and they are not contributory. There is, for example, no corresponding system of taxation relating to the possession of human rights. There is as yet no formal declaration of human duties – although there has been much discussion of such obligations. UNESCO encouraged an initiative for a charter of the duties and responsibilities of states, but these initiatives have yet to have much practical consequence.

The United Nations Declaration implies obligations, but they are not clearly or forcefully specified. While states enforce social rights, there is no sovereign power uniformly to enforce human rights at a global level.

Hannah Arendt presented a devastating criticism of "the rights of Man" in *The Origins of Totalitarianism* (1951) when she observed that these inalienable rights were supposed to exist independently of any government, but once the rights of citizenship with the support of a government had been removed, there was no authority left to protect people as human beings. Human rights without the support of a sovereign state, she argued, are merely abstract claims that cannot be enforced. It is almost impossible to define what they are or to show how they add much to the specific rights of citizens of nation-states. The right to rights only makes sense for people who are already members of a political community. Finally, she concluded bitterly and ironically that these arguments were compatible with conservatives like Edmund Burke who had argued that the rights of an Englishman were more secure and definite than the abstract rights of man.

The abuse of human rights is characteristically a product of state tyranny, dictatorship and state failure, as illustrated by civil war and anarchy; a viable state is important as a guarantee of rights. There is a valid argument, therefore, that the liberties of citizens and their social rights are better protected by their own national institutions than by external legal or political intervention. The often chaotic outcome of human rights interventions in East Timor and Kosovo might force us to the conclusion that any government that can provide its citizens with security, but with weak democracy, is to be preferred over anarchy. The ongoing internal security crises in Central Asia, Afghanistan and Iraq might also be added to the list of failed, or at least problematic, interventions. From a Hobbesian perspective, a strong state is required to enforce agreements between conflicting social groups. Another way of expressing this idea is to argue that we need to maintain a distinction between the social rights of citizens that are enforced by states, and the human rights of persons that are protected, but frequently and inadequately enforced, by both nation-states and international institutions.

CITIZENSHIP: THE LIMITS OF THE GLOBAL

There has been much discussion recently of the possibility of global citizenship and global governance. With the growth of the European Union, sociologists have considered the possibility of transnational citizenship.

Anthropologists have also explored the problem of identity in modern societies with the growth of transnational communities and diasporic cultures. Aihwa Ong has described "flexible citizenship" (1999) as "a strategy that combines the security of citizenship in a new country with business opportunities in the homeland". Consequently, existing paradigms of (national) citizenship have been criticized precisely because they cannot encompass these changes that result from globalization. While the sociological analysis of transnational identities is an important and interesting field of research, we argue that it is ultimately obfuscating rather than illuminating to use the concept of citizenship to describe these developments.

In fact citizenship can only function within the nation-state, because it is based on contributions and a reciprocal relationship between duty and rights, unlike human rights for which there are as yet no explicit duties. To employ the notion of citizenship outside the confines of the nation-state is to distort its meaning, indeed to render it meaningless. The idea of flexible citizenship is simply a political fiction. This criticism is not just a linguistic quibble. It implies that some terms are properly national and must remain so. There are limits to the idea of "sociology beyond societies" because some concepts are inherently not mobile, but necessarily fixed and specific. It does not follow that they are useless; it merely signifies that some institutions cannot become global. We should try to make "human rights" more serviceable for international research rather than transform the specific meaning of "citizenship".

Citizenship, the rights and duties of members of a nation-state, is a juridical status that confers a socio-political identity on persons, and determines how economic and other resources are redistributed within society. Its existence is confirmed by the provision of a passport. There are, broadly speaking, two dimensions of the social rights that constitute citizenship. In the strong version, citizenship is an important component of distributive justice, because it involves a contributory principle in which there must be some balance between an individual's contributions to society, typically through work, military service and parenting, and rewards such as welfare, education and subsidies, which such an individual might expect.

GLOBAL CITIZENSHIP

What solutions might be possible to this tension between the social rights of citizens and the human rights of people as such? We can simply accept the contradiction, and merely live with the fact that citizenship provides rights within territorially delimited political spaces and that human rights offer protection and security outside these limits, especially where states have failed to protect their own citizens. Whether these two sets of rights are in a condition of antagonism or mutual support becomes a largely empirical question. However, this modest answer is unlikely to be satisfactory. The real solution is to develop human rights in terms of human duties, and then to give these institutions significant political authority.

The key characteristic of the existence of citizenship in nation-states is the development of universal taxation and military subscription. A public political space can be said to exist once citizens contribute taxes to common purposes such as defence, education, road building and the maintenance of drains. When men are called upon to defend these utilities through military service, a state obviously exists in Max Weber's terms. Human rights are criticized by lawyers because they do not have these characteristics. Rights claims appear to have no corresponding set of duties, and hence they are often said to lack correlativity, and they are ultimately not justiciable.

In the United States, human rights are, in the popular imagination, seen to be the rights of foreigners who suffer from catastrophes of various sorts – droughts, famines and civil war. Americans by contrast have civil liberties and civil rights that are guaranteed by the Constitution. This view replicates the Burkean position that the rights of citizens – in his case Englishmen – are more real than the abstract rights of universal declarations. Human rights for many Western citizens do not impinge on their everyday world and are quite unlike the rights they enjoy as citizens. How do we make human rights more concrete and effective?

Human rights' enforceability can be strengthened through the United Nations, but it will realistically require greater economic commitment from the United States and other powerful nations. We also know that the exponential growth of non-governmental organizations in recent decades has also created a global civil society that impinges on people's local social reality. But the real necessity is to give ordinary people a sense of ownership over human rights and a clear understanding of how such global arrangements can contribute to social reform. In our view, until people start to contribute taxes to support human rights activities, human rights culture and institutions will continue to be remote. One model might be the Tobin tax as a basis for creating global responsibilities.

The underlying right of a global world is what may be called a "right of mobility". Many modern rights claims are implicitly or explicitly about crossing borders or creating new settlements – rights of migrant labour, rights to hold a passport, rights to enter a country, rights of asylum, rights of refugees and other rights of residence, rights to marry outside one's group, or the right to buy property in other societies. However, these rights to mobility do not appear to relate to any duties of mobility. A Tobin-type tax related to various forms of mobility may be proposed. The aim of the original taxation scheme proposed by the American economist, James Tobin (1978), was to stabilize national governments by getting greater control over international financial transactions. The original proposal was a stamp duty on foreign exchange trading. This basic idea was expanded to include other possibilities such as a global lottery. Tobin's original proposal was simple but radical, and it has the overwhelming merit of being global, but it does not reach far enough down into national populations. It is to some extent a tax on the rich and it does not therefore have sufficient breadth. We should look towards more general and widespread taxes on the movements of people – a tourist tax on petrol consumption or on air fuel, a mobility tax on people entering other countries by means of a passport, or a sports tax for people travelling overseas to watch sporting events, or even internal taxes on crossing state boundaries. These taxes would be small from the point of view of the individual but they could produce a substantial resource for UN agencies in the battle on poverty, illiteracy, poor health, pollution or civil unrest. However, the principle is that privileged people who benefit from globalization, such as tourists, should contribute to the global good.

There are obvious problems with such a global tax on human mobility. There would be considerable consumer resistance, because there would be arguments about getting some balance between contributions and receipts. Americans may feel that this is yet another tax on the rich to support countries that have failed economically or have authoritarian governments. However, a UN global tax would also make resources available to the residents of St Louis as relief from losses resulting from flooding and the incompetence of their own government. American citizens of Pakistani descent might approve of UN relief going to their relatives in northwestern Pakistan after the recent earthquake. In global terms, it would be more difficult to argue that human rights are only important when they provide a justification for US intervention in Iraq or Afghanistan. The argument would be that the mobility tax is a duty that applies in principle to everybody and that the resources create funding to meet the needs of rights claimers everywhere. This proposal involves a radical overhaul of the Tobin argument by creating a flat tax on global cosmopolitanism, thereby involving large numbers of people in global civil society.

Citizenship works partly because when people put investments into their societies (through work, military service or parenting) they can assume that they have a legitimate claim on that society when they fall ill, become unemployed or grow too old to support themselves. Their past investments in the community can now be used to make legitimate claims on the "commonwealth". They can see a connection between effort, reward and virtue. Citizenship in this way involves covertly an education in civic culture in which, because one is patriotically proud of the society to which one belongs, one is committed to defending its democratic culture. These relationships between individual, ethics and politics do not exist with respect to human rights. They do not contribute necessarily to civic education or indeed to ethics. If people started, albeit in a modest way, to pay for their rights and to contribute through taxation to the common good, human rights would become a more tangible part of everyday life, people would feel involved in global projects to prevent famine and drought, and they would start, however modestly, to see themselves as global citizens. Without a global taxation system, the UN will continue to be largely dependent on US funding and generosity. Without these changes, human rights will be subject to the criticism that they are fake rights because they do not correspond to duties. More importantly, the prospect of global governance and global citizenship without the development of a common set of institutions and values such as the redistribution of wealth through the Tobin tax will remain merely a political fantasy.

In this discussion on the development of a rights culture, the concepts of human vulnerability and institutional precariousness are employed both to understand the importance of human rights and to defend their universalism. Vulnerability defines our humanity and is presented here as the common basis of human rights. The idea of our vulnerable human nature is closely associated with certain fundamental rights, such as the right to life. The enjoyment of the rights that support life, health and reproduction are fundamental to human rights as such. It is, however, difficult to enforce human rights, and hence it is important to examine the complex relationship between the state, the social rights of citizens and the human rights of persons. Social institutions which are necessary for our survival are themselves fragile and precarious. Finally, because vulnerability has a close relationship to notions of suffering, on the one hand, and classical philosophical notions of virtue, on the other, any study of rights needs to examine more broadly their relationship to morality and religion, that is, to the conditions that make human society possible (Van der Ven et al., 2005).

It is important to reiterate the differences between the social rights of citizens and individual human rights. We might more precisely say that the development of national citizenship is definitively marked by the emergence of personal taxation and national armies. We will see in the course of this discussion, that there are many problems with this definition, but it will suffice at this stage as a minimal account.

This contrast between citizenship and human rights is often confused by the fact that in the United States the notion of "civil rights" is used as if they were equivalent to "human rights". For example, Martin Luther King's vision of political freedom and involvement in the civil rights movement, which had a direct impact on President Nkrumah at the time of Ghana's independence in 1957, is often regarded primarily as a human rights struggle rather than a movement for civil liberties. Why treat the struggle for black Americans to enjoy their full rights as citizens of the United States as a struggle for human rights? One implication of this elision is either that the American Constitution is in some sense a global legal framework or that globalization has made the distinction between human and social rights increasingly vague. If the American Constitution is to be regarded as a constitution of the world, then world citizens should have the right to vote in American elections, or alternatively we might want to regard the French Revolution as a global struggle. This notion of the global significance of revolutionary struggles for rights was an aspect of Leon Trotsky's argument that the Russian revolution could never be merely a "revolution in one country".

This tension between citizenship and human rights raises the question of the relationship between the enforcement of rights by nation-states that are sovereign, and by global institutions that have legitimacy by virtue of international agreements and hence are an aspect of global governance. Although many theorists of human rights, who are committed to the potential benefits of globalization, appear to welcome the erosion of national sovereignty, any historical overview of human rights in international and national politics brings us to the conclusion that effective human rights regimes actually require state stability and the institutionalization of national citizenship. Human rights abuse is often a consequence of state failure. There is a further difficulty that while most governments of nation-states typically claim some legitimacy (as a result of electoral success, for example), human rights can be said to have legality rather than legitimacy through the legislative activity of the United Nations. There is an argument, therefore, that the liberties of citizens and their social rights are better protected by their own national institutions than by external legal or political intervention. The often chaotic outcome of human rights interventions might bring us to the conclusion that any government that can provide its citizens with security, but with weak democracy, is to be preferred over bad and ineffective government.

UNIVERSALISM AND RIGHTS

The recent use of human rights conventions as a pretext for international intervention in the affairs of nation-states – Iraq, East Timor and the Balkans – has resurrected in an acute form the traditional debate about relativism and universalism. The legitimate intervention in societies where human rights abuse is endemic presupposes the universalism of human rights provisions. One aspect of contemporary globalization is the critique of the conventional arguments of social anthropology that human rights presuppositions cannot apply universally.

The universalistic perspective is consistent with Jürgen Habermas's defence of Enlightenment modernity (1987). There is of course one major difference: we attempt to establish the idea of a human community based, not on communicative rationality, but on our physical and moral vulnerability. Human beings experience pain and humiliation because they are vulnerable. While humans may not share a common culture, they are bound together by their vulnerability. Human happiness is diverse but misery is common and uniform, because we have a common ontological condition as vulnerable and intelligent beings. This need for ontological security provides a strong moral argument against cultural relativism, and offers an endorsement of rights claims for protection from suffering and indignity. Torture is, in this framework, the fundamental denial of human rights. Ontological insecurity indicates a cluster of salient rights (to reproduce and to family life, to health care and health rights, to a clean environment and protection from pollution, to protection from medical and technological exploitation) that are fundamentally connected with human embodiment. Our common vulnerability is the foundation of human rights.

12 MULTICULTURALISM, SOCIAL DIVERSITY AND GLOBALIZATION

INTRODUCTION: WE ARE ALL MULTICULTURAL NOW

Multiculturalism has been one of the most visible and contentious consequences of globalization. "Multiculturality" promises a progressive future for a society where difference is likely to be a source of social strength and cultural celebration, but it also runs the risk of constituting a source of conflict in society. With growing economic nationalism resulting from the current global economic crisis, peaceful inter-ethnic relationships may become frayed. Either as a result of the mobility of people or by growing political recognition of groups hitherto marginalized, a large number of national societies have become multicultural in both an objective as well as subjective sense. Hardly any society exists today that is not diverse in ethnic and religious terms. Echoing Nathan Glazer (1997), we can agree that "we are all multiculturalists now". Yet multiculturalism as an idea of political cultural accommodation or as a policy option remains embroiled in complex controversies.

Multiculturalism as political ideology bred in the context of democratic pluralism became visible in North America, Australia and Europe in the last quarter of the twentieth century. Much of the modern multicultural debate – mistakenly in our view – comes down to a narrow discussion of the inclusion of Muslim communities into a liberal framework. Today even a cursory survey of Europe and North America will reveal debates over the applicability of Sharia law or Islamic law in Britain as broached by the Archbishop of Canterbury (*The Times*, London, 8 February 2008; *The National*, Abu Dhabi, 24 February 2009), or controversies over the headscarf in France. Other aspects of the multicultural debate revolve around the need to protect the rights of indigenous groups in Canada, New Zealand or Australia or giving equal rights to the

54 or so ethnic groups in China, or the relationships among the ethnic minorities in the USA. In many different contexts, these separate cases reveal important and contentious features of multiculturalism which this chapter seeks to address.

In most global cities there is a Chinatown and a growing presence of Chinese food and culture, and in the USA there is a Chinatown bus service offering economical travel options between cities. In China, with rapid economic growth, there has been an influx of members of other nationalities from Europe to Australia with diverse ethnic and religious backgrounds. Shanghai has been the centre of gravity for a large number of expatriate professionals and business people, but this is by no means a new phenomenon. In the early part of the twentieth century, Shanghai was more cosmopolitan than many European cities. Many European Jews escaped from European cities in a bid to avoid persecution in the early twentieth century and found sanctuary in Shanghai which was a tolerant, cosmopolitan city.

Multiculturalism as a term may be new, but as a social process it has a long history. The historian William McNeil, Jr. tells us that cities in the Middle Ages were home to people from different nationalities and races since medieval cities were the loci of business and trade. Two of the oldest mosques were built in China – one in the port city of Guangzhou in the south and the other in Xian for the benefit of the Arab Muslim traders in the first millennium. The emergence of nationalism which developed in the nineteenth century subdued these pluralistic cityscapes. For example, Dhaka, the capital city of Bangladesh, was home to various nationalities in the eighteenth century. Foreign and Indian merchants, traders and bankers – Europeans, Armenians, Pathans, Turanis, Marwaris, and other up-country Hindus – came to Dhaka to do business. The English, French and Dutch established factories in the city. "Many strange nations resort to this city on account of its vast trade and commerce in great variety of commodities, which are produced in profusion in the rich and fertile lands of this region. These have raised the city to an eminence of wealth which is actually stupefying" (Ahmed, 2003: 15). In the twentieth century, Dhaka became less cosmopolitan. Shanghai as a cosmopolitan city was crushed by Mao's agrarian strategy and by his anti-bourgeois strategy, and it was only after 1978 that Shanghai revived as a global site.

Indian cities have a long history of multiculturalism. For example, when the Portuguese explorers went to India in the fifteenth century, they took some Arabic speakers with them who found Arab traders in Calicut. Columbus too included some Arabic speakers in his entourage, though his interpreters did not have much work on the coast of El Salvador, where he landed in 1493.

In the twentieth and twenty-first centuries, multiculturalism is often equated with the urban experience of European and North American cities and societies. It is not well known that there are four countries (Germany, the Gulf – UAE, Qatar and Kuwait) in the world where migrants form the majority. For example, Germany, which is often viewed as a relatively homogeneous society, is home to about 15 million people with an international background. They constitute about 18 per cent of the population. Germany is home to 3.2 million Muslims, most of whom are of Turkish origin. The growing number of teenagers of foreign origin who swell the population often resort to petty crime and delinquency. When such acts are committed by Germans their ethnicity does not come to the fore and they are viewed as juvenile delinquents, but when the same crimes are committed by Turkish or Greek teenagers the crimes are seen as examples of cultural alienation or even ethnic hatred. In other words, problems of multiculturalism and interethnic relations remain central in many European societies. Following the urban riots of 2006 and 2007 in suburban France, many writers used such phrases as the "Second French Revolution".

The modern state manages the social and political problems that can emerge from increasing religious diversity in societies that have large diasporic communities, a significant number of guest workers and multifaith civil societies, and an imbalance between majority and minorities where these groups have different religious and ethnic compositions. These policies range from a complete separation of state and Church in the liberal model, to states that declare that there is only one national religion, and states that attempt directly to regulate religious groups by only recognizing certain churches and suppressing what they regard as heretical cults or dangerous sects. In a number of Asian countries centuries of inter-ethnic and inter-religious tolerance have given way to tensions and conflicts in recent years. In some contexts, there are religious tensions arising from social diversity. These countries include the Philippines, Thailand, Malaysia, Indonesia, South Korea and Hong Kong (rather than mainland China as a whole), where we will examine the complex relationships between, in particular, Christianity, Buddhism, and Islam, but sects or cults such as Falungong and Aum Shinrikyo provide other examples. One can examine the evangelical activities of such groups as the Latter Day Saints and Pentecostalists. It is also worthwhile to consider the various political and legal arrangements that are created for what we call "the management of religions by the modern state". Most of the societies in Asia are confronted by these issues – the Philippines, with its history of communist and more recently Islamic insurgency, is no exception.

SECULAR CITIZENSHIP

Modern social diversity has in large measure resulted from international migration, and in turn migration has created greater religious
diversity alongside greater cultural complexity. The issues surrounding
religious tolerance have therefore been produced by globalization.
Cultural and religious diversities have become a political issue,
because we do not, in general terms, appear to have robust social policies and institutions to manage the social tensions that flow from cultural complexity, and the conventional liberal solutions, especially the
legacy of the Treaty of Westphalia of 1648 which is the foundation of
modern liberal policies in the West, appear to be in crisis. Here we
address the issues of multiculturalism and religious diversity in relation
to the state and the law, especially in the wake of the so-called war on
terror which followed the terrorist acts of 9/11.

The labour markets of advanced economies depend on high levels of
international migration, because they have ageing populations and
because their own labour force is either insufficiently mobile or reluctant
to take on unskilled or low-paid work. Global labour markets need
migrants, but democratic governments, often responding to electoral
pressures and negative media campaigns, cannot be seen to be overtly
lenient towards unrestrained migration. Since 9/11, there has been an
unfortunate tendency to conflate three categories of mobile persons:
migrants, refugees and asylum seekers. In a number of European countries, conservative or right-wing governments have successfully mobilized
electorates against existing liberal policies towards labour mobility and
porous frontiers, but even the social democratic countries of Scandinavia
and northern Europe have faced acute political difficulties over migration,
as we have seen in Denmark and the Netherlands. While migrants contribute significantly to economic growth, they are often thought to be
parasitic upon the host society. They do not fit easily into a welfare
model of citizenship and contributory rights. These problems are
endemic in a variety of countries ranging from Canada and Britain to
Australia and Indonesia.

The development of modern, secular citizenship is often regarded as
an important step towards reducing the likelihood of civil conflict, especially where generous criteria for naturalization are available to (legal)
migrants. However, governments have often been reluctant to give citizenship status to migrants without stringent criteria of membership, and
naturalization may be a slow and complex process. In the West, the
United States, Britain and the Netherlands have all been discussing the
desirability of increasing the difficulty of tests relating to history, law and

language which migrants would be expected to take as a preparation for citizenship. Furthermore, dual citizenship is often regarded as an anomaly and there is as a result an increasing level of social criticism directed against quasi-citizenship, dual citizenship and flexible arrangements, because these forms of citizenship are thought to undermine the hegemonic model of traditional political membership.

In the Middle East, especially in the Gulf, citizenship laws are rigid yet transparent. Migrants are temporary by law, with their residence visa tied to their work contract. This has created in many Gulf countries an ongoing temporary expatriate population. The citizenship issue is especially complex where the citizens are numerically a clear minority.

What has been the role of religion in this scenario? The globalization of the migrant labour market has been one cause of the globalization of world religions, especially Islam, and the creation of new diasporic religious identities. Religious identities tend to be transnational, and offer alternative matrices of self-definition that are not state-based. There is as a result a tension between the transnational identities of neo-fundamentalist religions (Christian, Muslim, Jewish, but also Hindu and Buddhist) and the state-based identities of national citizenship. In the traditional American pattern of assimilation, Protestant, Catholic and Jew became alternative identities within a common pattern of civil religion. There is little indication as yet that "American Muslim" will be an acceptable cultural identity providing full cultural assimilation. In Europe, there is no tradition of civil religion as such to which Muslim Europeans or Christian Europeans or Hindu Europeans could become attached. The idea of European common citizenship has been, at least for the time being, shattered by the rejection of the Constitution in the referenda in France and the Netherlands, and by the difficulty of enforcing a common economic policy. In many Asian countries, where national identity is often based on ethnic identity, minority groups have often been marginalized by the state or the majority, making the achievement of egalitarian citizenship problematic. This is especially true of Chinese diasporic business elites in the Philippines, Indonesia and Malaysia. We would anticipate that with the economic crisis of 2008–9 the possibility of racial aggression towards minorities will increase, especially if youth unemployment continues to grow in Europe.

The long-term solution to social conflict in culturally diverse societies must be the creation of a common legal and political framework, namely citizenship. Arguments in favour of flexible or global citizenship are problematic, unless they can resolve the relationship between rights and duties, namely the nature of social contributions. While human rights offer some protection to minority groups and to migrant workers through the convention on economic, social and cultural rights and through such institutions as the International Labour Organization, ultimately human rights (including freedom of religious expression) require the backing of states that promote active citizenship. The framework of citizenship is an important mechanism of democratic education and protection of rights. The paradox is that citizenship is in one sense an exclusionary institution, but the erosion of citizenship is also a threat to multiculturalism and cosmopolitanism.

Much of the negative view of cultural dialogue has been shaped by Samuel Huntington's article on "the clash of civilizations", in *Foreign Affairs* (1993). In the wake of 9/11, Huntington's bleak analysis of the development of micro fault-line conflicts and macro core-state conflicts influenced the interventionist assumptions of Western foreign policy in the era of the "war on terror". Huntington, of course, believed that the major division of civilizations was between the Christian West and the Muslim world, but after 9/11 he spoke even more openly about "the age of Muslim wars" and widespread Muslim grievance and hostility towards the United States (Huntington, 2003). Any attempt to engage with Islamic civilization is consequently set within the context of the war for Muslim minds.

Although Huntington's thesis might be seen as an extreme position, what seems to be beyond question is that cultural and religious complexity resulting from both legal and illegal migration creates new challenges for the state in a post-secular environment, because religious complexity creates new burdens on civil and political structures, and is a major test of the robustness of the institutions of social citizenship. Cultural and social diversity, including a trend towards legal pluralism, requires a vigorous defence of the rule of law if societies are to avoid social conflict and ultimately violence. There are many possible strategies for the management of ethnic diversity, but passive tolerance of migrants and arbitrary exclusion of asylum seekers does not constitute an effective political option.

RELIGIOUS DIVERSITY AND ETHNIC DIFFERENCES

Let us consider two controversial propositions. First, societies that are culturally and ethnically diverse are more difficult to govern than societies that are culturally homogeneous. Heterogeneity creates significant political problems that require explicit, decisive and clear solutions. Secondly, globalization, especially the globalization of religion, makes these problems increasingly endemic, global and potentially catastrophic. The growth of fundamentalism and neo-fundamentalism in Islamic, Christian, Jewish and Hindu traditions makes this political problem – how to sustain civil society in a context of religious diversity – increasingly difficult.

If these pessimistic views of globalization are valid, then it is imperative to consider what political and social measures might be explored to understand the conditions under which modern societies might be able to embrace multiculturalism (and with it religious diversity) without running the risk of communal violence, that is, the conditions under which they might be less precarious, and the lives of individuals less vulnerable.

Social and political approaches to cultural complexity cover, historically speaking, a wide spectrum of political strategies. At one extreme, fascism assumed the position that ethnic diversity undermines the quality of a population and the coherence of society, and hence that degenerate and deviant elements must be expelled or exterminated. At the other extreme, one might regard the liberal Westphalian strategy, as developed in recent political philosophy by John Rawls, as a solution that regards cultural differences as simply personal attributes that should not intrude on the public space, believes that the market can act as an arbiter between competing social groups and values, and seeks to create a consensus over liberal values. The liberal option of John Rawls in *The Law of Peoples* explores the problem of securing "an overlapping consensus of comprehensive doctrines". Rawls's argument concerning such a consensus of opinions can only work if the consensus of opinions is underpinned by an overlapping network of social groups (created by intermarriage, social capital, shared institutions and a common exchange of resources and goods). The problem in many modern societies may resemble what the British colonial administrator, J.S. Furnivall, reflecting on Burma in *Colonial Policy and Practice* (1948), called a "plural society", namely a society where people meet in the market place but do not have social connections elsewhere.

Contemporary social and political theory has been divided between a politics of difference that encourages us to recognize and accept cultural hybridity resulting from globalization, and a theory of global governance that attempts to identify new patterns of social solidarity. The emphasis on difference typically celebrates the diversity of cultural identities in a fragmented world by abandoning a strong commitment to principles of equality. Any emphasis on social equality – the basis of the Enlightenment tradition of citizenship – preserves some element of universalism in order to defend an idea of justice, but it has correspondingly great difficulty in formulating a satisfactory view of tolerance of difference. French republicanism was based on a formal principle of common citizenship, but the French tradition has run into difficulties over universalism in its confrontation with the Muslim community over the headscarf. The politics of identity implicitly abandons the emphasis on justice and equality in the republican notion of citizenship, and at the same time the idea of human rights is often perceived as inevitably Western and indifferent to local and specific demands for recognition and respect. Any sociological account of rights, migration and citizenship must grapple with the problem of cultural differences and recognition, on the one hand, and the quest for justice and equality in the conventional discourse of citizenship, on the other.

Because ethnic and religious conflicts in the modern world are exacerbated by globalization, social philosophers have engaged in debates about how tolerance and cosmopolitanism might be promoted. These concerns have spawned a rich ensemble of theories and concepts – cosmopolitan virtue, care, tolerance, and recognition ethics. Although these ideas are useful in the formulation of ethical orientations, they do not easily or immediately lead to empirical research strategies or to clear and effective social policies. However, two authors have been widely debated as offering intellectual solutions that can be translated into practical strategies. They are Will Kymlicka, who has developed a number of approaches to group rights as compatible with liberal constitutions, and Robert Putnam, whose notions of social capital and trust appear particularly relevant.

Putnam (1993) provides four reasons why general reciprocity has beneficial effects in terms of enhancing social cooperation: it increases the costs of defection; it fosters norms of cooperation; it improves communication; and it embodies past successes of collaboration, providing a model for future cooperation. More generally, economists have argued that social capital (or trust) reduces transaction costs. Social capital theories are attractive to sociologists because they show how voluntary associations and local non-government organizations can make a significant contribution to making the social glue that holds societies together. Philanthropy is good not only for recipients but also for society as a whole. One reason for the importance of religion in modern societies is that, in a neo-liberal economic environment where the state no longer supports a comprehensive welfare policy, religious groups and associations have filled the gap. This is particularly true of fundamentalist groups in Islam and Christianity, where they provide a safety-net of welfare services for their members or clients. The same can be said of Buddhist groups which in becoming socially active and in their search for a modern role have established many Buddhist philanthropic associations (for example in Singapore).

Critics of Putnam's social capital theory note that value consensus is not characteristic of modern societies, in which increasing social diversity destroys the cultural homogeneity of traditional societies, and where value diversity erodes social cohesion. It is useful to distinguish between sharing a common set of beliefs that are positively valued, and knowing about the beliefs that provide common expectations. In the cognitive sense of sharing, cooperative and predictable behaviour is guaranteed by the existence of social mechanisms whereby expectations converge towards actions that satisfy the requirements of mutual benefit (Knight, 2001). Cooperation with social norms affects an individual's attitudes towards how other people will cooperate, and in turn these expectations influence assumptions about future behaviour. This argument can be developed to make sense of Putnam's observation that social capital is a resource that increases with use. The growth of generalized trust is a function of everyday compliance with norms. Quite simply, the more individuals cooperate with each other, the more they trust one another. Past experience of reliable cooperative interaction tends to increase our general sense of the trustworthiness of others in the community. Conversely, lack of reciprocity tends to deflate trust. In societies with many transnational communities and many diasporas, if there is little reciprocity between social groups then there will be low trust, and consequently greater scope for misunderstanding, mistrust and conflict. The growth of mistrust in the face of growing competition between secular nationalists and Muslim parties has been characteristic of post-Suharto politics in Indonesia (Hasan, 2008).

From this pessimistic viewpoint, social diversity undermines community, and the erosion of common values and shared sentiments undermines trust (Lukes, 1991). Because ethnic and multicultural diversity is an obvious feature of most advanced societies, trust in such societies is difficult to sustain, because there are important differences of interest, of basic social ends, and of social beliefs and values. In culturally diverse societies, social groups will employ strategies of social closure to secure access to resources against outsiders who are seen to be competitors. Informal social regulation is unlikely to work effectively in social environments where social equality and fairness are manifestly absent. With inequality in resource allocation, there is a propensity for disprivileged groups to disrupt existing social arrangements. With social disadvantages, there is an incentive on the part of disprivileged groups to distance themselves from dominant groups. With relative deprivation, there is a probability that marginalized groups will respond positively to normative motivation to comply with existing social norms. Religiously diverse societies will become conflict-ridden, even with adequate legal safeguards, if material wealth is not only unequally distributed but also perceived to be unjustly allocated. Corruption in public life is thus a major factor in social unrest. The history of South African apartheid would be an extreme instance of injustice and relative deprivation, where the legitimacy of the system was constantly questioned, but social conflict between groups on the basis of ethnic classification and associated material inequalities remains an all too common aspect of political violence in contemporary societies. In recent history examples of ethnic conflict and ethnic cleansing are unfortunately both numerous and spectacular: Rwanda, Kashmir, Chechnya, Tajikistan, Sudan, Burma, and so forth. The post-Sukarno situation in Indonesia, which has been studied by Noorhaidi Hassan (2008), is perhaps more typical at least of religious conflict in modern Asia than more extreme examples from Darfur and Somalia. The crisis in the southern states of Thailand between Buddhists and Muslims may evolve into a more violent form of civil conflict (McCargo, 2007).

Liberal jurisprudence typically argues that without the rule of law there is little hope of sustaining social order and hence the task is to create a conception of the rule of law in socially diverse societies that satisfies the requirements of social order and cooperation and, as a by-product, creates the conditions for the emergence and maintenance of informal mechanisms, including trust. Achieving this desirable outcome is not easy. A pragmatic perspective treats the rule of law as a mechanism for satisfying the interests of different social groups in a differentiated social order. In order to accommodate the different interests of culturally distinct social groups, the law must develop a range of mechanisms that are not unduly conflictual and divisive. Legal proceduralism as a juridical principle underlines the importance of overt and predictable legal processes in the resolution of conflict. These legal procedures include adjudication, mediation, managerial discretion, contract and legislation, all of which can contribute to social cooperation. Pragmatism suggests that legal decisions have to satisfy a condition of equal respect and treatment for members of different social groups.

We should attempt to see the rule of law within a broader social and political framework, namely within the framework of social citizenship. The institutions of citizenship have been the principal mechanisms of social inclusion in contemporary society, and citizenship has played a major role in mitigating the negative consequences of income inequality and economic disadvantage in societies where markets are unregulated. In particular, social citizenship is important in containing and reducing the negative consequences of social class differences in capitalism. In European societies, citizenship evolved through the nineteenth and twentieth centuries as an amelioration of the negative effects of social class and the capitalist market. Citizenship provided individuals and their families with social security. One tension in British citizenship is that it assumed significant state intervention in the regulation of the market, but also emphasized individualism, initiative and personal responsibility. In the United States, where there has been political resistance to the growth of a universal welfare state, citizenship is associated with political membership, racial equality and individual freedoms rather than with social rights. The lack of centralized, bureaucratic government in America encouraged the growth of individual initiative and voluntary associations rather than state intervention to solve local community problems. While citizenship is often seen as a solution to social divisions, it is important to bear in mind that citizenship can assume many different forms.

One conclusion of this discussion of values or, more generally, cultural consensus as a foundation is that a legal framework, contrary to most sociological approaches, is a necessary precondition of social stability. Social capital may provide the glue of reciprocity to overcome ethnic division and conflicting interests, but social capital may also need the backing or precondition of formal rules and structures. How can states provide rights regimes that are sensitive to the (often conflicting interests) of minorities and majorities? Let us consider another set of arguments relating to rights. Will Kymlicka (1995) has defended the idea of group rights and cultural rights within a liberal framework (as a policy that has specific reference to multicultural societies such as Canada and Australia). Kymlicka (1995: 26) argues that liberal democracies that have accepted some form of multiculturalism typically make adjustments or accommodations to cultural pluralism through the mechanism of what he calls "group-differentiated rights". These are divided into three types.

First, there are rights to self-government. In multinational states, the component nations may demand some level of political autonomy or territorial jurisdiction. The right of self-determination has been sanctioned by the United Nations Charter – "all peoples have a right to self-determination" – but the charter does not define "peoples". In some societies, the demand for autonomy may lead to secession, but one common institutional response to the demand for autonomy has been federalism. In some respects, Kymlicka's argument may be specific to Canada, where federalism offers some solution to the demands of the Quebeckers within a federal structure.

The second accommodation is through the development of poly-ethnic rights. At a minimal level, these are merely rights to express cultural differences without exposure to prejudice. These rights are often expressed against so-called "Anglo-conformity" which has involved the dominance of Anglo-American values in the public domain, relegating minority cultural practices to the private sphere. More radical demands for these rights may entail the exemption of ethnic groups from laws and regulations that are seen to disadvantage them. The most obvious example has come from the Sikh community in Britain and Canada, where Sikh men are allowed to wear turbans as part of their official dress in public roles in the police force or military or schools. The point of these rights is to promote integration, whereas self-government rights are to secure self-government.

Finally, there is the creation of special representation rights in which minority or oppressed groups are given automatic or guaranteed representation in parliamentary and other democratic institutions. These rights can be regarded as a form of affirmative action, but they tend to be temporary. They are "kick-start" devices to ensure an evolution towards adequate participation, and they are subsequently abandoned once minority groups have entered the mainstream of the host community.

The theory of differentiated rights, while considered as a general legal framework, is often in practice specific to Canadian history and society. Canada is federal, and as a white-settler society it has first-nation communities with a problematic relationship to Canadian history and sovereignty. In addition, Canada has a substantial French-speaking community in the state of Quebec. Some aspects of the argument, however, can apply to Europe, where federalism could be a useful principle of accommodation. In addition, poly-ethnic rights already apply to certain social groups, but not to others. The case of the headscarf in French schools is the obvious illustration. However, one criticism of Kymlicka's general approach is the absence of any significant discussion of law. There is no attempt to connect legal pluralism with group-differentiated rights. Kymlicka's rights are in fact primarily cultural rights and hence the problem of legal sovereignty is not adequately broached, and yet, as various chapters in this collection demonstrate, the legal framework is a crucial ingredient of social harmony.

This contribution to liberal theory implies that societies can survive as effective democracies provided they are able to accommodate divergent cultures and identities. Other writers have been far more pessimistic about sustaining social order in the face of social diversity. As we have seen, cultural consensus in modern societies is unusual, because increasing social diversity undermines the cultural homogeneity of traditional societies. Cooperation with social norms affects attitudes towards how other people will cooperate, and in turn this expectation shapes assumptions about future behaviour. The growth of generalized trust is a function of everyday compliance with norms, and the more individuals cooperate with each other, the more they trust one another. Past experiences of reliable cooperative interaction tend to enhance our general sense of the trustworthiness of other people. In short, trustworthiness routinely generates trust, and, conversely, lack of reciprocity tends to deflate trust.

One consequence of cultural pluralism may therefore be legal pluralism. Some interesting work has been undertaken on legal pluralism in Asia (Burns, 2004; Peletz, 2002). If legal pluralism is an inevitable consequence of multiculturalism, it suggests that Kymlicka's group-differentiated rights are at present underdeveloped because they do not recognize the importance of legal self-determination. Legal pluralism would thus stretch the assumptions of liberalism to their limits. For example, the right to join or to leave a social group is central to liberalism. But in Islam there are traditional views that regard the right to opt out as parallel to apostasy and such arrangements could not be easily permitted. The notion that individuals can opt out of their own communities is therefore perhaps the most problematic aspect of individual rights. In the case of minorities, the survival of their cultures and traditions requires continuity of socialization and transmission – a process that has historically depended on women. Hence, women are typically subject to excessive (and at times brutal) subordination to group norms. But this fact offers no normative reason for supporting gender inequalities.

What is to be done? The social policy implications of these debates are numerous but also relatively simple. A successful society that is diverse and complex requires a strong legal framework and the institutions of citizenship to create a public environment in which overt racism is not tolerated and where assumptions about diversity are core elements of government business. Governments need such overt and explicit policies that convey to the public that the government does not favour one group over another, and hence minority rights are protected. Secondly, there must be sufficient economic growth and an adequate taxation system to redistribute wealth in such a way that second-generation children of migrants are not systematically disadvantaged. Educational policies are therefore fundamental to success. Thirdly, there must be social arrangements that allow for intermarriage, reciprocity and the growth of intermediate associations (clubs, churches and voluntary associations) to build up social capital as the underpinning of liberal values. These overlapping social groups are the supports that make possible an overlapping consensus of opinion and belief. Finally, there must be a cultural sphere (including sport and other leisure activities) where general values (an overlapping consensus) can counteract the tendency towards group loyalty, tribalism or sectarian solidarity.

13 RELIGION, MEDIA AND POPULAR CULTURE

INTRODUCTION

Marshall McLuhan, who coined the phrase "global village", underscored the importance of the role of the media in the process of globalization. The sociologists Beck (2000) and Giddens (1990) treat globalization as a "modernization of modernity" or "reflexive modernity" by equating globalization with the new role of the media in bringing the world together. We argue that the computerization of knowledge and the growth of the media are crucial developments in the creation of the knowledge society, which has opened windows of opportunity for less developed countries to share in the available global knowledge resources. The rise of new creative classes as indicated by Richard Florida is not likely to be confined to the developed countries; India and China provide interesting illustrations.

The emergence of the new globalized knowledge society has ramifications for the power/knowledge nexus, as suggested by Michel Foucault. The growing power of computer-mediated knowledge is best evidenced in politics. For example, shortly before the Iowa Presidential primary in January 2008, MySpace, a virtual web-based community, ran a survey that gave Barack Obama a lead over the other candidates, a result which was reflected in actual polling a day or two later (*Gulf News*, 4 January 2008).

The most visual aspects of the globalization process can be seen in the domains of media, sports and popular culture. These three domains have become interlinked owing to the expansion and intensification of globalization. While the global media have produced the global village, global processes, especially popular culture and sports, have given new significance to the media. The impact of such global sports as football, cricket and basketball will be discussed in this chapter. Why cricket became a popular and national sport can only be understood in light of the role of the media. Why are some post-colonial societies mad about basketball and others about cricket? Is the popularity of basketball related to the cultural hegemony of the United States, just as cricket or football was dominant with that of British colonialism?

Media and popular culture go together. In the late twentieth and early twenty-first century, the media created a globalized popular culture, a popular culture which hitherto has been confined to a specific location. It can be said that global popular culture is best expressed in terms of the three Ms: music, movies and McDonald's. In a substantial sense these three Ms represent modernization on a global scale. The disembedding of a local popular culture, whether in music, fashion, movies or food, was initiated by the forces of globalization.

Without the media it is unlikely that there could be global sports. Cricket would be played in various former British colonies, but without a transnational audience the game, as well as the revenue generated by the game on television, would dwindle, thus making the game less of a global sport. When the first World Wrestling Federation began only a handful of wrestling enthusiasts watched it at the rink; now the whole world can watch one wrestler beat the living daylights out of the other on TV.

Marshall McLuhan (1911–80) anticipated contemporary debates in his *Understanding Media* (1964) by popularizing the concept of the "global village". McLuhan argued that electronic systems of information delivery would abolish time and space; hence we are all living in a village. In contemporary sociology, the most general and important theory in this field has been developed by Manuel Castells. What are the implications of global knowledge for the economy, social networks and higher education? What are the implications of new forms of pedagogy for technologies of the self?

McLuhan is a much neglected social theorist. Influenced by Wyndham Lewis's manifesto in 1911 called *Blast*, McLuhan created the Centre for Culture and Technology in Toronto to study the social effects of new technologies. His works were popular and hence often dismissed by sociologists like Daniel Bell for allegedly trivializing the issues. His catch-phrases – such as "the medium is the message" – offered an imaginative understanding of the implications of print and electronic media as modes of communication. His media theory captured important technological changes and their implications for universities and education in general. Text-based knowledge required pedagogic techniques that would become obsolete in the electronic era of global communication. Technologies are extensions of the body. The book is an extension of the eye; the information media, of the nervous system. We can give a Foucauldian framework to McLuhan by asking what forms of "technologies of the self" are produced by different media of knowledge and information. Globalization involves the destruction of linear time and space by information technology.

Daniel Bell (b. 1919) developed the idea of post-industrialism in the 1960s and published the theory in his *The Coming of Post-Industrial Society* (1974) to describe a society in which the "axial principle" was the production of theoretical knowledge, the dominance of the service sector over manufacturing, the role of the university in organizing and developing scientific innovations for industry, the growth of a new managerial class, and the centrality of professional and technological occupations in the economy. Bell's work anticipated the debate about the globalization of knowledge and the dominance of the information and knowledge economy in the globalization of production. Universities are increasingly linked into global consortia that compete for science investment and postgraduate markets. The globalization of management degrees and accountancy courses illustrates the competition for status and dominance of the accreditation of service professionals. The globalization of knowledge has to some extent brought about the demise or at least the decentralization of research, design and investment through the privatization and corporatization of knowledge. Approximately 60 per cent of fundamental research takes place outside the university system through research institutions that are housed in the corporate sector. Universities are increasingly subject to globalized management systems including hot desks, open-plan offices and compliance audits.

J.F. Lyotard (1924–1998) invented the idea of the post-modernization of knowledge to describe the impact of computerization on knowledge and authority in the university. New systems of knowledge would be reflexive, fragmentary and post-disciplinary. Lyotard used Bell's notion of post-industrialism to take the argument one step further. How could knowledge be effectively legitimized? Lyotard's post-modern questioning of legitimate knowledge (scepticism about grand narratives) raises questions about how the forms of authority can operate. Linearity was the main principle of the age of print. Print requires linear learning techniques, separate disciplines, and hierarchy. The queue is a basic principle of linearity in the print age. Webs and nets are principles of organization in global knowledge societies. Access and exit can have many different points in the net. There are no linear principles of pedagogy – no accumulation, hierarchy or structure. Plagiarism and simulation cannot be monitored. There is no authorship. Hence these educational systems are post-disciplinary (Turner, 2003a). Post-modern global classification would appear to be characterized by incompleteness, instability (categories are fluid), allegorical reasoning (knowledge is endlessly self-referential), and randomness (entry and exit points are arbitrary).

Web knowledge creates critical problems of a political variety, namely, how to protect knowledge sites from vandalism, fraud and force. Hence, there are serious problems about the feasibility of global knowledge parks in new information systems. As we move from book cultures to a paperless global economy, how can the authenticity of knowledge be underpinned? New systems that are not based on print knowledge will require new types of social systems and technologies of the self (Lash, 2002).

Manuel Castells has argued that the globalization of knowledge is driven by the contradictions, and competition by the conflicting interests, of three elites, namely, the military, business and academics (Castells, 1996, 2001). From the perspective of communications theory, globalization includes: the emergence of ubiquitous mobile telecommunications and computing links; the consolidation of electronically integrated, global financial markets; the expansion of an interlinked, cohesive capitalist economy; the shift in the labour force from primary and manufacturing industries to knowledge, information and communication industries; and the emergence of "real virtuality" in the hypertexting of cultural and economic relations (Turner and Rojek, 2001). The network society was created by the contradictory competition between the three elites who sought to control the new communication systems. Business elites wanted to keep websites open and free in the interests of the free expansion of business. Academics wanted free access to information for idealistic reasons. While military and government elites would prefer regulation of networks, business and academic pressure groups for very different reasons want open access. While the net creates opportunities for heterogeneous movements from global Nazi sites to women's cooperatives, Castells argues optimistically that the net embraces two values. These are horizontal free communication and self-directed networking.

While traditional forms of hierarchical power operated through chains of command between people, the network society operates through data rather than people. These chains of authority are somewhat different from the chains of authority in Islamic traditions in which the Hadith (sayings and customs of the Prophet) are regarded as legitimate where they have a continuous chain of known persons to verify their legitimacy. Data do not possess the identity to resist, and they do not have a focus to oppose. Power is not necessarily embodied; it is a switch-point in the information flow. While Castells recognizes that the dominant managerial elites claim national control of informational flows, the logic of networking is that control cannot be concentrated for long at any single switch-point in the system. A further aspect of the network society is the emergence of "real virtuality" to illustrate the prolific quality of cultural exchange. Castells has identified a cultural system in which electronic representation establishes symbolic and discursive parameters of social interaction.

The development of a global network society has also triggered powerful opposition groups. Feminism and green environmentalism are two such instances of global opposition, but a variety of movements (from Zapatistas to the Japanese Aum Shinrikyo) can be seen as forces in opposition to standardization and routinization. Castells's argument suggests that contemporary struggles are struggles over the control of information. The result is a new informational class system with divisions between informational workers and generic labour, the social exclusion of large segments of the labour market and the separation of the market logic of global network flows and the human experience of workers' lives. Castells also recognizes major global divisions between the American/European/Asia-Pacific bloc and other regions that are informational black holes such as Africa and Latin America.

Castells's work can be elaborated to suggest a dialectic between localized struggles that employ networks to gain some control over their lives and spaces, and global network power systems that seek to centralize and monopolize control by employing the same technologies. These struggles have been a constant feature of the network society through its history, for example the struggle between hackers and network managers for access to information. The network society is the site of struggles where hacking, cracking and viruses mark the new boundaries of such power conflicts. However, Castells argues that "the Internet was born at the unlikely intersection of big science, military research and libertarian culture" and that all three have interests (business, military and social) in the development of open, free and cheap communication (Castells, 2001: 17). The openness of the communications architecture of the Internet is its main strength as users become both producers and shapers of the technology. The future of this openness will be an effect of the relations of struggle and competition between what Castells identifies as four cultures and four elites: the techno-meritocratic culture, the virtual communitarian culture, the hacker culture and the entrepreneurial culture. For different reasons, these cultures require open access, and hence democratic opportunities are built into the technology of communication. Castells has therefore identified two norms that emerge from these technological requirements. These are freedom of horizontal communication and access to e-knowledge, and the right to unimpeded self-steering. In some respects these two freedoms of access and movement reflect the liberal rights of the market place. Individuals should have the right to unrestricted access to the net (market of information), and they should be free to negotiate their way through the net without (undue) interference. These "net rights" resemble the liberal rights of non-interference and emerge from the technical opportunities of information exchange. They are a product of the technological characteristics of the net and the contradictory interests of the elites who attempt to own and manage the global flow of knowledge. They are features of an e-democracy that makes possible a global democratic discourse, while also providing ideal conditions for child pornography, global crime and terrorism.

The network society brings with it complex questions about intellectual property, patents, ownership and control. In particular, this set of questions about the globalization of knowledge converges on the problem of authority: who or what might exercise authority in an emerging system of global knowledge? In terms of Weber's theory of authority, it is clear that the authority and legitimacy of information cannot be subsumed under traditional or charismatic authority. E-democracies are not traditional, and make no claim to traditional legitimacy. The network is not charismatic because it cannot be legitimized by a single person, and no routinized charisma could significantly influence the web. We live in a world of manufactured celebrity, not charisma; the dominance of Britney Spears in terms of hits on her Internet site illustrates her ephemeral attraction as a celebrity, but it is not an illustration of charismatic power. The new forms of authority are not, however, legal-rational, because the authority of a site of information is not the product of the hierarchical organization of a set of offices giving commands in a linear chain of officers. The authority of the net is devolved, dispersed and diffused. There is therefore a connection between net rights, devolved systems of delivery and access, and a global civil society. As an ideal type, the virtual authority of the net requires the unimpeded operation of access, dialogue and steering. These conditions will not guarantee the truth or validity of communications, but they establish essential criteria for democratic conversations on the web. In this sense, they match the criteria of communicative rationality in Jürgen Habermas's theory of communicative action. The authority and legitimacy of communication can only be secured in terms of the adequacy of the two critical net rights.

TRADITIONAL SOCIETY AND RECITATION

Although the global net has transformed modern societies, there is an important interaction between global communication and traditional knowledge. Traditional forms of authority continue to dominate local communities in Islam, where memorization and recitation continue to play a central role in religious revivalism and in sustaining the cohesion of local communities. There has been an Islamic revival in Indonesia in which collective memorizing and reciting of the Qur'an play an important role in the creation of religious communities that are in many ways resistant to the emergence of secular knowledge-based societies. Traditional forms of learning through memorizing, recitation and collective performance continue to be important, because they train children in the collective expectations of the community, they sustain an emotional bond between the self and the collectivity, and they reward a particular type of personality. Traditional pedagogies are important because in the Muslim world they sustain an ethical and aesthetic order that is encapsulated in the Arabic notion of *adab* or rectitude, meritorious behaviour or ethical comportment. These traditional patterns of ritualized learning are changing, but they remain important for the Islamization of societies. To understand the problem of authority in Islam, we must attend to these basic pedagogies of Qur'an knowledge.

To illustrate some central issues in modernization and the media, it is instructive to return to Daniel Lerner's classic but much criticized *The Passing of Traditional Society* (1958). Lerner argued that there is a global logic to the growth of democracy or participatory society. In Lerner's developmental model, increasing urbanization results in enhanced literacy, partly because mass education becomes economically feasible with increasing population growth and density. Literacy is an important condition for mass exposure to the impersonal messages in newspapers and television, and a system of mass communication facilitates a wider political participation in democratic politics and greater economic participation through acquiring a desire for consumption through advertising. Lerner's theory used sociological notions about the systematic connections between education, literacy and political participation, and psychological ideas about character types and empathetic engagement with processes of social change. Lerner was particularly interested in transitional personalities or people who were departing from the hierarchical and personal society of the traditional village to the participatory, urban and impersonal society of an urban, democratic, capitalist society. Lerner's principal criticisms of Middle Eastern societies were that they were "societies in a hurry" in which the sequencing between the various dimensions of participant society were out of joint. In Middle Eastern societies, the state interfered in the free flow of information, and used the media not as technologies to enhance participation but as means of social control. For example, Lerner (1958: 67) complained that authoritarian Arab states were issuing radios *gratis* to their populations to facilitate social control rather than individual participation in society.

While Lerner had his mind focused on the problem of television as a medium of nationalism, the problems of media in relation to culture in the contemporary world are somewhat different. Music videos, delivered by satellite channels, are the only form of popular culture in the Middle East that is not censored. Fundamentalists and conservative politicians regularly protest against such forms of degradation of the young, but with little effect. The region now has many privately owned music channels. Occasionally student groups will protest (as they did recently at the University of Alexandria), but there is little that can be done while these channels attract enthusiastic audiences.

Lerner's model presented a simple evolutionary development from traditional to modern society, in which traditional forms of communication were expected to disappear inevitably with the introduction of modern technology (Turner, 1978). What Lerner may not have anticipated is that electronic and other media such as cassettes have allowed traditional ideas and values to be circulated nationally and globally. The transition to a participatory society does not mean that traditional cultures are destroyed. The religious word, the prayer and the sermon can be preserved by the media and become more effective as means of global communication, but they often sit alongside and compete with alternative religious pedagogies.

Sociologists have argued that the dominant characteristic of modernity is that it is reflexive (Giddens, 1990: 38). Social practices are constantly examined and critically evaluated by secular knowledge and by expert systems, and hence these social practices are constantly transformed. We would argue that the new media create what we might call "reflexive traditionalism" in which traditional norms and practices are examined and modified by new technologies, but they are not necessarily abandoned, because there is a profound distrust of the (Western) media. Where there is distrust of the modern media, traditional learning appeals (to fundamentalists) because it is thought to come from a reliable source. Conventional religious training creates a powerful affective loyalty to the community and deep-rooted motivational commitments to religious discourses. Reflexive traditionalism is, however, constantly exposed to the open and discursive characteristics of the electronic public sphere that erodes traditional authority.

This modern world of "cool" communication does not reflect the world of Islamic revivalism in which intensive exposure to the Qur'an through memorizing and chanting verses produces a disciplined personality in terms of Michel Foucault's "technologies of the self" (Foucault, 1991), but it also involves community building. Qur'an learning takes place typically in religious schools, involves public recitation of passages and a competitive desire to achieve status as a pious pupil. In her study of the revival of Islam in Indonesia, Anna Gade (2004) in *Perfection Makes Practice* examines the emotional bonds that connect learning, status and spirituality. Learning involves the production of a controlled self, but it is also an intensely communal or social activity that involves what she aptly calls a "technology of the community". Daily repetition of the Qur'an from memory is a central act of piety and a necessary requirement of prayer. Communal involvement in memorizing not only safeguards the individual from lapses of memory but creates a collective effervescence, to use Émile Durkheim's vocabulary. To memorize the Qur'an is not to repeat it once, but to maintain the memory of it in its entirety. This challenge requires constant practice and discipline that is centred around the pious notion of *adab*. In order to achieve this disciplined subjectivity, the memorizer must have moral as well as intellectual strength. Anna Gade points out that the Arabic lexical root for "memory" and "intelligence" is the same (*dh–k–r*) and also carries the connotation of strength. The one who has the moral discipline of intelligent repetition also has spiritual strength – and standing in the community. These processes of memorizing typically involve reading through the written text of the Qur'an, memorizing alone, peer learning with others and repeating the text before a teacher.

In the 1990s, there was some experimentation with "modern" methods of Qur'an learning that involved national competitions and engendered an enthusiasm for learning among young people. In Indonesia, therefore, the introduction of traditional forms of religious learning led eventually to the transformation of such practices, for example by the creation of national recitation competitions. Nevertheless these collective technologies of the community produce powerful emotions and have the consequence of consolidating the coherence of the religious community, and contributing to Islamic revivalism.

ISLAM, DIASPORIC COMMUNITIES AND AUTHORITY

Although Lerner's study of the modernization of the Middle East contains some fatal assumptions, his attempts to connect the use of media technologies with psychological changes in personality contained an important thesis, similar to McLuhan's slogan that the medium is the message. New technologies, including media technologies, require different operating practices and different pedagogical assumptions. In turn, different pedagogical environments produce different personalities. For example, in fundamentalist Islam generally the social movement of Deobandism has been particularly important. This Sunni revivalist sect emerged in British India in the nineteenth century, and it has played an important part in the radicalization of Islamic thought in Pakistan and Afghanistan. Pakistan's Deobandi *madrassas* or religious schools played an important part in the training of the radical Taliban. The Deobandi tradition came into existence around 1867 to defend Islamic traditions in a society dominated by Hinduism. As a strategy of cultural survival, they developed a strict interpretation of Islam, including strict control over women. By the 1980s the Deobandi community found itself in conflict with Shi'ites in Pakistan and Iran. In part this was an economic conflict in which impoverished Sunnis found themselves in conflict with rich Shi'ite landowners. The Deobandi movement has employed the idea of *jihad* to attack any group such as the Ismailis, who are considered to be *kafirs*. The Deobandi *madrassas* were influential in creating powerful social solidarity through an intimate dependency between students and their *ulama*. Deobandi pedagogy emphasizes the memorization of Qur'an verses, repetitive learning and strict obedience to teachers. It creates a disciplined self that is very different from the spontaneity and shallowness that is associated, for example, with surfing the net. The generation that came out of the Pakistani Deobandi *madrassas* became the Taliban, whose name means '*madrassa* pupils'. These pupils became the jihadist militants of the 1990s (Kepel, 2002: 103).

For Islam, and many other cultures, globalization has meant migration and then the creation of diasporic communities. The Internet provides an obvious method for dialogue within and between such diasporic groups, but the unintended consequence is often that diasporic politics and their intellectual elites come to depart radically from tradition, building up their own internal notions of authority, authenticity and continuity. The Internet holds the diasporic community together across space and then challenges traditional authority, which is often oral, and print authority. Although the new media have had important consequences for the Middle East as a region, it is often in the diaspora that the democratic effects of the media have their most important effect. Perhaps the most useful recent discussion of Muslims, diaspora and the information superhighway is to be found in Peter Mandaville's *Transnational Muslim Politics* (2001). Many young Muslims bypass their *ulama* and *imams* in order to learn about Islam from pamphlets and sources in English, for example *The Muslim News* and *Q-News*. The majority of Muslim users of the Internet are in Europe and North America. These diasporic Internet users are typically Muslim students in Western universities undertaking technical degrees in engineering, chemistry and accountancy. There is an important affinity between their scientific backgrounds and their fundamentalist interpretations of Islam. Because Internet access is often too expensive to be available in peasant communities in the Middle East and Asia, it is again students in Western universities who access the net for religious and political communication. There is little real evidence that the net is used by radical activists to promote terrorism against the West. By contrast, the net tends to promote reasoned argument in a context where everybody can in principle check the sources for themselves. "In the absence of sanctioned information from recognized institutions, Muslims are increasingly taking religion into their own hands" (Mandaville, 2001: 168). Much of this net discussion is about the proper conduct required by a "good Muslim" in a variety of contexts and circumstances. Muslim sites tend to provide opportunities for discussion and discourse outside the official culture. It is for this reason that the net is a means of bypassing the traditional gatekeepers of Muslim orthodoxy. The net also has a democratizing effect in the sense that it levels out power differences between social groups; for example, the Ismailis can appear to be as mainstream as other movements in Shi'ism.

A major issue on the web, as we have seen, is the problem of authority. Within the American diaspora, for example, because the educated sheikhs of the Al-Azhar mosque are physically absent, any young student in California can turn himself into a teacher by setting himself up with a website and provide rulings on various questions relating to Muslim conduct in the diaspora. These email *fatwas* are not yet recognized by Sharia courts as admissible evidence, but they clearly have an influence within the diaspora. They become authoritative because users can check these rulings against other sites and e-*fatwas*. In conclusion, Mandaville (2001: 170) argues that the net is an important technology for creating an imagined community for individuals and groups who are separated from their homeland and existing in alien (often secular) cultures that are hostile to Islam.

E-DEMOCRACY AND CIVIL SOCIETY

Expectations about the beneficial effect of the Internet prompted Howard Rheingold (1993) in *The Virtual Community* to imagine a new global community held together online by common interests in unrestricted communication, and that the dispersed thin communities on the net might also spill over into face-to-face networks. Electronic city halls were developed in North America and in Europe, for example

Italy, to experiment with direct voting on public issues and interests. There is ample evidence that social movements such as anti-globalization campaigns have not only used electronic communication in political action but their communities are built up by the net. Electronic interaction has played a major role in sustaining diasporic politics.

Web-based information and social action based on the Internet have an important feature in common: they challenge traditional forms of authority, namely, those forms of authority based on textual or book-based learning. Three illustrations are important: the role of health websites for people with long-term, expensive chronic illness such as cystic fibrosis has been important for care givers to bypass medical or expert knowledge monopolies; the disability movement has used the web effectively in the mobilization of its members; and the Internet has played a major part in integrating Muslim diasporic communities. But these examples all show how lay use of expert knowledge undermines the text-based book knowledge of professional hierarchies. In the case of Islam, traditional understanding of the Qur'an and *hadith* of the Prophet has been challenged. In conclusion, the consequences of globalization of information technology are contradictory: they open up opportunities for participation and also contribute the systems of surveillance. Amnesty International in 2004 accused Microsoft, along with Nortel Networks and Cisco Systems, of selling technology to the Chinese government to censor the Internet, resulting in a dramatic increase in the number of people detained or sentenced for Internet-related offences, namely circulating material offensive to the government.

CONCLUSION: ENLIGHTENMENT THROUGH ELECTRONIC KNOWLEDGE

Our thesis is that the information society cannot be easily regulated either by Western governments who cannot control the flow of information on TV channels, newspapers or the web, or by traditional religious groups who would want to impose some control over the content of the media. In this sense, multimedia entertainment and communication systems challenge the authority of Western governments and the religious authority of the world religions. In this argument, the "new media" refers to web-based information systems – websites, email channels, chat rooms, internet cafés, blogging networks, and so forth. We can also include in this category, in deference to McLuhan's notion of media fertilization, the use of videos, cassette tapes, digital imaging and telephone chat lines. The great contradiction of the knowledge society is that governments and corporations embrace an ideology of the free flow of information, while simultaneously trying to control knowledge through patents and intellectual copyright laws.

These new technologies have contradictory effects, but they provide alternative, deregulated, devolved and local opportunities for debate and discussion, and hence they make an indispensable contribution to a democratic civil society. The new media are important politically and sociologically, because they have the unintended effect of corroding traditional forms of authority that are either based on oral transmission or on print-based forms of textual learning, that is linear, hierarchical and repetitive. Knowledge based on oral transmission and memory, on the one hand, and print-based knowledge, on the other, are associated with traditional forms of authority and certain pedagogical technologies that produce a disciplinary self.

Modern religions have benefited considerably from modern technology. Mel Gibson's *The Passion of the Christ* probably did more for the revivification of Christian commitment in America than innumerable Sunday sermons, and also did much to revive Christian anti-Semitism. A new brand of Christianity has emerged, particularly in America, that is based on TV evangelism and the commodification of the Christian message, and fundamentalist Islam has been assisted by the use of cassettes to record and transmit the sermons of radical clerics. Although modern fundamentalism benefits considerably from the global communication media, there are important differences, as McLuhan warned us, between a world constructed on print-based knowledge and learning, and a social environment in which texting is probably the most important means of communication for young people. A traditional library was typically organized on linear Dewey principles, constructed around university disciplines, and organized by subject matter. The modern reader surfing the net has multiple choices about how to use knowledge sites, and a complex array of possible pathways. Entry points into the net are ad hoc and temporary. Every site is continuously under construction. There can be no single authority, because no site, entry or file can be controlled by a single editor or authority. It is difficult to define plagiarism and, for similar reasons, intellectual property rights are difficult to enforce. There are many free-riders, hackers and crackers.

How can the authority of authors or the final authority of an editor be enforced? Global information technologies and their associated cultures undermine traditional forms of religious authority, because they open up opportunities for debate and for the emergence of alternative visions. Global network society and its pedagogy undermine traditional

Islam and simultaneously promote the conditions for political Islam, but the new media are essentially democratic in terms of access. The new media can have corrosive consequences for those professions associated with text-based learning, such as religious clerics and clergy. While fundamentalist groups in Islam, Christianity and Judaism employ modern forms of communication, the net promotes open discussion and hence prevents forms of closure that were the basis of traditional authority. The democratization of global Islam as a network of diasporic communities is facilitated by the new information society in ways that bring into question the traditional structures of learning and training.

But the implications for Western societies are equally radical. While there has been a profound concentration of media ownership and power, no single corporation or state can control the global flow of information. The recent invasion of Iraq is a classic illustration. Within the US media, there was little critical analysis of the war, but there was a virtual storm of critical information and discussion available outside the US sphere of media influence. While the concentration of ownership in newspapers and television is well documented, there has also been an important integration between mass culture entertainment industries, communication systems and news. These giant corporations oversee the mass production of symbols that are distributed globally through diverse outlets including theme parks, sporting events, TV, video games, CDs, DVDs and so forth. These media giants have contributed to the trivialization of news gathering and public debate in a context where news gathering and film making intersect as entertainment.

Despite these tendencies towards a monopolization and trivialization of information and knowledge, the USA finds it very difficult to control the flow of information, because the technology relies upon freedom of access through the Internet, and as a result it cannot easily establish any global control over these flows. Hence its political legitimacy as a global policeman is constantly under review. To take one example, Al-Jazeera continued to provide independent views and information about the wars in Afghanistan and Iraq despite US tank attacks on its offices, coming under fire in the Palestine Hotel in Baghdad, and being expelled from Iraq. While the American press was largely mute about civilian casualties, figures on civilian deaths and damage to public utilities and civilian areas are debated and circulated online. Although journalism depends almost entirely on "official sources", the net provides endless opportunities for unofficial news gathering.

The opportunities for democratic discussion via these new knowledge sites are infinite and difficult to control or contain. Because the business world depends on open, free and unrestrained access to e-knowledge, it is difficult to see how governments or security agencies can exercise surveillance or control over this global chatter. These electronic sites do not require the corporeal presence of the participants. They are not like conventional public meetings, protest marches or sit-ins. Electronic democratic forums provide relatively safe sites for virtual meetings; they are safe because bodies do not need to enter into them. Website discussions and protests cannot be controlled with the same efficiency as, for example, the police can bring to bear in controlling public protests or student marches. However, it is important not to become romantic about e-democracy. Information technology provides opportunities for "cyber affairs", but it also facilitates the spread of pornography, sex tourism, terrorism and political violence. In Britain in 2004, the Home Secretary came under pressure to close a fascist website connected to Redwatch that provides the home addresses and personal details of public figures who have opposed racism in northern constituencies. To prevent police intervention, Redwatch is hosted on three different websites that are based outside Britain. The open-access nature of the website makes the control of fascism difficult, but for the same reason it makes the control of democracy difficult. The net is cheap, open and (relatively) safe.

During the Rangoon uprising in September 2007, in the face of a government ban on foreign media and strict censorship of official media, it was through the Internet that observers outside Burma had a window on the level of oppression by the Burmese military. The spread of information technology, especially the Internet and its impact on finance, economic development, education and the military, has received considerable attention in academic as well as popular discussion.

Our argument is that the principal issue in the debate about the electronic globalization of knowledge is about its implications for a global civil society and democracy. The implications of global communication are contradictory. There are two contradictions. First, it creates expanded opportunities for the growth of civil society, and at the same time it creates commercial opportunities for trivialization and standardization. Second, electronic systems democratize because they can overcome the issue of access (despite the digital divide), but they corrode the conditions by which communications can be made authoritative.

14 CONCLUSION: PERPETUAL PEACE OR PERPETUAL WAR?

INTRODUCTION: POST-GLOBALIZATION

In the course of this study, we have become familiar with ideas such as anti-globalization and de-globalization. In this final chapter, perhaps it is appropriate to return to the issue of post-globalization which we raised briefly in Chapter 1. This notion refers to a period in which many of the changes over the last half century were reversed or at least halted and we entered a period of protectionism, social closure, blocked labour markets, bureaucratic restrictions on travel and repatriation of migrant labour. There are signs in 2009 of these developments or at least talk about such possibilities as the major economies slow down. However, we would argue that post-globalization is in fact an impossible outcome, since the Internet, international legal system and global institutions such as the UN and human rights will survive these economic changes. Other twentieth-century developments such as the emergence of hybrid cultures, mega-cities and diasporic communities will not be undone by post-globalism. We anticipate episodes of de-globalization but not post-globalization.

The global economic crisis of 2008–9 raised some demands for a return to economic nationalism. While the economic crisis may come to an end towards the close of 2010, the questions will linger on. Standing in the first decade of the twenty-first century, one has to confront an unavoidable question: is the world in the twenty-first century going to be more rational, more peaceful and more democratic than it was in the twentieth century? Although the last century was in many respects a century of perpetual war, an optimistic assessment of the global situation today would be overwhelmed by the bleak prospects caused by the financial crisis, deep troubles in the world ecological system, and the strain on non-renewable resources. This depressing picture would be deepened by recognition of ongoing wars, fear of terrorist attacks, endemic poverty, periodic pandemics and disasters, racial, religious, and ethnic conflicts, gender discrimination and the generalized climate of both intolerance and indifference. However, these pessimistic assessments of the world were also confounded on 4 November 2008 by the outbreak of global euphoria following the landslide victory of Barack Obama in the US presidential election. The expansive expectations surrounding Obama are likely to give way to disappointments, because the financial crisis will certainly continue for several years and the crippling ecological system cannot be fixed overnight. Nevertheless the Obama effect which is felt globally has restored faith in democracy, a political institution that gives even the most improbable candidate a chance to hold the highest office in the world's most powerful country. While one of the legacies of US President George W. Bush was to besmirch the presidency by carrying out wars that were often inept, futile and unavoidably tragic in the name of spreading democracy, the electoral victory of President Obama rekindled trust in democratic institutions and created hope that long-standing racial divisions could be modified or mitigated.

Despite regular and daunting setbacks, there are more democratic countries in the world today than at any other time in the past: by the end of 2006, according to Freedom House (2008), 123 out of the 200 or so countries of the world were classified as electoral democracies. Freedom House (2008) judged 90 countries as "free", 60 as "partly free", and 43 countries as "not free". Since 1974, more than 90 countries have made the transition to democracy. Freedom House (2008) struck a less optimistic note, however, in stating that "the year 2007 was marked by a notable setback for global freedom. The decline was most pronounced in South Asia, but also reached significant levels in the former Soviet Union, the Middle East and North Africa, and sub-Saharan Africa."

In another – perhaps more refined – analysis the Economist Intelligence Unit (2007) classified the countries of the world as follows: full democracies 28; flawed democracies 54; hybrid regimes 30; and authoritarian regimes 55. Thus, about half the countries of the world can be said to be democratic. If we measure by counting people rather than countries, then the majority of the world's population can be plausibly recognized as living under democracies.

However, it is better to see democracy as a process rather than a system as such, since many countries are in a tug of war between democracy and authoritarian one-party rule. Towards the end of the first decade of the twenty-first century, a number of countries were being transformed from democracy to authoritarianism and several others could only be called democratic if we accept a fairly elastic definition of what counts as a democracy. Following Eric Hobsbawm (2007: 100), it can be said that "in the age of the common man, all government is government of the people and for the people, though patently it cannot in any operational sense be government by the people". The rise and fall of democratic governments is another illustration of the unending tensions in the present global situation. Any attempt to overlook the factions, frictions and dangers that can easily derail the process of democratic progress is obviously naïve.

Yet there are other grounds for optimism. The point is that it would be a colossal mistake to allow oneself to entertain the delusion of the end of history and the permanence of liberal democracy and capitalism. However, the Enlightenment project is a work in progress, allowing oneself not to surrender completely to pessimism and cynicism and thus to live in a world of nihilism would be a mistake of equal proportions. Major changes in human society are explained by the economic, technological and cultural transformations of the social structure, but no less important is the willingness on the part of people to undertake collective action. In short, any sociological explanation of social change must also take into account the possibilities of collective human action for change. The lessons of social movements, be it the movement to end slavery in the nineteenth century, the women's movement in the twentieth century or the ecological movement in the late twentieth and the early twenty-first centuries, illustrate the importance of collective action and the power of social connectivity across national borders. The optimism invested in the discussions of global democracy and the dialogue among civilizations and cultures through the framework of global civil society is not misplaced. From a sociological point of view, there are at least three ways of formulating social frameworks of democracy as participatory politics. These are social capital, citizenship and civil society. Sociologists have looked at the social "investments" or "capital" that people are willing to put into society and have argued that such capital contributes trust in society. Without trust, institutions cannot work. Then citizenship can provide the necessary "social glue" for society to function, and finally civil society itself is the necessary foundation of the polity. But perhaps all of these sociological views of participatory democracy come back eventually to the question of whether rights are implemented or not.

Whether democracy remains sustainable or not, rights and human rights, once fought for and achieved, cannot be easily undone and rolled back. The acceptance and defence of human rights have spread to more and more countries around the world. The great expansion of human rights legislation and culture over the last century has been a consequence of the mechanization of warfare, the growing number of civilian casualties in both civil and international wars, and the potential dangers of biological and chemical warfare. Historical accounts of the growth of human rights typically concentrate on the evolution of rights as such, but in this book we also wanted to suggest that the rise of the notion of "humanity" as such is paradoxically a consequence of the globalization of the technical means of violence. We need to understand the growth of human rights against this broader historical context of the idea of humanity.

The analysis of rights has until recently been predominantly the province of lawyers and philosophers rather than social scientists, and the intellectual contributions of anthropology and sociology to the study of rights have, if anything, been negative. Philosophers have not, on the whole, welcomed the intervention of social science for two reasons. First, social science approaches are seen to promote cultural relativism, and hence they make moral assessment problematic by questioning any universalistic account of moral claims. Second, the causal arguments of the social sciences appear to preclude any recognition of human intentionality and responsibility (Morgan and Turner, 2009). By contrast, any "rights talk" must, it is alleged, assume the moral autonomy and rationality of social actors. The classic criticism of both socialism (as a political ideology) and sociology (as a social science) came from Isaiah Berlin (1978) in his "Does political theory still exist?", in which he condemned the legacy of Marxism for denigrating the role of ideas and intentions in human history. Berlin insisted that historical analysis involved moral evaluation, and as such it could not ignore the autonomy of the individual as a moral agent. In this respect, war crimes tribunals presumably agree with Berlin and not with historical materialism.

One important feature of this distinction between sociology and politics is that political philosophy, but less so political science, has been primarily concerned with the question of justice, and hence the analysis of rights arises necessarily from a concern with the justice and legitimacy of political regimes. By contrast, sociology often portrays itself as "value neutral", and hence it does not easily raise normative questions about such matters as justice. Sociological studies do, however, approach these normative issues indirectly, for example through the study of inequality. The paradoxical consequence of this concentration on empirical studies of income inequality is that sociology typically does not study equality directly. Equality is merely the absence of inequality and not, as it were, a topic worthy of independent study. Because anthropologists and sociologists have typically been either positivists in epistemology or relativists in ethics, they have not developed any systematic analysis of justice and rights, and as a result they have failed to engage with the most significant institutional revolution of the twentieth century – the growth of universal human rights. In our estimation, the growth of human rights world-wide is one of the most important aspects of globalization.

HUMAN RIGHTS AND COSMOPOLITAN DUTIES

The mass killing of civilians in the twentieth century was probably the most important cause of human rights legislation and the modern development of human rights. Paradoxically, crimes against humanity have led to a greater social awareness and acceptance of the notion of a common humanity. Treating other human beings as members of a common community is a radical historical development. In this conclusion, we want to connect these juridical developments with the debate about cosmopolitanism. Can sociology develop a "cosmopolitan vision" (Beck, 2006; Holton, 2009) to match the current transformations of societies? Taking human rights seriously reflects an ethic of cosmopolitanism that can be associated with the Enlightenment. Specifically, we conclude by arguing that cosmopolitanism is the single most important project that brings the West and the East together in a common purpose. The cosmopolitan philosophy of the German Enlightenment, for instance in the work of Gottfried Wilhelm Leibniz (1646–1716), evolved with a clear fascination for the outside world and especially with Chinese civilization. Similarly, the ideas of modern Indian cosmopolitan thinkers such as Rabindranath Thakur (Tagore) and Gandhi were shaped by their appreciation of the encounter between and among the civilizations of the world.

Although the European Enlightenment is most frequently associated with Immanuel Kant, there is a strong case to connect the "Age of Reason" with Leibniz. At first sight Leibniz might appear to be an unlikely candidate as the father of human rights principles, yet in our view he lays out the essential ethical ingredients for human rights as not only a juridical institution but also a shared culture. Leibniz is characteristically associated with the concept of "theodicy" (which says that we live in the best of all possible worlds). His critics claimed that this notion provides a justification for the acceptance of violence and suffering in the world because it requires us also to accept the rationality of empirical reality. However, this interpretation fails to recognize the radical nature of his commitment to cosmopolitanism. For Leibniz, living in the best of all possible worlds meant not that all forms of injustice are part of a divine plan, but rather that a perfect world was one in which diversity had been fully and completely developed, and was also reconciled with order. Because something rather than nothing exists, there is a principle of perfection or the maximization of being. The astonishing diversity of cultures existing in the world is an aspect of this order-in-diversity principle. Leibniz wanted not only to recognize this diversity but also to celebrate it. This is an important point, because from Leibniz's philosophy it is not enough, for example, to accept multiculturalism simply as a fact – the inevitable outcome of globalization. Multicultural diversity has to be celebrated as part of the plenitude of modern life.

Leibniz lived at a time when contact with other cultures was beginning to expand people's horizons. China was a topic of growing interest, especially among Jesuit missionaries who had established contact with the imperial court. In this expanding world, Leibniz argued that just as there was a commerce of exchange (of commodities), so there ought to be what he called a "commerce of light" in which ideas were easily and eagerly exchanged between different societies. Leibniz, like Spinoza and Locke, supported tolerance towards other cultures, but he went much further to advocate "an imperative to learn from diversity ... [and he] is the only modern philosopher to take serious interest in Europe's contact with other cultures" (Perkins, 2004: 42). Even more remarkably, Leibniz recognized in his concept of the "monads" that this appreciation of the world's diversity could not occur simply from the perspective of an abstract mind separated from its body, but that our relationship to the world is always mediated through our own embodiment. Human embodiment means that perceptions of the world are always differentiated and limited. Embodiment in creating differences also creates the need for exchange, and as a result it also lays the foundation for a commonality of human beings. Cultural exchange is ontologically necessary, and it is made possible because our shared embodiment forms the basis of a shared culture, and furthermore we share a number of innate ideas that make communication possible. The intersection of these common realms makes possible a sympathetic understanding of other people and other cultures, while still preserving the notion of infinite cultural diversity.

Of course we can still ask how, in the best of all possible worlds, cross-cultural misunderstanding occurs. Why do shared embodiment, a common vulnerability and innate ideas not make cultural disagreements unlikely? Leibniz argued, reasonably in our view, that misunderstanding exists because human beings have freedom of action in recognizing or not recognizing others. Without this cognitive and moral autonomy, human beings could not act as moral agents. They would not in fact be able to live a virtuous life. In this respect we sympathize with

Berlin's hostility to much social science, with its often bleak adherence to a uniform notion of structural causation, historical materialism or technological determinism. A science of society needs also to preserve the notion that human beings are confronted by choice and that moral action involves making choices between alternative options – often where the options look unpromising or undesirable. In his recent exhaustive biography of Max Weber, Joachim Radkau shows that Weber believed that "freedom of will" is not as it were an inherent aspect of human nature, but exists when we behave rationally in the light of adequate empirical knowledge of a situation. However, he also points out that the "sense that historical actors mean to give to their actions is not unimportant, but it is not identical with the final outcome" (Radkau, 2009: 253). Choice is central to the philosophy of human action, but sociology is also concerned to understand the unintended consequences of actions. While we can spell out the moral character of cosmopolitanism, we also need to pay attention to the unintended consequences of human behaviour. The celebration of diversity may have the effect of isolating those social groups that cannot participate in diversity and for whom diversity can be threatening.

With this caveat in mind, Leibniz's positive celebration establishes the philosophical foundation for modern cosmopolitanism and in his inter-cultural ethic there is a more general recipe for "virtue ethics". In this notion, following Aristotle, the moral subject is placed at the core of ethical life and it follows that in order to flourish as ethical beings we need to cultivate and protect a set of virtues (Turner, 2000a). These virtues are ultimately grounded in human nature, by which we mean simply that we are embodied, and hence virtue ethics attempts to take account of the psychological, sociological and biological features of human beings. Virtue ethics constitutes the most appropriate ethical system for human rights as a set of legal injunctions. In placing Leibniz's cosmopolitanism at the core of virtue ethics, we can recognize that the minimal components of cosmopolitan virtue are as follows: irony both as a method and as a value in order to achieve some emotional distance from our own culture; intellectual reflexivity with respect to other cultural values; scepticism towards the grand narratives of modernity; care for other cultures; and finally, acceptance of cultural change.

Cosmopolitan virtue specifies a set of duties that can be seen to correspond to human rights. The right to life has a duty to care for others; the right to participate in the cultural life of the community has a corresponding duty to care for other cultures. From Leibniz's standpoint, we might argue that there is a duty to sustain cultural diversity and respect for other cultures. These rights and duties can be derived from the need for cultural exchange, and from the needs arising from human embodiment for sustenance, care, respect and dignity. This picture of life is unashamedly an optimistic theodicy, but, despite its recognition of diversity, it is an important argument against relativism.

How might we incorporate Leibniz's normative endorsement of cultural diversity into a sociological view of society? In his *Reflections on the Causes of Human Misery*, Barrington Moore (1970) argued that, while some weak version of cultural relativism was inevitable for social science, there is a well-developed consensus against tolerating human suffering. He argued wisely that while there is a diversity of happiness, there is a unity of human misery. Thus "a general opposition to human suffering constitutes a standpoint that both transcends and unites different cultures and historical epochs" (Moore, 1970: 11). If human rights exist to offer us some protection from suffering, why not argue that there are universal human obligations to oppose human misery, to respect the cultures of other peoples and to condemn governments that fail to protect human rights? Scepticism and a degree of distance from one's own culture can provide the basis for a duty of care and stewardship for other cultures.

This description of cosmopolitanism and virtue ethics as a set of obligations flows from a recognition of the vulnerability of persons and the precariousness of institutions. It is intended to take a stand against relativism and awaken the recognition of similarities between the prospect and problems of cosmopolitan understanding and an ecumenical commitment to dialogue with other cultures, especially religious cultures. The argument is not that contemporary cosmopolitanism can be simply a return to classical cosmopolitanism or religious universalism. Cosmopolitan irony protects us from that possibility, because irony is generally incompatible with these forms of nostalgia. We believe that our contemporary global dilemmas, which are very many and deeply daunting, cannot be solved simply by a naïve return to origins. Fundamentalism – whether political or religious – cannot help us settle the problems of the modern world, because the fundamentalist mentality is too rigid to respond effectively to the complexity of the modern world.

The cosmopolitanism of the Stoics was an attempt to come to terms with the cultural diversity of the classical world. We recognize that classical cosmopolitanism was an inevitable product of Roman imperialism, but contemporary globalization cannot be easily or effectively dominated or orchestrated by a single political power. Contemporary cosmopolitanism is a consequence of social changes that are associated with globalization. These changes include: the partial erosion of national sovereignty and the growth of post-national citizenship; the emergence of global markets, especially a global labour market, and a corresponding growth of diasporic communities; and cultural hybridity as an aspect of mainstream political life. These global political communities require ironic and reflexive membership, if the modern world is to escape from the vicious cycle of ethnic conflict, revenge and retribution. Cosmopolitan virtue may well turn out to be an ethic of exile for people who are no longer attached to a permanent homeland (Turner, 2000b). The more the modern world becomes an enclave society, the less prospect there is for cosmopolitan understanding and the greater the risk of sectarianism and violence.

HUMAN RIGHTS AND CITIZENSHIP IN A GLOBALIZED WORLD

We have explored the growth of human rights and cosmopolitanism as aspects of contemporary globalization. It may be argued by some that the expansion of national citizenship from around 1890 has come to an end with globalization, the erosion of the sovereignty of the nation-state and modern patterns of migration. We have argued, however, that "global citizenship" may be desirable but not feasible. Discussions of "global citizenship" and "flexible citizenship" ignore the fact that citizenship can only function in the context of the nation-state. Modern citizenship evolved with the nation-state, the creation of nationalism, the growth of the passport, the development of national systems of education and the evolution of conscription as a duty of the citizen. This historical development also illustrates the difference between citizenship and human rights. While citizenship entails reciprocal relations between duties and rights, for human rights there are no corresponding duties. The nation-state to which the idea of citizenship is organically linked remains a powerful and meaningful institution in the context of globalization and shows no sign of withering away. Citizenship, as a product of nationalism and the rise of the nation-state, is a system of contributory rights, in which there must be a relatively close relationship between rights and duties, and therefore citizenship is tied to the sovereignty of the nation-state. Hence the growth of European citizenship within the European community will be a slow and painful process partly because a federal Europe must compromise the sovereign status of the respective states and there is little evidence that states would surrender their sovereignty over key issues such as taxation and defence.

There are several arguments against this position. First, the very existence of dual citizenship might suggest that the relationship between sovereignty and social rights is not as close as we have claimed. Second, there is often a lack of fit between duties and rights, for example in the case of children's rights. Citizenship tends to assume a healthy and intelligent person who is capable of undertaking their civic duties, or at least capable of gainful employment. The physically disabled cannot always fulfil such expectations. As we have already argued, citizenship thus contrasts sharply with human rights since the latter do not presuppose any relationship between rights and duties.

These hypothetical objections may in fact strengthen our argument. Generally speaking, states are reluctant to admit dual citizenship, precisely because it creates divided loyalties and ambiguous identities, and it is seen as a clear challenge to sovereignty (Montgomery and Glazer, 2002). The lack of fit between rights and duties in the case of disabled persons accounts for the fact that they are discriminated against and often treated as second-class citizens. The elderly, while also discriminated against, are regarded as having retrospective claims on the state for past contributions. The absence of a relationship between rights and duties in these cases only serves to reinforce the notion that citizenship is based on contributory rights. In the case of the United States, where there has been a relatively weak development of welfare institutions, the underlying assumption of citizenship entitlements is that citizens will serve in the military, pay their taxes, raise children and generally contribute to the common good.

A citizen was originally the denizen of a city, and citizenship can be traced historically back to the classical world of Rome and Greece via the Renaissance cities of northern Italy, but modern citizenship is fundamentally the product of political revolutions, especially the English Civil War, the French Revolution and the American War of Independence (Turner, 1986). The notion of citizenship then spread in the late nineteenth century from Europe to Japan and China (Goldman and Perry, 2002). In the process of nation-building, nineteenth-century citizenship incorporated the urban working class into capitalism through welfare institutions and social rights, primarily under the umbrella of "social security" (Mann, 1987). Welfare states achieved the pacification of working-class radicalism with relatively little concession to basic inequalities of class, wealth and power. While welfare capitalism avoided the revolutionary conflicts that were predicted by Karl Marx, there were significant variations between capitalist regimes in terms of their relationship to democracy and authoritarianism.

Citizenship and welfare have been profoundly altered by the global neo-liberal revolution of the late 1970s, which created a political environment in which governments were no longer committed to the universalistic principles of social citizenship, a comprehensive welfare state and full employment. These economic changes – reduction of state intervention, deregulation of the labour and financial markets, implementation of free trade, reduction in personal taxation, fiscal regulation of state expenditure – were a reflection of the New Right doctrines of F.A. Hayek, Karl Popper and Milton Friedman. New Right theorists argued that the spontaneous order of the market must not be regulated by the state, and that judgements about human needs should be left to the operation of the market. The neo-liberal revolution has converted the citizen into a passive member of consumer society, where conservative governments understand "active citizenship" as a method of regulating the efficiency of public utilities such as the railways. But these changes in the global economy have not produced the global citizen.

It is possible to take a cynical view of the growth of welfare rights in the post-war period by arguing that welfare states and the growth of civil liberties were an aspect of the Cold War, in which Western states wanted to demonstrate their liberal values against bleak atheism and authoritarian communism. The right to free speech was particularly important, especially in the case of internal struggles within Czechoslovakia and Poland for the right of artists and intellectuals to publish creative works. In the post-Cold War environment, there has been less pressure to uphold those liberal rights, and after 9/11 there have been increasing restrictions on personal liberties with the passing of the Patriot Act in the United States and increasing restrictions on mobility in Europe, where Britain, Spain and Italy have sought greater control over and surveillance of asylum seekers, refugees and migrants, especially from North Africa. The attempt to impose greater security measures internally is clearly a response to the specific threat of terrorism when governments have to balance the preservation of civil rights against effective security measures (Ignatieff, 2004).

Although these political and legal developments can be connected directly with the perceived threat of terrorism, there is a more general political movement to limit the growth of multiculturalism. In the United States, conservative critics claim that multicultural education programs have distorted the historical truth of America's cultural origins and have undermined national unity by the effective Balkanization of the American republic (Glazer, 1997). Liberal intellectuals had historically believed that Americanization was unproblematic, because ethnic minorities would be culturally assimilated and eventually benefit from growing economic prosperity. However, this optimism was shaken by the fact that black progress appeared to have stalled in the 1970s. The neo-conservative response to alienated black youth was unsympathetic, if not hostile. Black youth was presented with a stark choice: either continue to experience social alienation, unemployment, low wages and resort to criminal careers to satisfy their needs, or passively accept limited social inclusion into American society on white terms. These developments in Europe and the United States suggest that citizenship is not a flexible institution, and that it is tied inextricably to the sovereignty of the nation-state.

Despite the institutional rigidity of many aspects of citizenship as an institution, we must continue to explore the possibility of creating new forms of social and political participation in modern societies – what are the opportunities for social action, religious involvement and political practice in contemporary civil societies? As we have already indicated, much of the modern debate about social participation appears to focus on the merits or otherwise of three concepts: social citizenship, social capital and civil society. The concept of civil society is best understood in terms of the legacy of Antonio Gramsci, who claimed that civil society is that space between the coercive state and the dull compulsion of the economy in which social and political action is possible. Without a vibrant civil society, the state is merely a coercive instrument and the economy blindly rules the lives of people. Civil society is that domain in which moral leadership can be formed, and, in the specific context of Italy, Gramsci argued that the Communist Party would have to challenge the moral hegemony which the Catholic Church exercised over the working class. While Gramsci's world may appear remote from our world, we do not think so, in the sense that we also need to ask what can offset the coercive nature of state politics and how moral (religious, aesthetic) leadership can be exercised in our time. These questions are the central issues of modern Western politics, but they also bear directly on Asian societies, especially those suffering most from the current economic crisis such as the Philippines, Vietnam and Thailand. Even Hong Kong witnessed significant street protests in July 2009 against rising unemployment and what were seen as failures in economic and political management of the crisis.

The concept of civil society has gone through many transformations. For Hannah Arendt the rise of mass society meant the destruction of the possibility of politics, and she complained that sociology was itself a sort of manifestation of the erosion of responsibility for our actions. She famously argued against David Riesman about the nature of individualism and the other-directed personality, and the failure of sociology to understand the conditions that gave rise to totalitarianism. The debate about civil society has recently once more assumed a dominant position in modern social science because the global neo-liberal revolution, in reducing government expenditure on public utilities, education and welfare, can be said to have contributed to the decline of public life, the rise of (what Durkheim called) egoistic individualism, and rampant consumerism.

Despite their importance, the problem of defining such concepts as civil society and public sphere has bedevilled political philosophy for centuries. While the definitional problems remain, we need a vital concept of civil society as the "civil sphere" (Alexander, 2006), that is, a field of values and institutions, in order to create a space for social criticism and democratic integration. Such a sphere depends for its very survival on social solidarity, including a substratum of emotions such as affective sympathy for others. Since social solidarity is *par excellence* the subject matter of sociology, the analysis of civil society or the civil sphere remains a core interest of the discipline. Indeed, the importance of sociology as a critical discipline can be said to be hitched to the survival of the civil sphere (Turner and Rojek, 2001).

For sociologists such as Jeff Alexander the civil sphere is bounded by what he calls the "non-civil" institutions of religion, family and community, which are seen to be particularistic and sectional rather than universalistic and societal. The hierarchies within these arenas often conflict with the processes of building solidarity in the wider sphere of civil life. Kinship loyalties can easily undo the transparency and effectiveness of public institutions. The solidarity of the public domain is inevitably fragile and because these solidarities within the civil sphere constantly fail, there is an important role for what Alexander calls "civil repair", namely those social and political acts that function to rebuild confidence, solidarity, hope and trust. For example, the demand for justice, especially in modern social movements from the black civil rights campaigns and the women's movement onwards, is an important component of civil repair. For Alexander, Rawls's *Theory of Justice* (1971) is a turning point in the development of modern political philosophy. However, Rawlsian theories of justice can be criticized because they are often blind to the underpinning of empirical sociological research. In *The Law of Peoples* (Rawls, 1999), the idea of an "overlapping consensus" of comprehensive doctrines is a significant dimension of his theory of a liberal society, but he offers little evidence about this consensus and identifies no empirical processes that might produce such a consensus. Some obvious processes would be high rates of intermarriage between minority and host communities, or the absence of residential segregation based upon ethnicity, or the access to public spaces and utilities such as parks or municipal swimming pools, or a common taxation system. In other words, an overlapping consensus would require significant inter-group solidarity resulting in social capital and trust. One obvious danger and one unintended consequence of multiculturalism and the acceptance of group rights is the growth of social enclaves divided by separate schooling, distinctive clothing and separate jurisdiction. One example is from Ontario in Canada where the use of Sharia law was authorized in civil arbitrations, provided decisions in religious tribunals do not conflict with or contradict secular Canadian law, but critics fear that the 600,000 Muslims living in Canada will be increasingly isolated from mainstream multicultural Canada. In short, there will be no overlapping consensus because there is little overlapping social world.

There are numerous issues confronting actually existing civil societies and Alexander argues that the reinvigoration of sociological theories of civil society cannot be simply a return to the classical political economy of Smith, Ferguson and Hegel. His principal theme is that we should conceive civil society as "a solidary sphere, in which a certain kind of universalizing community comes to be culturally defined and to some degree institutionally enforced" (Alexander, 2006: 31). The economic forces of neo-liberal capitalism are not the only or most damaging threat to this civil sphere, which is all too frequently undermined by racial hatred, misogyny, patriarchy, or by the monopolistic power of political elites and experts within impenetrable state bureaucracies. In these situations, social movements demanding a restoration of justice or a defence of civility and solidarity against the dominant themes of economic efficiency and hierarchy of expertise can result in civil repair.

CONCLUSION: IS GLOBAL MULTICULTURALISM POSSIBLE?

For many political theorists, such as Thomas Hobbes, we can only achieve some degree of security if we surrender a modicum of our own freedom in order to establish the sovereignty of the state. Herein lies the great intellectual puzzle of political philosophy. Politics can never be wholly universal, because it is essentially about the struggle for particular resources between conflicting groups whose motivation is to achieve power. Politics involves the contradiction between the state which needs to achieve some level of legitimacy in order to function and the struggle for power which appears to take place outside the framework of law, which is necessary for the continuity of the state.

In this account of democracy, human rights and the civil sphere, we have associated the legitimacy of the state with the provision of security for its citizens. We have assumed an irreconcilable tension between any human rights regime which is universal, and the legitimacy of government, which is particular and exclusive. Yet this tension between the state and citizenship, on the one hand, and global governance and human rights, on the other, may turn out to be more apparent than real.

The attacks on New York, Madrid, London, Bali and Mumbai have shaped the more general debate about the nature of terrorism, human rights and the role of the state. The American and British governments have been anxious to change the law, which was often seen to be unduly generous in protecting the civil liberties of individuals and groups whose beliefs are seen to be hostile to Western liberal culture. In these circumstances, there is little room for optimism, and the idea of cosmopolitanism appears to be increasingly out of step with contemporary political sentiment, which is to protect national interests. In these circumstances, what is the difference between terrorist violence and counter-terror measures? The coercive force which is available to the state is legitimate, if it is subordinate to legal norms, namely to the rule of law. Michael Ignatieff (2004) argues that state violence is legitimate only as a "lesser evil" – only if it is ultimately restrained and made accountable as a consequence of the due process of law. In the twentieth century, therefore, the legitimacy of the state came to depend increasingly on the extent to which both the domestic and foreign policies of powerful states were compatible with international human rights standards. The legal difficulty for the coalition forces in Iraq has been that the original invasion and subsequent treatment of prisoners do not appear to be consistent with UN requirements or human rights objectives. The notion that terrorism creates exceptional circumstances which permit states to act outside human rights norms is likely to be counterproductive. Such actions merely give further credibility to terrorist ideologies, and continue the erosion of the credibility of the UN and other international institutions. Human vulnerability sits therefore at the heart of human rights principles, because security is a necessary condition for containing our vulnerability, and legality and legitimacy are preconditions of human security. The political world has become increasingly precarious, and the contemporary international crisis is not well served by academic arguments supporting moral relativism. Recognition of our common vulnerability is the only starting point for the construction of a peaceful global community in which security might be restored.

In writing this conclusion, we are faced, on the one hand, with genuine optimism from New York to Jakarta about the prospects for the world system with the election of President Obama, as a result of which American foreign policy may become more cooperative and less coercive. On the other hand, we are faced with the economic constraints on social development that will be a consequence of the credit crisis. While the election of Obama is a tribute to the robust nature of American democratic institutions, the problems facing his administration are enormous. It is almost certain that the inflated expectations surrounding his presidency and the realities of the world economy will collide, resulting in frustration and disappointment. Although the price of a barrel of oil declined during the early months of 2009, in the long run we expect the cost of basic food-stuffs and energy to rise, with dire consequences for the global poor. We see no solution to the Arab–Israeli conflict or an end to the war in Afghanistan nor to the political instability in Pakistan, and hence political Islam will remain a potent ideology among alienated youth. In bringing this study to a close in 2009, we appear to be witnessing a sudden upsurge in refugees from Burma, Sri Lanka, Pakistan and Afghanistan who, crowded into leaky boats, try to enter Malaysia and Indonesia as stepping stones towards illegal entry into Australia, where they will encounter a Labour Government that is reluctant to appear "soft" on illegal migration.

Nevertheless we have sought to avoid a pessimistic assessment of the prospects of social development or any simplistic anti-globalization standpoint, because globalization has brought many benefits with it – human rights, the Internet, a global consciousness, the sharing of the notion of humanity, cosmopolitan cultures and so on. We have also attempted to avoid equating globalization with Americanization. If McDonald's is *par excellence* the symbol of American cuisine, we would argue that fast food was invented in Asia. After all, what are noodles for? We have, finally, attempted to avoid instant pessimism, since we observe that, despite the problems of warfare, the credit crunch and soaring commodity prices, democracy is a resilient system of politics. We pin our hopes (for our children rather than for ourselves) on the survival of democratic institutions, the emergence of an awareness of our common humanity based on human vulnerability and the growth of cosmopolitanism as a system of virtues relevant to globalization. Whether our hopes are reasonable and our aspirations well grounded are simply empirical questions. While democratic aspirations may be easily overwhelmed by empirical realities, the Enlightenment possibility of perpetual peace is a worthy aspiration.

BIBLIOGRAPHY

Abaza, M. and Stauth, G. (1990) "Occidental reason, Orientalism, Islamic fundamentalism: a critique", in M. Albrow and E. King (eds), *Globalization, Knowledge and Society*. London: Sage.

Adhikari, R. (2007) "Combating girl-trafficking and sex slavery", *Nepal Monitor*. www.nepalmonitor.com/2007/06/cpmbatting_goriltraffi.html (accessed 28 July 2009).

Ahmad, A. (1992) *In Theory: Classes, Nations, Literatures*. London: Verso.

Ahmed, S.U. (2003) *Dhaka: A Study in Urban History and Development 1840–1921*. Dhaka: Academic Press and Publishers Limited.

Alavi, H. (1972) "The state in post-colonial societies: Pakistan and Bangladesh", *New Left Review*, 1/74 (July–August).

Alexander, J. (2006) *The Civil Sphere*. Oxford: Oxford University Press.

Altman, D. (2001) *Global Sex*. Chicago: University of Chicago Press.

Anderson, B. (1983) *Imagined Communities. Reflections on the Origin and Spread of Nationalism*. London: Verso.

Antoun, R. (2008) *Understanding Fundamentalism*, 2nd edition. Lanham, MD: Rowman & Littlefield.

Anwar, Z. (2001) "What Islam, whose Islam? Sisters in Islam and the struggle for women's rights", in R.W. Hefner (ed.), *The Politics of Multiculturalism. Pluralism and Citizenship in Malaysia, Singapore and Indonesia*. Honolulu: University of Hawai'i Press, pp. 227–52.

Appadurai, A. (1996) *Modernity at Large: Cultural Dimensions of Globalization*. Minneapolis: University of Minnesota Press.

Arendt, H. (1951) *The Origins of Totalitarianism*. New York: Harcourt Brace.

Armstrong, K. (2001) *The Battle for God. Fundamentalism in Judaism, Christianity and Islam*. London: HarperCollins.

Bales, K. (1999) *Disposable People: New Slavery in the Global Economy*. Berkeley: University of California Press.

Bales, K. (2005) *Understanding Global Slavery. A Reader*. Berkeley: University of California Press.

Barbalet, J.M. (1998) *Emotion, Social Theory and Social Structure*. Cambridge: Cambridge University Press.

Barber, B. (1996) *Jihad vs. McWorld*. New York: Ballantine.

Barkawi, T. (2006) *Globalization and War*. Lanham, MD: Rowman & Littlefield.

Bauer, J.R. and Bell, D.A. (eds) (1999) *The East Asian Challenge for Human Rights*. Cambridge: Cambridge University Press.

Bauman, Z. (1989) *Modernity and the Holocaust*. Ithaca, NY: Cornell University Press.

Beck, U. (1992) *Risk Society. Towards a New Modernity*. London: Sage.

Beck, U. (2000) *What is Globalization?* Cambridge: Polity.

Beck, U. (2006) *Cosmopolitan Vision*. Cambridge: Polity.

Beck, U. and Beck-Gernsheim, E. (1995) *The Normal Chaos of Love*. Cambridge: Polity.

Beckford, J. (2003) *Social Theory and Religion*. Cambridge: Cambridge University Press.

Beckford, J. and Luckman, T. (eds) (1989) *The Changing Face of Religion*. London: Sage.

Bell, D.(1974) *The Coming of Post-Industrial Society*. New York: Basic Books.

Bell, D. (1987) "The world and the United States in 2013", *Daedalus*, 116 (3): 1–31.

Bellah, R.N. (1957) *Tokugawa Religion*. Glencoe, IL: Free Press.

Benedict, R. (1946) *The Chrysanthemum and the Sword: Patterns of Japanese Culture*. Boston: Houghton Mifflin.

Benveniste, E. (1973) *Indo-European Language and Society*. London: Faber.

Berger, P.L. (ed.) (1999) *The Desecularization of the World*. Grand Rapids, MI: William B. Eerdmans Publishing Co.

Bergesen, A. (ed.) (1980) *Studies in the Modern World System*. New York: Academic Press.

Berlin, I. (1978) "Does political theory still exist?", in *Concepts and Categories. Philosophical Essays*. London: Hogarth Press, pp. 143–72.

Beyer, P. (1994) *Religion and Globalization*. London: Sage.

Bhabha, H. (1994) *The Location of Culture*. London and New York: Routledge.

Bhagwati, J. (2007) *In Defense of Globalization* (2nd edition). Oxford: Oxford University Press.

Binder, L. (1988) *Islamic Liberalism*. Chicago: University of Chicago Press.

Black, J. (1998) *War and the World 1450–2000*. New Haven, CT: Yale University Press.

Brandt, W. (1980) *North–South, A Program for Survival*. London: Pan Books.

Brown, D.A. (1971) *Bury My Heart at Wounded Knee: An Indian History of the American West*. New York: Holt, Rinehart & Winston.

Burns, P. (2004) *The Leiden Legacy: Concepts of Law in Indonesia*. Leiden: KITLV Press.

Cai, H. and Treisman, D. (2006) "Did government centralization cause China's economic miracle?", *World Politics*, 58 (4): 505–35.

Castells, M. (1996) *The Rise of the Network Society*. Oxford: Blackwell.

Castells, M. (2001) *The Internet Galaxy*. Oxford: Oxford University Press.

Castles, S. and Miller, M. (1993) *The Age of Migration: International Population Movements in the Modern World*. New York: Guilford Press.

Chanda, N. (2007) *Bound Together: How Traders, Preachers, Adventurers and Warriors Shaped Globalization*. New Haven, CT: Yale University Press.

Chin, Y. and Vasu, N. (2006) "Rethinking racial harmony in Singapore", IDSS Commentaries. www.rsis.edu.sg/publications/Perspective/IDSS0542006.pdf (accessed 30 July 2009).

Chomsky, N. (1994) *World Orders: Old and New*. New York: Columbia University Press.

Clinton, H. (2009a) "Remarks at release of the Ninth Annual Trafficking in Persons Report alongside Leaders in Congress", 16 June. www.state.gov/secretary/rm/2009a/06/124872.htm (accessed on 2 July 2009).

Clinton, H. (2009b) "Partnering against trafficking", Op-Ed, *Washington Post*, 17 June.

Constable, N. (1997) *Maid to Order in Hong Kong: Stories of Filipina Workers*. Ithaca, NY: Cornell University Press.

Constable, N. (1999) "At home but not at home: Filipina narratives of ambivalent returns", *Cultural Anthropology*, 14 (2): 203–28.

Cox, H. (2003) "Christianity", in M. Juergensmeyer (ed.), *Global Religions: An Introduction*. Oxford: Oxford University Press, pp. 17–27.

Darnton, R. (2000) "An early information society: news and the media in eighteenth-century Paris", *American Historical Review*, 105 (1): 1–35.

DeParle, J. (2005) "What happens to a race deferred", *New York Times*, 4 September.

Derrida, J. (1998) "Faith and knowledge: the two sources of 'religion' at the limits of reason alone", in J. Derrida and G. Vattimo (eds), *Religion*. Cambridge: Polity Press, pp. 1–78.

Dirlik, A. (1997) *The Postcolonial Aura*. Boulder, CO: West View Press.

Dubos, R. (1960) *The Mirage of Health*. London: Allen & Unwin.

Dynes, R.R. (2000) "The dialogue between Voltaire and Rousseau on the Lisbon earthquake: The emergence of a social science view", *International Journal of Mass Emergencies and Disasters*, 18 (1): 97–115.

Earth Summit report (1987) *Our Common Future*. New York: Oxford University Press.

The Economist (2009) "A Special Report on aging populations", 27 June.

Economist Intelligence Unit (2007) *The World in 2007*. www.economist.com/media/pdf/Democracy_Index_2007_v3.pdf (accessed 24 July 2009).

Elias, N. (2000) *The Civilizing Process*. Oxford: Basil Blackwell.

Esposito, J. and Mogahed, D. (2008) "Who will speak for Islam?", *World Policy Journal*, 25 (3): 47–57.

Evans, P. (1995) *Embedded Autonomy: State and Industrial Transformation*. Princeton, NJ: Princeton University Press.

Evans, P. (1997) "The eclipse of the state?", *World Politics*: 50 (1): 62–87.

Fandy, M. (1999) "CyberResistance: Saudi opposition between globalization and localization", *Comparative Studies in Society and History*, 41 (1): 124–47.

Faw, B. (2005) "Katrina exposes New Orleans' deep poverty", 1 September. www.msnbc.msn.com/id/9163091/ (accessed 12, November 2008).

Figes, O. (2002) *Natasha's Dance: A Cultural History of Russia*. New York: Metropolitan Books.

Flexner, A. (1910) *Medical Education in the United States and Canada*. New York: Carnegie Foundation for the Advancement of Teaching.

Florida, R. (2003) *The Rise of the Creative Class*. New York: Basic Books.

Florida, R. (2005) "The world is spiky", *Atlantic Monthly*, October, pp. 48–51.

Foucault, M. (1991) "Governmentality", in G. Burchell, C. Gordon, and P. Miller (eds), *The Foucault Effect*. London: Harvester Wheatsheaf, pp. 87–104.

Freedom House (2008) *Freedom in the World 2008*. www.freedomhouse.org/template.cfm?page=395 (accessed 27 September 2008).

Friedman, T. (2005) *The World is Flat*. New York: Penguin.

Fries, J.F. (1980) "Aging, natural death and the compression of morbidity", *New England Journal of Medicine*, 303: 130–5.

Fukuyama, F. (2002) *Our Posthuman Future. Consequences of the Biotechnology Revolution*. New York: Farrar, Straus & Giroux.

Furnival, J.S. (1948) *Colonial Policy and Practice*. Cambridge: Cambridge University Press.

Gabriel, R.A. (2005) *Empires at War*. Westport, CT: Greenwood Press.

Gade, A. (2004) *Perfection Makes Practice*. Honolulu: University of Hawaii Press.

Gamburd, M.R. (2008) "Milk teeth and jet planes: kin relations in families of Sri Lanka's transnational domestic servants", *City & Society*, 20 (1): 5–31.

Garrett, L. (1995) *The Coming Plague. Newly Emerging Diseases in a World out of Balance*. London: Virago.

Geertz, C. (1968) *Islam Observed. Religious Development in Morocco and Indonesia*. Chicago: University of Chicago Press.

Giddens, A. (1990) *The Consequences of Modernity*. Stanford, CA: Stanford University Press.

Giddens, A. (1994) *Beyond Left and Right*. Cambridge: Polity Press.

Giffin, K. and Lowndes, C. (1999) "Gender, sexuality and transmissible diseases: a Brazilian study of clinical practice", *Social Science and Medicine*. 48 (3): 283–92.

Giulianotti, R. and Robertson, R. (2004) "The globalization of football: a study in the glocalization of the 'serious life'", *British Journal of Sociology*, 55 (4): 545–68.

Glazer, N. (1997) *We Are All Multiculturalists Now*. Cambridge, MA: Harvard University Press.

Global Commission on International Migration (2005) *Migration in an Interconnected World: New Directions for Action*. www.gcim.org/en/finalreport.html (accessed 25 September 2007).

Goldman, M. and Perry, E. (2002) *Changing Meanings of Citizenship in Modern China*. Cambridge, MA: Harvard University Press.

Goonatilake, S. (1995) "The self wandering between cultural localization and globalization", in J. Nederveen Pieterse and B. Parekh (eds), *The Decolonization of Imagination*. London: Zed Books.

Green, A., Day, S. and Ward, H. (2000) "Crack cocaine and prostitution in London in the 1990s", *Sociology of Health and Illness*, 22: 27–39.

Habermas, J. (1987) *The Philosophical Discourse of Modernity*. Cambridge: Polity.

Hammami, R. (1997) "From immodesty to collaboration: Hamas, the women's movement, and national identity in the intifada", in J. Beinin and J. Stork (eds), *Political Islam: Essays from Middle East Report*. Berkeley: University of California Press.

Hannerz, U. (1992) *Cultural Complexity: Studies in the Social Organization of Meaning*. New York: Columbia University Press.

Hannerz, U. (1996) *Transnational Connections: Culture, People, Places*. London and New York: Routledge.

Hardman, J.B.S. (1930) "Terrorism", in D.C. Rapoport (ed.), *Encyclopedia of the Social Sciences*, Vol. 14. New York: Macmillan.

Hardt, M. and Negri, A. (2000) *Empire*. Cambridge, MA: Harvard University Press.

Hardt, M. and Negri, A. (2004) *Multitude: War and Democracy in the Age of Empire*. New York: Penguin.

Harvey, D. (1989) *The Condition of Postmodernity*. Oxford: Blackwell.

Harvey, D. (2000) *The Spaces of Hope*. Berkeley: University of California Press.

Hasan, N. (2008) "State, religion, and the dynamics of transition: repertoire of violence in post-Suharto Indonesia" in B.S. Turner (ed.), *Religious Diversity and Civil Society*. Oxford: Bardwell Press.

Held, D., McGrew, A., Goldblatt, D. and Perraton, J. (1999) *Global Transformations*. Cambridge: Polity.

Hirschman, A.O. (1970) *Exit Voice and Loyalty. Responses to Decline in Firms, Organizations, and States*. Cambridge, MA: Harvard University Press.

Hobsbawm, E. (2007) *Globalisation, Democracy and Terrorism*. London: Little, Brown.

Hodgson, M.G.S. (1974) *The Venture of Islam*. Chicago: Chicago University Press.

Holton, R.J. (2009) *Cosmopolitans. New Thinking and New Directions*. Basingstoke: Palgrave Macmillan.

Hunt, S. (2005) *Religion and Everyday Life. The New Sociology*. London: Routledge.
Huntington, S.P. (1993) "The clash of civilizations", *Foreign Affairs*, 72 (3): 22–48.
Huntington, S.P. (1997) *The Clash of Civilizations and the Remaking of World Order*. New York: Touchstone.
Huntington, S.P. (2003) "America in the world", *The Hedgehog Review*, 5 (1): 7–18.
Huxley, A. (1946) *Brave New World*. New York: Harper & Brothers.
Ignatieff, M. (2004) *The Lesser Evil: Political Ethics in an Age of Terror*. Princeton, NJ: Princeton University Press.
ILO (n.d.) www.asian-migrants.org/index/php (accessed 3 March 2009)
ILO (2009) *The Cost of Coercion*. Geneva: International Labor Organization.
James, P. (2005) "Arguing globalizations: propositions towards an investigation of global formation", *Globalizations*, 2 (2): 193–209.
Jarvie, I.C. (1983) "Rationality and relativism", *British Journal of Sociology*, 34: 1.
Jessop, B. (2002) *The Future of the Capitalist State*. Cambridge: Polity.
Juergensmeyer, M. (ed.) (2003) *Global Religions. An Introduction*. New York: Oxford University Press.
Kant, I. (1960) *Religion within the Limits of Pure Reason*. New York: Harper & Row.
Kass, L. (2002) *Life, Liberty and the Defense of Dignity: The Challenge for Bioethics*. San Francisco: Encounter Books.
Kaufmann, J. and Patterson, O. (2005) "Cross-national cultural diffusion: The global spread of cricket", *American Sociological Review*, 70 (1): 82–110.
Kaufmann, D., Kraay, A. and Mastruzzi, M. (2007) *Governance Matters VI*. Washington, DC: World Bank.
Kennedy, P. (1990) *The Rise and Fall of the Great Powers. Economic Change and Military Conflict from 1500 to 2000*. London: Unwin Hyman.
Kepel, G. (2002) *Jihad: The Trail of Political Islam*. London: I.B. Tauris.
Kertzer, D. and Laslett, P. (eds) (1995) *Aging in the Past: Demography, Society and Old Age*. Berkeley: University of California Press.
Keynes, J.M. (1967) *The General Theory of Employment, Interest and Money*. London: Macmillan.
Khondker, H. (1985) "Governmental response to famine: A case study of the 1974 famine in Bangladesh". PhD Thesis, Department of Sociology, University of Pittsburgh, USA.
Khondker, H. (1989) "The 1984–85 Ethiopian famine", in U. Rosenthal, M. Charles and P. Hart (eds), *Coping with Crises*. Springfield, IL: Charles C. Thomas Publishers, pp. 278–99.
Khondker, H. (1992) "Floods and politics in Bangladesh", *Natural Hazards Observer*, 16 (4): 4–6.
Khondker, H.H. (2008) "Globalization and state autonomy in Singapore", *Asian Journal of Social Science*, 36 (1): 35–56.
Kibria, N. (2008) "The 'New Islam' and Bangladeshi youth in Britain and the US", *Ethnic and Racial Studies*, 31 (2): 243–66.
Kiely, R. (1998) "Globalization, post-Fordism and its contemporary context of development", *International Sociology*, 13 (1): 95–115.
Kim, D.J. (1994) "Is culture destiny? The myth of asia's anti-democratic values", *Foreign Affairs*, November/December, pp. 189–94.
Knight, J. (2001) "Social norms and the rule of law: fostering trust in socially diverse societies", in K. Cook (ed.), *Trust in Society*. New York: Russell Sage Foundation Press, pp. 354–73.

Kohli, A. (ed.) (1988) *India's Democracy: An Analysis of Changing State Society Relations*. Princeton, NJ: Princeton University Press.

Krasner, S.D. (1999) "Globalization and sovereignty", in D.A. Smith, D.J. Sollinger and S.C. Topik (eds), *States and Sovereignty in the Global Economy*. London and New York: Routledge.

Krugman, P. (2008) *The Return of Depression Economics and the Crisis of 2008*. New York: Penguin.

Kymlicka, W. (1995) *Multicultural Citizenship. A Liberal Theory of Minority Rights*. Oxford: Oxford University Press.

Lash, S. (2002) *Critique of Information*. London: Sage.

Laslett, P. (1965) *The World We Have Lost*. London: Methuen.

Laslett, P. (1995) "Necessary knowledge. Age and aging in the societies of the past" in D. Kertzer and P. Laslett (eds), *Aging in the Past. Demography, Society and Old Age*. Berkeley: University of California Press, pp. 3–77.

Laszlo, E. (ed.) (1993) *The Multicultural Planet: The Report of a UNESCO International Expert Group*. Oxford: Oneworld.

Leibfried, S. and Wolf, D. (2005) "Europeanization and the unravelling European nation state: dynamics and feedback effects", *European Foreign Affairs Review*, 10 (4): 479–99.

Lerner, D. (1958) *The Passing of Traditional Society: Modernizing the Middle East*. Glencoe, IL: Free Press.

Lieven, P. (1936) *The Birth of Ballets-Russes*. London: G. Allen & Unwin.

Luckmann, T. (1967) *The Invisible Religion. The Problem of Religion in Modern Society*. New York: Macmillan.

Lukens-Bull, R. (2005) *A Peaceful Jihad. Negotiating Identity and Modernity in Muslim Java*. New York: Palgrave Macmillan.

Lukes, S. (1991) *Moral Conflicts and Politics*. Oxford: Clarendon Press.

Mandaville, P. (2001) *Transnational Muslim Politics. Reimagining the Umma*. London and New York: Routledge.

Manila People's Forum on APEC Declaration (1996) www.asian-migrants. org/index.php (accessed 3 December 2007)

Mann, M. (1987) "Ruling class strategies and citizenship", *Sociology*, 21 (3): 339–54.

Mann, M. (2004) *Fascists*. Cambridge: Cambridge University Press.

Markoff, J. (1996) *Waves of Democracy: Social Movements and Political Change*. Thousand Oaks, CA: Pine Forge Press.

Markoff, J. and Montecinos, V. (1993) "The ubiquitous rise of economists", *Journal of Public Policy*, 13 (1): 37–68.

Marshall, T.H. (1950) *Citizenship and Social Class and Other Essays*. Cambridge: University of Cambridge Press.

Mattson, K. (2005) *When America Was Great. The Fighting Faith of Postwar Liberalism*. New York: Routledge.

McCargo, D.J. (ed.) (2007) *Rethinking Thailand's Southern Violence*. Singapore: National University Press.

McGeown, K. (2005) "Criminals target tsunami victims", 4 January. http://news.bbc. co.uk/2/hi/asia-pacific/4145591.stm (accessed 15 September 2005).

McKeown, A. (2004) "Global migration, 1846–1940", *Journal of World History*, 15 (2): 155–89.

McLuhan, M. (1964) *Understanding Media. The Extensions of Man.* London: Routledge & Kegan Paul.

McLuhan, M. (1967) *The Medium is the Massage.* San Francisco: Hardwired.

Meeker, M. (2002) *A Nation of Empire: The Ottoman Legacy of Turkish Modernity.* Berkeley: University of California Press.

Meyer, J.W. (1980) "The world polity and the authority of the nation-state", in A. Bergesen (ed.), *Studies of the Modern World System.* New York: Academic Press, pp. 109–37.

Meyer, J. and Hannan, M.T. (eds) (1979) *National Development and the World-System.* Chicago: Chicago University Press.

Meyer, J. et al. (1979) *School Knowledge for the Masses.* Washington: Falmer Press.

Meyer, J.W., Kamens, D.H. and Benavot, A. (1992) *School Knowledge for the Masses: World Models and National Curricula Categories in the Twentieth Century.* London: Falmer.

Migdal, J. (1988) *Strong Societies and Weak States.* Princeton, NJ: Princeton University Press.

Migdal, J., Kohli, A. and Shue, V. (eds) (1994) *State Power and Social Forces.* Cambridge: Cambridge University Press.

Milani, F. (1999) "Lipstick Politics in Iran", *New York Times,* 19 August.

Miliband, R. (1970) *The State in Capitalist Society.* London: Weidenfeld & Nicolson.

Miliband, R. (1973) "Poulantzas and the capitalist state", *New Left Review,* 82: 83–92.

Mittelman, J. (ed.) (1996) *Globalization: Critical Reflections.* Boulder, CO: Lynne Rienner.

Mittelman, J. (2004) *Whither Globalization?* London and New York: Routledge.

Mohanty, S.P. (1989) "Us and Them: On the philosophical bases of political criticism", *Yale Journal of Criticism,* 2 (2): 1–31.

Montgomery, J. and Glazer, N. (eds) (2002) *Sovereignty Under Challenge: How Governments Respond.* New Brunswick, NJ: Transaction.

Moore, B., Jr. (1970) *Reflections on the Causes of Human Misery and upon Certain Proposals to Eliminate Them.* London: Allen Lane, Penguin Press.

Moore, W.E. (1966) "Global sociology: The world as a singular system", *American Journal of Sociology,* 71 (5): 475–82.

Moreland, W.H. (1923) *From Akbar to Aurangzeb: A Study in Indian Economic History.* London: Macmillan.

Morgan, R. and Turner, B.S. (eds) (2009) *Interpreting Human Rights. Social Science Perspectives.* London: Routledge.

MSNBC (2005) "Calling Katrina survivors 'refugees' stirs debate". www.msnbc.msn.com/id/9232071/#storyContinued (accessed 15 September 2005).

Münkler, H. (2005) *The New Wars.* Cambridge: Polity.

Najita, T. (1993) "Japan's industrial revolution in historical perspective", in M. Miyoshi and H.D. Harootunian (eds), *Japan in the World.* Durham, NC: Duke University Press.

Nasr, S.H. (2003) "The achievements of Ibn Sina in the field of science and his contributions to its philosophy", *Islam and Science,* December.

Nayar, B.R. (2003) "Globalisation and India's national autonomy", *Commonwealth and Comparative Politics,* 41 (2): 1–34.

Nettl, J.P. (1968) "The state as a conceptual variable", *World Politics,* 10: 559–92.

Nettl, J.P. and Robertson, R. (1968) *International Systems and the Modernization of Societies.* New York: Basic Books.

Newby, H. (1996) "Citizenship in a green world: global commons and human citizenship", in W.M. Bulmer and A.M. Rees (eds), *Citizenship Today: The Contemporary Relevance of T.H. Marshall*. London: UCL Press, pp. 209–21.

Ohmae, K. (1994) *The Borderless World*. London: Harper Collins.

Okakura, K. (2001) *Book of Tea*. New York: Dover.

Ong, A. (1999) *Flexible Citizenship. The Cultural Logics of Transnationality*. Durham, NC: Duke University Press.

Ong, A. (2004) "Citizenship", in D. Nugent and J. Vincent (eds), *A Companion to the Anthropology of Politics*. Oxford: Blackwell, pp. 55–68.

Paddock, W. and Paddock, P. (1967) *Famine 1975!* Boston: Little, Brown.

Parrenas, R.S. (2001) *Servants of Globalization*. Stanford, CA: Stanford University Press.

Pearson, M.M. (2005) "The business of governing business in China: institutions and norms of the emerging regulatory state", *World Politics*, 57 (2): 296–322.

Peletz, M. (2002) *Islamic Modern: Religious Courts and Cultural Politics in Malaysia*. Princeton, NJ: Princeton University Press.

Perkins, F. (2004) *Leibniz and China: A Commerce of Light*. Cambridge: Cambridge University Press.

Petras, J. (1993) "Cultural imperialism in the late 20th century", *Journal of Contemporary Asia*, 23 (2): 139–48.

Pew Global Attitudes Project (2007) "World publics welcome global trade – but not immigration". http://pewglobal.org/reports/display.pup?Report ID=258 (accessed 5 October 2007).

Pieterse, J.N. (1995) "Globalization as hybridization", in M. Featherstone, S. Lash and R. Robertson (eds), *Global Modernities*. London: Sage, pp. 45–68.

Polidano, C. (2001) "Don't discard state autonomy: revisiting the East Asian experience of development", *Political Studies*, 49: 513–27.

Popkin, B. (2008) *The World is Fat*. New York: Penguin.

Population Reference Bureau (2008) *2008 World Population Data Sheet*. www.prb.org/pdf08/08WPDS_Eng.pdf (accessed 29 July 2009).

Poulantzas, N. (1969) "The problems of the capitalist state", *New Left Review*, 58: 67–78.

Poulantzas, N. (1973) *Political Power and Social Class*. London: New Left Books.

Putnam, R. (1993) *Making Democracy Work*. Princeton, NJ: Princeton University Press.

Qaysi, M.I. (1986) *Morals and Manners in Islam*. Leicester: Islamic Foundation.

Radkau, J. (2009) *Max Weber. A Biography*. Cambridge: Polity.

Rawls, J. (1971) *A Theory of Justice*. Cambridge, MA: Belknap Press.

Rawls, J. (1999) *The Law of Peoples*. Cambridge, MA: Harvard University Press.

Rheingold, H. (1993) *The Virtual Community*. Reading, MA: Addison Wesley.

Rhodes, T. and Cusick, L. (2000) "Love and intimacy in relationship risk management: HIV positive people and their sexual partners", *Sociology of Health and Illness*, 22: 1–26.

Ritzer, G. (2000) *The McDonaldization of Society*. Thousand Oaks, CA: Pine Forge Press.

Robertson, G. (2002) *Crimes against Humanity. The Struggle for Global Justice*. New York: New Press.

Robertson, R. (1987a) "Globalization and societal modernization: A note on Japanese religion", *Sociological Analysis*, 47 (30): 35–42.

Robertson, R. (1987b) "Globalization theory and civilizational analysis", *Comparative Civilizational Review*, 17 (Fall): 1–19.

Robertson, R. (1990) "Mapping the Global condition: globalization as the central concept", *Theory, Culture and Society*, 7: 2–3.

Robertson, R. (1992) *Globalization. Social Theory and Global Culture*. London: Sage.

Robertson, R. (1995) "Glocalization: Time space and homogeneity–heterogeneity", in M. Featherstone, S. Lash and R. Robertson (eds), *Global Modernity*. London: Sage.

Robertson, R. (2007) "Open societies, closed minds? Exploring the ubiquity of suspicion and voyeurism", *Globalizations*, 4 (3): 399–416.

Robertson, R. and Chirico, J. (1985) "Humanity, globalization and worldwide religious resurgence: a theoretical exploration", *Sociological Analysis*, 46 (3): 219–47.

Robertson, R. and Lechner, F. (1985) "Modernization, globalization, and the problem of culture in world-systems theory", *Theory, Culture and Society*, 2 (3):103–17.

Robertson, R. and Khondker, H. (1998) "Discourses of globalization", *International Sociology*,13 (1): 25–40.

Rodrik, D. (1997) *Has Globalization Gone Too Far?* Washington, DC: Institute for International Economics.

Roof, W.C. (1993) *A Generation of Seekers: The Spiritual Journeys of the Baby Boom Generation*. San Francisco: Harper.

Roof, W.C. (1999) *Spiritual Marketplace. Baby Boomers and the Remaking of American Religion*. Princeton, NJ: Princeton University Press.

Rotberg, R.I. (ed.) (2003) *State Failure and State Weakness in a Time of Terror*. Washington, DC: Brookings Institution Press.

Roy, O. (1994) *The Failure of Political Islam*. Cambridge, MA: Harvard University Press.

Roy, O. (2004) *Globalised Islam. The Search for the New Ummah*. London: Hurst & Co.

Sassen, S. (1999a) "Embedding the global in the national: implications for the role of the state", in D.A. Smith, D.J. Sollinger and S.C. Topik (eds), *States and Sovereignty in the Global Economy*. London and New York: Routledge.

Sassen, S. (1999b) *Guests and Aliens*. New York: New Press.

Sassen, S. (2001) *The Global City* (2nd edition). Princeton, NJ: Princeton University Press.

Savage, M., Bagnall, G. and Longhurst, B. (2005) *Globalization and Belonging*. London and Thousand Oaks, CA: Sage.

Scheper-Hughes, N. (2001a) "Neo-cannibalism: the global trade in human organs", *Hedgehog Review*, 3 (2): 7–52.

Scheper-Hughes, N. (2001b) "Commodity fetishism in organs trafficking", *Body & Society* 7 (2–3): 31–62.

Scholte, J. (2000) *Globalization: A Critical Introduction*. New York: Palgrave.

Sen, A. (1982) *Poverty and Famines*. Oxford: Clarendon Press.

Sen, A. (1993) "India and the West", *New Republic*, 7 June, pp. 27–34.

Sen, A. (2002) "How to Judge globalism", *American Prospect*, 13 (1): 1–14.

Sen, A. (2005) *The Argumentative Indian*. London and New York: Allen Lane.

Shaw, M. (2003) *War & Genocide*. Cambridge: Polity.

Shibutani, T. (1961) *Society and Personality*. Englewood Cliffs, NJ: Prentice Hall.

SIPRI (2008) *SIPRI Yearbook 2008: Armaments, Disarmament and International Security*. Oxford: Oxford University Press. Available at: http://yearbook2008.sipri.org65.

Skocpol, T. (1985) "Bringing the state back in: strategies of analysis in current research", in P. Evans, D. Rueschemeyer and T. Skocpol (eds), *Bringing the State Back In*. London: Cambridge University Press.

Smith, J. (1999) *Islam in America*. New York: Columbia University Press.

Smith, N. (1997) "The satanic geographies of globalization: uneven development in the 1990s", *Public Culture*, 10 (1): 169–89.

Soros, G. (2002) *On Globalization*. New York: Public Affairs.

Soros, G. (2008) "The economy fell off the cliff", interview in *Spiegel*, 24 November.

Spellman, K. (2004) *Religion and Nation: Iranian Local and Transnational Networks in Britain*, New York: Berghahn Books.

Spinner-Halev, J. (2005) "Hinduism, Christianity, and liberal religious tolerance", *Political Theory*, 33 (1): 28–57.

Spiro, M.E. (1970) *Buddhism and Society. A Great Tradition and its Burmese Vicissitudes.* Berkeley: University of California Press.

Stiglitz, J. (2002) *Globalization and Its Discontents.* New York: W.W. Norton.

Stiglitz, J. (2007) *Making Globalization Work.* New York: W.W. Norton.

Stiglitz, J. (2008) "Global crisis – made in America", interview in *Spiegel*, 12 November.

Stiglitz, J. and Bilmes, L. (2008) *The Three Million Dollar War: The True Cost of the Iraq Conflict.* New York: W.W. Norton.

Stone, M.S. (1998) *The Patron State. Culture and Politics in Fascist Italy.* Princeton, NJ: Princeton University Press.

Strange, S. (1996) *The Retreat of the State.* Cambridge: Cambridge University Press.

Sunderland, J.T. (1900) "The cause of Indian famines", *New England Magazine*, 23 (1): 56–64.

Sztompka, P. (1990) "Agency and progress: the idea of progress and the changing theories of change", in J. Alexander and P. Sztompka (eds), *Rethinking Progress.* Boston: Unwin Hyman.

Tanner, A. (2005) "Some evacuees see religious message in Katrina". www.redorbit. com/news/general/229921/some_evacuees_see_religious_message_in_katrina/ (accessed 29 July 2009).

Tedjasukmana, J. and Cangkring, T. (2006) "Indonesia's skin wars", *Time International*, 10 April, 167 (14): 22.

Therborn, G. (1995) "Routes to/through modernity", in M. Featherstone, S. Lash and R. Roberston (eds), *Global Modernities.* London: Sage.

Therborn, G. (2000a) "At the birth of second century sociology: times of reflexivity, spaces of identity, and nodes of knowledge", *British Journal of Sociology*, 51 (1): 37–57.

Therborn, G. (2000b) "Globalizations", *International Sociology*, 15 (2): 151–79.

Therborn, G. (2000c) "The pole and the triangle: US power and the triangle of the Americas, Asia and Europe", in V. Hadiz (ed.), *Empire and Neoliberalism in Asia.* London: Routledge, pp. 23–37.

Therborn, G. and Khondker, H. (eds) (2006) *Asia and Europe in Globalization.* Leiden: Brill.

Theroux, P. (2007) "The golden man", *New Yorker*, 28 May: 54–65.

Tobin, J. (1978) "A proposal for international monetary reform", *Eastern Economic Journal*, 4: 153–9.

Tomlinson, J. (1991) *Cultural Imperialism: A Critical Introduction.* Baltimore, MD: Johns Hopkins University Press.

Tomlinson, J. (1999) *Globalization and Culture.* Cambridge: Polity.

Torpey, J. (1998) "Coming and going", *Sociological Theory*, 16 (3): 239–59.

Turner, B.S. (1978) *Marx and the End of Orientalism.* London: George Allen & Unwin.

Turner, B.S. (1986) *Citizenship and Capitalism. The Debate over Reformism.* London: Allen & Unwin.

Turner, B.S. (1998) *Weber and Islam.* London and New York: Routledge.

Turner, B.S. (2000) "Cosmopolitan virtue: loyalty and the city", in E. Isin (ed.), *Democracy, Citizenship and the Global City.* London: Routledge, pp. 129–47.

Turner, B.S. (2001) "The erosion of citizenship", *British Journal of Sociology*, 52 (2): 189–209.

Turner, B.S. (2000b) "Edward Said and the exilic ethic: on being out of place", *Theory, Culture & Society*, 17 (6): 125–9.

Turner, B.S. (2002) "Cosmopolitan virtue, globalization and patriotism", *Theory, Culture & Society*, 19 (1–2): 45–63.

Turner, B.S. (2003a) "McDonaldization: linearity and liquidity in consumer cultures", *American Behavioral Scientist*, 47 (2): 137–53.

Turner, B.S. (2003b) "Historical sociology of religion: politics and modernity", in G. Delanty and E.F. Isin (eds), *Handbook of Historical Sociology*. London: Sage, pp. 349–63.

Turner, B.S. (2006) *Vulnerability and Human Rights*. University Park: Pennsylvania State University Press.

Turner, B.S. (2007) "The enclave society: towards a sociology of immobility", *European Journal of Social Theory*, 10 (2): 287–304.

Turner, B.S. (ed.) (2009) *Handbook of Globalization Studies*. London and New York: Routledge.

Turner, B.S. and Rojek, C. (2001) *Society and Culture. Principles of Scarcity and Solidarity*, London: Sage.

United Nations (2009a) UN Report of the Commission of Experts of the President of the United Nations General Assembly on Reforms of the International Monetary and Financial System. www.un.org/ga/president/63/interactive/financialcrisis/PreliminaryReport210509.pdf (accessed 1 July 2009)

United Nations (2009b) *World Economic Situation and Prospects 2009. Updates as of mid-2009*. www.un.org/esa/policy/wess/wesp.html (accessed 1 July 2009)

Urry, J. (2000) *Sociology Beyond Societies*. London: Routledge.

US Department of State (2007) *Trafficking in Persons Report*, June. www.state.gov/documents/organization/82902.pdf (accessed 28 July 2009).

Van der Ven, J., Dreyer, J.S. and Pieterse, H.J.C. (2004) *Is there a God of Human Rights? The Complex Relationship between Human Rights and Religion. A South African Case*. Leiden: Brill.

Wade, R. (1990) *Governing the Market: Economic Theory and the Role of Government in East Asian Industrialization*. Princeton, NJ: Princeton University Press.

Wahid, A. (2006) "Extremism isn't in Islamic law", *Washington Post*, 23 May.

Wallerstein, I. (1974) *The Modern World-System*. New York: Academic Press.

Wallerstein, I. (1999) "States? Sovereignty? The dilemmas of capitalists in an age of transition", in D.A. Smith, D.J. Sollinger and S.C. Topik (eds), *States and Sovereignty in the Global Economy*. London and New York: Routledge.

Walzer, M. (1994) *Thick and Thin*. Cambridge, MA: Harvard University Press.

Waters, M. (1995) *Globalization*. London: Routledge.

Weber, M. (1948) *From Max Weber: Essays in Sociology*, translated and edited by H.H. Gerth and C.W. Mills. London: Kegan Paul.

Weber, M. (1996) *The Sociology of Religion*. London: Methuen.

Weber, M. (2002) *The Protestant Ethic and the Spirit of Capitalism*. London: Penguin.

Weiss, L. (2000) "Globalization and state power", *Development and Society*, 29 (1): 1–15.

Wolferen, Karel van (1989) *The Enigma of Japanese Power*. New York: Knopf.

World Bank (2009) Press Release No. 2009/414/DEC. Seoul, 22 June.

Young, L. (ed.) (1997) *Rational Choice Theory and Religion*. New York: Routledge.

Zabala, S. (ed.) (2005) *The Future of Religion*. New York: Columbia University Press.

Zakaria, F. (1994) "Culture is destiny: A conversation with Lee Kuan Yew", *Foreign Affairs*, March/April, pp. 109–27.

Zolberg, A. (2006) "Managing a world on the move", *Population and Development Review*, 32 (Supplement): 222–53.

INDEX

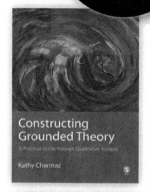

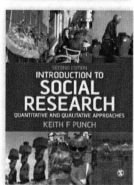
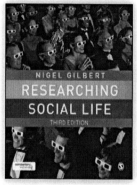
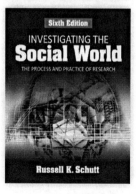

The Qualitative Research Kit

Edited by Uwe Flick

Read sample chapters online now!

Doing Ethnographic and Observational Research — Michael Angrosino — The SAGE Qualitative Research Kit

Using Visual Data in Qualitative Research — Marcus Banks — The SAGE Qualitative Research Kit

Doing Focus Groups — Rosaline Barbour — The SAGE Qualitative Research Kit

Designing Qualitative Research — Uwe Flick — The SAGE Qualitative Research Kit

Managing Quality in Qualitative Research — Uwe Flick — The SAGE Qualitative Research Kit

Analyzing Qualitative Data — Graham Gibbs — The SAGE Qualitative Research Kit

Doing Interviews — Steinar Kvale — The SAGE Qualitative Research Kit

Doing Conversation, Discourse and Document Analysis — Tim Rapley — The SAGE Qualitative Research Kit

www.sagepub.co.uk

Research Methods
Books from SAGE

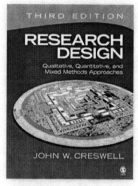

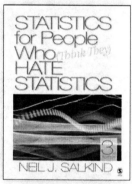

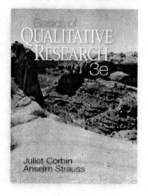

Lightning Source UK Ltd.
Milton Keynes UK
UKOW05f2148210115

244866UK00001B/28/P